Josiah Martin

Miniature portrait of Governor Josiah Martin painted by Jeremiah Meyer, miniaturist to George III from a private British collection.

Josiah Martin

The Last Royal Governor of North Carolina

Vernon O. Stumpf

Carolina Academic Press
for the Kellenberger Historical Foundation
Durham, North Carolina

ISBN 0–89089–305–5 (cloth)
0–89089–304–7 (paper)

LCC No. 85–73112

Carolina Academic Press
P. O. Box 8795
Durham, North Carolina 27707

For

*Marie Dawson and
Oral B. Stumpf,
Anne Koehler and
Joseph L. Magrum.*

Contents

royal governors, such as John R. Alden's study of Lieutenant Governor Robert Dinwiddie and Bernard Bailyn's study of Thomas Hutchinson. These scholars have demonstrated the wisdom of special study of the royal governors, for the British monarchy gave much attention to the appointment of the more than 300 individuals who held the office in the Atlantic coastal and Caribbean colonies. The office became the model for the later offices of governor in the American states and, together with the British monarchy, one of the few models for the American presidency. A study of the royal governors is also of special importance for trying to recapture those moments when the American colonies threw off their allegiance to the crown and became states. The United Colonies declared their independence on July 4, 1776, but that was the beginning of independence only in retrospect. In their own minds many of the subjects of George III slowly became citizens of independent states long before July 4, 1776 while others realized their independence when the royal authority disappeared from their colonial capitals. That change was dramatized when the royal governors left their posts.

In the history of North Carolina the change from a colonial government to an independent state can be seen in the administration of the last royal governor, Josiah Martin. The state's founding fathers made their patriot governor a figurehead; they stripped him of all power, including the much abused veto power. Martin did not leave his post quietly as many governors did; he transferred to a British warship and laid plans to recover his lost office.

Josiah Martin never attained a higher office than governor of North Carolina. Except for his plans for the crown to reconquer the southern colonies, submitted to the secretary of state for the colonies, Josiah Martin had little part in the great decisions of his time. He did participate in the two British invasions of the southern colonies. In following Martin's career one can gain insight into the supreme fact of the Revolution—the disappearance of one authority and its replacement by another.

This study was researched and written in London, New York, Washington, Durham, and in Harnett County, North Carolina. It seems fitting to have written most of this study in Harnett County, for the county is named after the great radical leader of the North Carolina Revolution. Nearby is the county seat of Lillington, named for one of the heroes of the Battle of Moore's Creek. Close at hand is the road down which Cornwallis and Martin marched toward Wilmington after the victory of Guilford Court House and on their way to defeat.

Chapter I of this book in a different version, was published earlier in *The North Carolina Historical Review*, volume LIII, January, 1976. Chapter V was previously published in a different version in the Lower Cape Fear Historical Society, Inc., *Bulletin*, volume XIX, October, 1975, and February, 1976.

The author is indebted to many individuals and institutions for support and guidance in this study. Among those who gave support and direction were John R. Alden (who suggested that I study the governor) and Calvin D. Davis of Duke University; H. G. Jones, curator of the North Carolina Collection, University of North Carolina Library, William S. Powell and Hugh T. Lefler of UNC-Chapel Hill; Robert M. Calhoon of UNC-Greensboro; W. Conard Gass of Campbell University; Hugh Buckner Johnston of Atlantic Christian College, and many others. I am indebted to Florence Blakely and Mary Canada of Perkins Library, Duke University; Martha Beals, Catherine Pollari, and Karen Dickerson of the Campbell University Library; and librarians of the Library of Congress, Manuscript Division; the Massachusetts Historical Society; the New York Historical Society; the staff of the Department of Archives and History of the State of North Carolina; and the British Museum Manuscripts Division; and the Institute of Historical Research, University of London. Sir Frances Loyd and his staff of London House in England provided a home away from home. The writer received the Don Clayton Award for Research Overseas and Travel and a grant from the Z. Smith Reynolds Foundation. The grant from the Kellenberger Historical Foundation to publish the book is very much appreciated.

Finally, I would like to express special gratitude to the students who helped me with the research of this book. They are

Josiah Martin

Douglas Carter, Edith Coggin, Vickie Jordan, Kenneth Knust, Christopher Mays, Edmund Miller, Leslie Parker, Steven Smith, David Whitby, Robert B. Wiggins, Jr., and Iris Williford.

Vernon O. Stumpf

Chapel Hill, November 1985

Josiah Martin

I. Martin and the Search for Success

As Great Britain expanded into the Atlantic world and prospered, so did the fortunes of the gentry families which staffed the bureaus, held colonial offices, and provided officers for the British armed forces. Many such families sought wealth and preferment within the emerging British empire by investing their energies in imperial development, administration, and property. This is the story of one gentry family, the Martins of Antigua in the West Indies in the eighteenth century, and in particular the story of Josiah Martin, the last royal governor of North Carolina.

The Martin family gave its allegiance to the Crown as early as William the Conqueror recognizing that through service to the Crown it could gain property, power, and prestige. They possessed critical insights and skills, and they gave each other support and inculcated in their children a sense of their own ability and importance which the empire encouraged and rewarded.

The coat of arms of the Martin family declared its devotion to the Crown with the motto "Pro Patria." A family tradition claims that the founder of the English branch of the family was Martin of Tours who accompanied William the Conqueror to England in 1066. He was neither the saint nor the French bishop, but was a neighbor of the Conqueror near Bayeux in Normandy. He fought at Hastings and was granted estates in Devon, Somerset, Cornwall, Buckinghamshire, Lincoln, Dorset, and Wiltshire.

The Martin family was fruitful, and members prospered on their various estates. One of the descendants of the Aethelhampton branch of the Martin family went to Long Melford in Suffolk; and from him was descended the branch that went to Ireland in the sixteenth century and to Antigua in the seventeenth century. An earlier Josiah Martin settled in County Dublin on an estate called Greencastle. His grandson, another Josiah, accompanied

3

Lord Essex to Ulster to suppress a rebellion during the reign of Queen Elizabeth I. Governor Martin's great-grandfather, Colonel George Martin of Whitehouse, was elected mayor or "the Sovereign of Belfast," Ireland, in September, 1649. He was a noted royalist who, according to family tradition, sent men and money to aid Charles I when he was fighting Cromwell in the north of England. After the civil war, Cromwell confiscated Colonel George's estates in Ireland. Fleeing Cromwell's wrath, Colonel George settled in Surinam on the northeast coast of South America, where he died before 1667. Family tradition further relates that Charles II gave Colonel George portraits of himself and Charles I. Although there is no mention of the estates in Ireland and England being restored to the family, an assumption can be made that part or all of them were returned to the family because they were held by the descendants of Colonel George in the eighteenth century.[1]

After England ceded Surinam to the Dutch in 1667, Colonel George's oldest son, Major Samuel Martin, went to Antigua and became a prosperous planter. His plantation was called Greencastle, after the Dublin estate and he derived his title from the island militia. He became speaker of the assembly in 1689 and a member of the royal council in 1693. Major Samuel made judicious investments in land and wise marriages to three wealthy women who had important political connections. The records indicate that Major Samuel was not the kindest master to his slaves; he deprived them of their traditional holiday when he ordered them to work on Christmas Day, 1701. Early on Christmas morning, the slaves broke into the house at Greencastle and murdered him in his bed. His wife, Lydia Thomas, escaped with her young children by hiding them in the sugarcane fields; the oldest child was Samuel who was about seven and one-half years old, his brother Josiah, and the two babies, William Thomas and an unidentified daughter.[2]

The brave and beautiful Lydia Thomas Martin was a true daughter of Colonel John Thomas, a military hero at the capture of the island of St. Christopher (St. Kitts) in 1690. She aroused the neighboring planters, who succeeded in reestablishing order. In 1708 Lydia Thomas Martin married Colonel Edward Byam, governor of the Leeward Islands. Her children by her first marriage approved of her second marriage, because Byam as a Christian name was given to some of their children. The murder of his father may have been one of several reasons why Colonel Samuel Martin spent time later converting his numerous slaves to Christianity and probably accounts for his kindly attitude toward his slaves.

Colonel Samuel Martin of Greencastle, Antigua, inherited large landholdings, both in Antigua and the British Isles. Janet Schaw, who visited Colonel Samuel, described the Martin family as one of the oldest in Antigua, noting that it had for "many generations enjoyed great power and riches. . . . " Colonel Samuel was a commander of the island militia and speaker of the assembly in the decade 1753-1763. When he was fifteen years old, he was sent to Cambridge University. On his way to the university the young Samuel had his portrait painted by the studio of Sir Godfrey Kneller. Like many of his relatives, Colonel Samuel had several fine miniature portraits made of himself at different stages of his life.[3] Both Samuel Sr. and his brother Josiah inherited plantations from their father and presumably Josiah and his younger brother, William Thomas Martin, who became an M.D., were given a comparable education. Colonel Samuel's only sister, who has not been identified by name, married a Colonel Chester of the royal army. His oldest brother, Josiah married a young widow, a Mrs. Chester, and by her he had a surviving daughter named Elizabeth. Josiah Martin operated a plantation on Antigua and he was president of the royal council there, 1748-1750. Later he emigrated to New York where he lived on his estate, Rock Hall, Far Rockaway, Long Island. After the death of his first wife, he returned to Antigua where he married Mary, daughter of William Yeamans, lieutenant governor of Antigua. By Mary he had at least four sons and two daughters; his son, Dr. Samuel Martin, is the best known of his children. Josiah Martin returned to Long Island and was a member of the New York royal council in 1754-1755, and aide-decamp to the governor, and a member of the first board of trustees for King's College (now Columbia University) in 1754.

The first wife of Colonel Samuel Martin of Greencastle was Frances, the daughter of John Yeamans, onetime attorney general of Antigua. By Frances, Colonel Samuel had a daughter Henrietta, and a son, Samuel, Jr. That son later became an influential member of Parliament, a consultant for the Crown's advisers, and an efficient expediter for the careers of his half-brothers, Henry, Josiah, and William Byam Martin. After the death of Frances, the colonel married Sarah Wyke Irish on May 1, 1728. Sarah was the daugher of Edward Wyke, the second governor of the island of Montserrat, and the widow of William Irish. By Sarah, the colonel had four surviving children, all of them sons. The oldest son, George, died when he was nineteen years old; the second son, Henry, rose to become the comptroller of the royal navy, was made a baronet, and was elected as a member of Parliament. The future governor, Josiah, was the third son by Sarah; he was born in Dublin, Ireland, on April 23, 1737. The youngest son, William Byam, was educated at Eton and joined the civil service in India. A friend of Warren Hastings, he rose rapidly to be commissioner of Calcutta; and in 1778 he was appointed Resident to the Mogul Court at Delhi, remaining there until 1781. He returned to England and settled on his estate Whiteknights in Berkshire. He was High Sheriff of the county in 1787. A perusal of the places where the children of Colonel Samuel Martin were born indicates his extensive traveling and business interests. Some of his children were born in Antigua, others in London, Essex, Dorsetshire, and Josiah in Dublin.

Colonel Samuel Martin noted in his family Bible that he had twenty-one children by his two wives; only five of them were alive in 1748. The proliferation of Josiahs, Samuels, and Henrys either reflected the Martin family pride in ancestors or a lack of imagination in naming their sons, or perhaps both. The two most influential men in molding the young Josiah's life were his half-brother Samuel, and their father, Colonel Samuel Martin. Samuel, Jr., was educated at Westminster School, London; and then in 1729, like his father, he attended Trinity College at Cambridge University. He received his legal education at the Inns of Court, Inner Temple, beginning in 1729 and was called to the bar in 1736. In London, he served as deputy agent for the island of Antigua in 1742-44; as agent for Montserrat in 1742-49, and for the island of Nevis in 1744-50. He took the opportunities afforded him by his position as agent for those sugar islands to move into the inner circles of the imperial advisors to the Crown. Samuel Jr. was made senior bencher or senior governing member of the Inner Temple in 1747. In the same year he was elected to the House of Commons and served his constituency in Camelford until 1768, when he was elected from Hastings, a treasury borough, where he served until his retirement in 1774. He was secretary to the chancellor of the exchequer from April, 1754, to November, 1755. As secretary of the treasury, Samuel held one of the key offices of the civil service. He served in the treasury on two occasions: November, 1756-April, 1757, and April, 1758-April, 1763. He also served as treasurer to the dowager princess of Wales (the mother of George III) from October, 1757, to February 8, 1772. On May 1, 1772, he was granted a pension of £1,200 for life. Samuel Martin, Jr., was said to have had great charm, singular good looks, and administrative ability; and he had an income of £10,000 a year.[4]

Samuel, Jr., the dedicated financial expert and public servant, seems to have attracted public attention on matters that suggest scandal on three separate occasions. First, Samuel sired an illegitimate son; second, after 1751, he joined the Pelham political party and in 1754 stood for election at Camelford on the government interest, with the alleged help of secret service money, against the Duke of Bedford's candidate; third, after George III became king in October, 1760, Samuel was involved in the differences between the new court and the Duke of Newcastle over the financing of the Prussian phase of the Seven Years War. Lord Bute retired as chief-minister in April, 1763. Samuel departed with Lord Bute (the king's former tutor and chief adviser); but by keeping up with Bute and retaining his position in the household of the dowager princess of Wales, he became a target for invective in the campaign waged against his patron. Following an attack by John Wilkes in the *North Briton*, Samuel spoke out against Wilkes in the debate in the House on November 15, 1763. That outburst led to a duel in which Wilkes, the self-proclaimed defender of the freedom of the press, was wounded. Both men fled to France; Wilkes to escape prosecution and Martin in case Wilkes died of his wound. In Paris both hotheads exchanged sober civilities.[5]

7

Thus far, it can be said that the Martin family had given allegiance to the crown, and later to the empire, beginning with their ancestor's adventure with William the Conqueror. They were aggressive in securing and defending property, prestige, and power. Moreover, they had the intelligence to prepare for and recognize opportunities when they occurred. They made judicious investments in land; and they married wealthy women who brought them land, slaves, and political connections within the empire. They exercised political and military power in their provinces and in some cases on the imperial level. They carefully husbanded their property to serve as a financial base for their political ambitions. Whenever they lost political power they managed to recoup and gain back their estates. Like many other gentry families, the Martins realized that their fortunes and their lives were best protected by their allegiance to the Crown and the empire.[6]

The economic base that supported the family of Colonel Samuel Martin was his plantation called Greencastle in Antigua and income from his estates in England and Ireland. The plantation produced sugar, molasses, and rum. In 1768, Colonel Martin estimated the value of the 605-acre plantation to be £43,333 (approximately $1,083,325). The estimate included 304 slaves; sugar works, including windmills, boiling house, curing house, rum distillery, and cisterns; dwelling house; stables; hospital house; coach house; 115 head of mules, oxen, cows, calves, bulls, and steers; and 6 wagons and carts, and the estimated value of his current sugar cane crop. The plantation was not always prosperous in the earlier years of the colonel's life because he was absent from Antigua on numerous occasions. He and his family often visited the British Islands and lived there for periods from two to ten years at a time. Most of the period from 1729 to 1748 was spent in England, and during that time his plantation was supervised by relatives and friends. He thought that the last two hired managers had cheated him for "they grew rich as I grew poor."[7]

Returning to Antigua in 1750, the colonel found his Negroes reduced to a small number, his stock of cattle decreased, his sugar works "all tumbling down," and his land "ten fold worse than it was naturally." He began a program of reconstruction to restore his plantation to its former productivity. However his restoration program required large outlays of capital to rebuild the sugar works and increase his supply of Negroes and cattle. He reinvested profits and borrowed funds; gradually his plantation once more was productive, although he admitted in 1776 that it was not yet restored to its former fertility.

Out of his experience in restoring his plantation to a profitable venture, Colonel Martin published a pamphlet describing his innovating methods in management, humane use of slaves, improvement in the breed of his livestock, and new methods in manuring and restoring the fertility of the soil. Martin belonged to that fraternity of contemporary gentlemen farmers in England who applied science to agriculture so as to increase their wealth and later their followers invested their profits in the emerging industrial revolution. The gentlemen farmers in England were Robert Bakewell, Jethro Tull, and Charles "Turnip" Townshend. Their methods were printed and publicized by Arthur Young. Martin adapted the principles of the "new husbandry" methods to his plantation and sugar factory. He seems to have been moving toward what is called in the twentieth century efficient management ideas of men and materials, capital investment, labor-saving techniques, and the creation of a superior product because his sugar commanded premium prices in the English market. His innovating ideas made him unique in the sugar culture of the West Indies.

All of Martin's agrarian ideas can be seen in his popular pamphlet, *An Essay upon Plantership, humbly inscribed to his Excellency George Thomas, Esq., Chief Governor of All the Leeward Islands, As a Monument to Ancient Friendship*, which was written in Antigua and first published there in 1755. The pamphlet went through seven editions and several reprints in England and the West Indies, and it was influential in persuading many British farmers and planters to use Martin's new ideas. Samuel Martin's essay reached an even larger audience when Arthur Young reprinted it in *Annals of Agriculture and Other Useful Arts*, in England in 1792. Besides the popularity of his pragmatic pamphlet, Martin's ideas were also spread by his numerous apprentices who carried copies of the essay with them when they left to become

successful planters. Colonel Martin was a kindly man but no fool;
if his apprentices proved to be honest and diligent he agreed to
teach them the arts of plantership, and evidently treated them as
he would the members of his large family.

Colonel Martin invested his profits in the plantation and the
education of his children. He was an intelligent and loving father
who studied his children and knew their strengths and weak-
nesses. The colonel planned the education of each of his sons and
helped prepare them for their careers in the emerging British empire. He was ably supported in this endeavor by his eldest son,
Samuel, the M.P., although there are hints in the extant correspondence that Samuel, Jr., did not always want to have a younger
sibling underfoot to hamper his busy schedule. Samuel, however,
would often walk and talk with his younger brothers in Hyde Park,
near his lodgings, when they were on a school holiday. They would
talk about the youngsters' needs and consider the possibility of careers in law, medicine, the imperial bureaus, and as officers in the
armed forces. There is also other evidence to indicate that Samuel
gave loving support to his father and his younger brothers. Young
Henry and Josiah attended an academy in England just as their
father and Samuel had done before them. Their mother, Sarah
Martin, died of fever and childbirth while they were in school; and
their father asked Samuel in May, 1748, to inform the youngsters of
her death with "the utmost prudence & tenderness." Young Henry
and Josiah admired their older brother for his success in the imperial city of London, and they adored their father. He often reminded them that Samuel, Jr., was "ye prop" of the family.[8]

The colonel wanted Josiah to enter the mercantile business and
help him supervise his plantation on Antigua. He consulted with
Samuel, Jr., on the proposal to return Josiah home when he
thought the younger boy was of "fit age, as much to his own, as to
your advantage and that of the family." The father suggested that
if Josiah were industrious, he might acquire enough money to purchase "a pretty settlement in ye delightful climate of North America, where he may carry on a trade and factorship" to and from Antigua, after establishing his reputation and gaining general
experience in the business. While Josiah was building a fortune in

trade, he could be of great service to the family and a great comfort "in my old age." In November, 1752, Josiah returned to Antigua with his tutor. Although his father thought that Josiah was happy with his plans to make him a merchant-planter, Josiah was not. He dreamed of being a dashing, young officer in the army and probably charming every desirable nubile maiden in the city of London. While he persisted in his dream, Josiah humored his father by continuing his studies in Antigua. In December, 1752, the fifteen-year-old Josiah asked his brother Samuel to send copies of "a Latin Tacitus," and "your translation of Tully's Orations." He advised his brother that their father wanted him to send "a cheap edition of Pope's Works, a Livy, a pocket Common Prayer for each of us," and "Psalms by Sternhold & Hopkinson." Besides the indication that they were Anglican, the request for the works of classical and modern writers suggested the cultivated tastes of the Martin family. It is probable that his father had asked his tutor to expose Josiah to the belles-lettres system of education, popularized by the English translation of Charles Rollin's essays that had had Voltaire's approval.[9]

The colonel continued his reports to Samuel on the progress of Josiah's education. In April, 1753, Josiah was very studious and interested in studying law, in August his temper, "behaviour, and knowledge" had improved; but at the end of January, 1754, his father observed that he was naturally indolent, "mulish in his temper, and tending much to ye vanity of dress and extravagance." By February the frustrated Josiah appealed to his older brother Samuel for help and advice, hoping that he would intercede for him. In a display of juvenile theatrics, Josiah described himself "dragging on a miserable & loathsome life for 3 or 4 years longer in this odious place & so that under my present circumstances Death is preferable." Despite that appeal, his brother did not encourage Josiah's aspiration for the army. Not only his dominating father's attitude toward him, but the weather led to Josiah's frustration. Antigua had a rainy season that began about July and ended in December; the dry season was from January through June. As an adult Josiah complained about the weather in Antigua; he never liked tropical weather because it affected his health. Much of the first fifteen years of his life was spent either in Dublin or near London, both relatively cool cities. Moreover, parochial St. John's was rural compared to the metropolitan centers, Dublin and London.[10]

Whenever Josiah looked at the Kneller portrait of his father at the age of fifteen, he was reminded that his father, at that age, had more freedom than he did. Moreover, The early death of Colonel Samuel's father freed him from a dominating father. Perhaps that was one of the reasons the colonel eased the pressure on Josiah and allowed him to visit London during the summer of 1754. In preparation for his visit, Josiah ordered a "cock hat" with silver lace; a visible sign that the seventeen-year-old, would-be dandy considered himself a man. In London, the handsome lad had an opportunity to sample the earthly delights of the metropolis as well as to have long talks about his future career while walking with Samuel in Hyde Park. After his return to Antigua, Josiah continued to try to persuade Samuel to become his advocate in convincing their father to let him enter the army.

Josiah's campaign to persuade his father to allow him to enlist in the army resulted in a compromise. He joined the Antigua militia, a mounted troop of gentlemen, in 1754. His father thought that Josiah was seized with a "military madness" but once he was in the militia, Josiah's studies began to show progress. He read Greek with facility, "and the Latin Classicks with haste, as well as Mr. Locke." He made "good progress in Euclid under a good Tutor, with whom I intend he shall read Astronomy and Opticks."[11]

Although Colonel Martin derived his title from the local militia, he did not approve of the regular army as a career for Josiah. He dropped his plans to make Josiah a merchant-planter and instead urged Josiah to study law in London. Persuaded by his father and older brother, Josiah finally agreed to study at the Inns of Court. Colonel Martin asked Samuel if he could secure any "genteel little post" in the Exchequer or Treasury which Josiah could fill at the same time he studied law. His farsighted father believed that Josiah's talents were good enough to ensure success in the law, "but if he should not have occasion to enter wholly into practice, yet it would be a qualification which may entitle him to hold some office in ye state, which he cannot hold with any grace as a mere layman." With the way prepared for him by his father and brother, Josiah Martin arrived in London early in 1756 to study law. Samuel's position on the governing board may have helped Josiah for on March 1, he was admitted to the Inner Temple.

After studying law for several months, Josiah returned to Antigua, still dreaming of an army career. The French and Indian War had spread to Europe and had become a world war. Britain and Prussia formed an alliance against France and Austria; Britain declared war on France on May 15, 1756. The new war encouraged Josiah's "military madness" and both his father and his brother sought to temper it by securing for Josiah an honorary ensign in the regiment stationed at Antigua. On December 17 Josiah joined the Fourth Foot Regiment as an ensign. When he wrote Samuel to congratulate him on his appointment as secretary of the treasury, he also thanked his brother for helping him secure his army commission. In two years Josiah was commissioned a lieutenant, and early in 1759 he was on the expedition to Martinique. His father hoped that the fatigues of the voyage and the hard camp life would cure his son of his "soldier-mania." He hoped his experience with the army would "give him a turn to civil life, and a better sphere of action." Late in December, 1759, Josiah returned to Antigua after participating in the campaign to take the French island of Guadeloupe. Apparently the Guadeloupe expedition and Josiah's success as a "spirited good Soldier in every important attack" convinced his father that an army career might be a stepping stone to a civil office for his son. Moreover, the colonel was elated that his son Henry was recently promoted to captain in the navy.[12]

When Samuel learned that Josiah was in Canada, he wrote their father in August that he hoped Josiah had joined with "General Amherst in time to reap a share in the glory of compleating the reduction of Canada." With the fall of Montreal on September 8, 1760, the governor of Canada, the Marquis de Vaudreuil, surrendered Canada to the British. From Montreal Josiah described to his brother the reduction of Canada. Amherst assigned Martin's regiment the task of rebuilding the fortifications of Ft. St. Frederic, which had been renamed Crown Point. Exhilarated by the success of British arms, the twenty-three-year-old Josiah described the Canadians "as a hardy race of people far beyond the people of our colonies in point of Stature." He noted that the Canadians had established "a certain equality among them" which he thought extraordinary. He believed that it would be easy to subvert their equality by allowing these "Poor Settlers to become the prey of the more opulent & ambitious." Martin's elitist attitude toward foreign commoners was a view shared by many Britons. [13]

While Josiah was participating in the conquest and reconstruction of Canada, the colonel and Samuel were trying to advance his career. His father suggested that the money from the sale of Josiah's subaltern commission be used for "the purchase of a Majority, and then ye post of Lieut. Colonel, with the remainder of ye fortune I intend for him, . . . in obtaining these promotions, as speedily as money, and your vigour can effect it." The father saw military promotion as a stepping stone "to ye Government of New York, or some other of less value." Moreover, the promotions might help Josiah "to captivate a Lady of Character and good fortune at New York, where there are many heiresses to vast Estates (which are now likely to rise much in value) who seem fond of our military men." If Josiah were so lucky as "to catch such a Gold Finch, it will facilitate his rise in ye army, and to a Government: if not it will be a noble retreat, under all other disappointments." In the eighteenth century marriages of the upper classes were seldom made in heaven, but often they were arranged to preserve and develop wealth and landholdings. Both Josiah's father and grandfather made several prudent marriages which greatly increased their family fortune. [14]

While stationed at Crown Point, Josiah visited his uncle, Josiah, and his family at their estate, Rock Hall, in the Far Rockaways on Long Island. There he renewed friendship with numerous cousins and met many of the New York gentry. Young Josiah's frequent visits to Rock Hall gave him an opportunity to court his own cousin, Elizabeth. On January 8, 1761, Josiah wrote his brother that he planned to marry Elizabeth and the young couple were married a few days later. The marriage occurred long before Samuel received Josiah's letter. Both Samuels, father and son, were offended and disappointed because Josiah had not asked his father for permission to marry. Obviously Josiah did not know that his father and brother had plans for his possible marriage to an heiress. In July the disappointed colonel wrote to Samuel: "Your brother Josiah has foolishly married his Cousin Bettsey Martin, against her father's consent and mine." Then followed a revealing comment about Josiah: "Yet as good Providence produces good out of human folly, I hope that will cure him of two vices, that of women, and extravagance."[15]

Uncle Josiah gave the young couple some money and possibly slaves and horses, because he stated in his will that he had already "paid to her husband her fortune, as may be seen by my book." In his will Uncle Josiah left two of his daughters £1,000 each with some horses, and slaves; possibly Elizabeth received a dowry of similar value. Five months after his marriage, Josiah asked his father for forgiveness for "this single deviation." It should be noted that both Josiah and Elizabeth defied convention when they married for love.[16]

The growing awareness of the financial obligations of marriage caused Josiah to search for ways in which to increase his income. Elizabeth was carrying their child, the future Mary Elizabeth. Josiah again turned to his father and brother, as they had both anticipated he would and asked for their help in purchasing a commission of major. His father approved a proposed trip to England to purchase the commission, although he commented to Samuel that Josiah had departed for England leaving his "wife big with child." Nevertheless, the kindly father had continued Josiah's annual allowance of £100. According to one historian, a gentleman in the English colonies needed £100 annually to live in comfort. For a man to maintain a higher standard of living, an income of £450 per annum was essential. Josiah obviously needed more income if he were to live in the manner of the New York gentry.[17]

In London, Captain Josiah recruited soldiers, visited his brother Henry's wife, Eliza Anne, and consulted with Samuel

15

about advancement in the army. The faithful Samuel secured two fairly rapid promotions for him. When Josiah Martin returned to New York he served as a major in the 103rd Regiment or the Volunteer Hunters with Charles Lee of American Revolution fame. On December 24, 1762, Martin was commissioned lieutenant colonel of the Twenty-second Regiment of Foot, later called Gage's Regiment.[18]

Although Josiah received help from his father in purchasing a commission, Colonel Samuel reminded him that Elizabeth had not brought much of a dowry to him. He added: "This is always ye consequence of hasty marriages for which people may mark themselves, and you must do ye best you can" by economizing. His father continued: "I cannot without injustice make a difference among my children of equal merit, yr. eldest bro. excepted, who is ye prop of the family." Josiah thought that if his father saw Elizabeth and their child he might approve of the marriage. He promised that they would visit him in the next few months.[19]

With the peace settlement of the Seven Years' War in February, 1763, Josiah realized that opportunities for advancement in the army would be limited. Although Martin knew that he and his family could stay with his aged father on the Antigua plantation, he wanted to live on his own place. About that time he was transferred to the Sixty-eighth Regiment which was stationed in Antigua. Once more Josiah turned to his brother for advice. He visited Samuel in London in the summer of 1764, but could find no satisfactory solution for his financial problems. While in London, Josiah had a miniature portrait of himself painted by the fashionable Jeremiah Meyer, enamel-painter to the king. Realizing that he could not find opportunities for advancement in London, and lonely for his family, Josiah borrowed from his brother £200 to pay his debts so he could return to Antigua. He was reunited with his family and his father on September 15, 1764.[20]

Snug on his island retreat on the edge of the empire, the young Josiah was aroused to passionate declarations by the Stamp Act crisis that inflamed the mainland colonies as well as the sugar colonies. The first direct tax ever levied by Parliament upon America, the stamp tax, was passed on March 8 to become effective November 1, 1765. When the protest on the American mainland spread to Antigua, the Martin family was directly affected. Writing to his brother about the repeal of the Stamp Act, Josiah said:

Do not ye friends of Americans begin now to see that it was highly impolitic to grant to the *Contumacy* of this people, such a triumph as they did by absolutely repealing ye Stamp Act? If they are so willfully blind as to maintain ye propriety of that measure I will venture to pronounce without the Gift of prophecy, that their posterity will long rue their dastardly concession. The unnatural jealousy of the Mother Country still subsists & the leading people continue to encourage the consumption of her Manufactures by precept & example.[21]

Josiah's irritation about the stamp tax crisis was exacerbated by the New York assembly's refusal for full compliance with the provisions of the Quartering Act as requested by General Thomas Gage. Gage, commander of all British forces in America, had his headquarters in New York City. When the assembly refused full compliance, protests and violence ensued which soon equated, in the minds of the colonists the Quartering Act with the Stamp Act as instruments of British oppression. Tension continued to grow and the assembly was prorogued on December 19. Finally, on June 8, 1767, the assembly voted £3,000 for Gage.

From New York Josiah complained to his brother Samuel about the colonists and their defiance of Parliament:

This country is much alarmed by the late proceedings of the H of C & fearfully expects the arrival of a Packet which it is conjectured will bring the result of its deliberations upon the Contumacious resistance of this Province to the measures of Govt. Under this apprehension however, I perceive no disposition to compliance among the people. The most moderate of their politicians, holding the opinion, that by receiving the Act of P. for billetting troops, they will not only admit its supreme authority over the Colonies in the present instance but yield to it the right of having taxes upon America; a Power which they cannot consent should reside in Great Britain, who hath lately so flagrantly invaded their liberty, by requiring their contribution, to the support of a state, to which they are indebted for nothing, but their lives, Liberty & Property.[22]

Josiah was critical of some American newspapers for their scurrilous and "inflammatory misrepresentations" that helped to develop "a spirit of independence." He may have had in mind John Holt's press that vigorously supported the local Sons of Liberty in their successful efforts to persuade many New Yorkers of the unconstitutionality of the Stamp Act. Martin thought a crisis was at hand "when Britain must vigorously assert her sovreignty as resign it to a weak, timid, licentious mob, wished by a few affected Patriots." Martin believed the bold triumph of America "in the repeal of the Stamp Act, hath so inspired this people with ideas of their power & importance" that they would "dispute the Authority of Britain in every case" in the future. He thought it was time for coercive measures to bring the Americans to reason, and that once the "spirit of Govt." was shown to them they would cease their resistance. Thus, Martin was arguing for coercive measures against the colonies almost seven years before Parliament passed the Coercive Acts in response to the Boston Tea Party.[23]

Resistance had spread to Antigua and its sister islands. Josiah, who was living in Antigua at the time of the Stamp Act crisis, described the defiance of the Antiguans: "The uproar of the colonies against the Stamp Act hath inspired the little West Indian Communities with like jealousies, & apprehensions." He declared that the assembly of Antigua had proved to him "that the bond, liberty hath not less the power of intoxication, in a Country supported by barbarian bondage" than in other parts of the empire. The guard of the king's regiment suffered daily insults. Instead of employing a "Peace officer to act in conjunction with the King's Troops," the Antiguan assembly resolved that hiring a peace officer would be an infringment of "the Subjects' liberty in the person of the Constable." That opinion Josiah thought repugnant to common sense and established practice, but it was "cherished by many people who knew better." As lieutenant colonel of the local regiment, the Sixty-eighth, Josiah saw the Antiguan protestors opposing him "as servant of the Crown." The island protests continued and tensions grew which caused the assembly to support the stamp tax. The only member to oppose the assembly in this matter was Josiah's father, Colonel Samuel. Josiah told his brother "my Father singly held a contrary opinion & treated their objections with desired ridicule." Like his powerful political friend, Lord Bute, Samuel,

Jr., had opposed repeal of the Stamp Act; and on February 22, 1766, he had voted against the repeal measure. Josiah and Samuel, Jr., supported a strictly legal philosophy in the Stamp Act crisis, whereas their father supported the protestors; a reversal of the usual classic behavioral pattern of father and sons.[24]

During and after the Stamp Act crisis, Josiah continued to seek ways to increase his income and free himself from financial dependence on his father. His experience with the Antiguan protestors as they harassed his regiment increased his disillusionment with army life. Moreover, he strongly disapproved of abuses within the army. He complained to his brother Samuel about what he called "surplusages in the soldiers' pay that they did not receive," a reference to a common practice in the British army in which colonels of the various regiments were given allotments for the pay of their troops, their clothing, and their hospital expenses. Those colonels had a "pecuniary advantage" when they were given money to clothe and equip their men out of the net "off-reckonings; that is from the total pay of the non-commissioned officers and men of their regiments," after subsistence pay had been given and the customary deductions had been made. Depending on the size of their regiments, the colonels could manipulate allotments for clothing and equipment by making arrangements with suppliers so that each colonel could realize a substantial profit for himself. On January 21, 1766, from Antigua, Josiah sent a letter to his brother Samuel by a fellow officer, a Captain Munro, who was paymaster of the Sixty-eighth regiment. The letter carried by Munro would explain, Josiah said, the colonels' surplusage money scandal as represented to Lord Barrington, the secretary for war.[25]

Josiah had hoped that his brother and his powerful friends could have persuaded Lord Barrington to alleviate the abuse of the off-reckonings money which he called the "surplusages." Barrington apparently ignored the request for a reform, for Josiah later criticized Barrington for his lack of interest and his unwillingness to pay the regimental surgeon 100 guineas. The rates of pay for the soldiers had been set in the reign of William III when the first act of Parliament was made for regulating the army. The surgeon's rate was £20. 13s. 1d. a year, over £80 less than what

Josiah wanted for surgeons. In all probability Barrington did not see Josiah Martin's letter concerning the colonels and regimental payments, because it first crossed the desk of Samuel Martin, Jr. Samuel knew the political power of the colonels who were members of Parliament, and he understood Lord Barrington's potent friendship with George III. The conservative Samuel may have dismissed Josiah's reforming spirit and impatience with corruption and procrastination in the army as a problem that could not be solved by anyone. Nevertheless, Josiah's reforming spirit suggests that he was a true son of Colonel Samuel, who also abhorred inefficiency and waste and practiced ethics in his everyday life.[26]

Disillusioned with the army, Josiah's future looked bleak. His lieutenant colonelcy did not provide enough income for his growing family. Moreover, his brother Samuel was considering retiring from his seat in Parliament. Josiah advised his brother that if he did retire he wanted him to sell his commission, because he could expect nothing more in the army "after your secession from Parliament." Josiah added that he would forsake "with great concern a profession to which I have rooted myself near ten years."[27]

On July 11, 1766, his father's intimate friend, Governor George Thomas of Antigua, gave Josiah a temporary appointment to the royal council. His brother Samuel, tongue-in-cheek, called the council the "Sugar Cane Peerage." Prestigious locally, the appointment was not financially rewarding, but it did give Martin experience in colonial government. Josiah continued to explore ways to improve his financial position. He told his brother Samuel that he did not know where he would get enough money to support his family. He confided that he had gotten over his juvenile admiration of the army with its "gawdy charms." He wanted to sell his commission and buy lands in the conquered islands of the Caribbean. Samuel's delay in answering Josiah's letters may have been due to his busy schedule, but he may have been procrastinating so as to encourage his brother to consider a number of alternatives.[28]

Colonel Samuel told his eldest son: "Poor Joe is much down in spirits by the fatigues in his Regiment, by getting Children fast, and having no hopes of farther advancement in his profession. He talks of selling his Commission and settling in one of ye new Islands as a Planter: a sorry alternative. I advised him against it, at least till he has your concurrence." The colonel had earlier proposed a plan to Samuel that he should help his father gain a governorship in the conquered islands so that he could favor his sons by granting them crown lands. The colonel had visited St. Vincent and Dominica in 1765. Colonel Samuel's interest in a colonial governorship may have been one of several factors in his later enthusiastic support for Josiah's appointment to the governorship of North Carolina. What the father failed to do, the son accomplished. Later both the colonel and Josiah changed their minds about the alleged attractions of plantation life in the conquered islands. Josiah determined that the northern provinces of North America were more desirable than the Caribbean, not only because of the temperate climate, but because of the possibility of securing a civil office. He asked his brother to help him get "an office of emolument, such as Collector of New York or Boston," or the office of secretary of a colony "which is a Patent Office" and should be profitable.[29]

Josiah decided to move in the spring of 1767 to New York where economic opportunities might be more plentiful than in Antigua. Preparing for his move, Josiah ordered from London medicines, hunting rifles, some magnificent silver service, and a splendid library. Books on his list included works by Julius Caesar, Thucydides, Longinus, Xenophon, Plutarch, Terence, Bolingbroke, Clarendon, Milton, Addison, Fielding, Pope, Swift, Montaigne, Newton, Rousseau, Robertson, Rollins, Ben Jonson, Rabelais, Sidney, and Grotius. He also ordered Burn's *Justice of the Peace*, and volumes of the *Spectator*, *Tatler*, and *Guardian*. For Elizabeth his wife, he ordered the "Compleat Housewife by E. Smith." His order also included "Boyer's French Dictionary," "Martinieri's Geographic Dictionary," "Lilly's Grammar," and Vauban's "Treatise of Fortification." Josiah Martin's book order is indicative of his knowledge of French, Latin, and Greek and his taste for classical and modern literature.[30]

Josiah asked his brother Samuel to secure a mandamus on the New York council for a land grant that was available to him as an army officer. Samuel was to pay the charges out of the sale of Josiah's army commission. Samuel reprimanded Josiah for wanting to be an "exciseman," a collector of the customs. Josiah admitted "inconsistency of my first project of transplanting myself to St. Vincent," which resulted from the alluring description given him by a friend and from his own "vexed mind." Josiah assured his brother that his plan to "retreat to N. America was the offspring of a deliberate view" because of the impossibility of achieving any financial success for his family in Antigua. Another urgent reason he gave was his family's ill health; Elizabeth has miscarried of twins in the spring of 1767.[31]

As an officer Josiah had to secure the king's permission before he could go to New York, and that Samuel obtained for his brother. Josiah arranged for a fellow officer in Antigua to look after his regiment. He and his family arrived in New York on May 20, 1767. There he discovered that the office of adjutant general of the British army on the continent had been taken by a Lieutenant Colonel Maitland, but the office of deputy quartermaster general was still vacant. Pleased with the climate, but unhappy with country living, Martin explored every rumor that he heard about vacancies in the army and the civil provincial offices. When he learned that all staff officers subordinate to the commander in chief in North America were paid only ten shillings per diem, his interest in staff offices disappeared at once. In the meantime, Samuel tried to persuade Lord Granby to appoint Josiah to the quartermaster office for North America. Granby refused the request, but agreed to transfer Josiah from Antigua to North America when the first lieutenant colonelcy became vacant. Samuel cautioned his brother that if the vacancy did not soon materialize he should return to Antigua before his leave expired. He added that he was reluctant to sell Josiah's commission for him.[32]

Josiah faced a difficult situation when he arrived in New York with his family and his father, because he was concerned about his father's declining health and the health of Elizabeth. He did not wish to be dependent upon his father's income; he wanted to make his own way in the bureaucratic world of the empire. The difficulty was that his father preferred the warmer climate of Antigua and Josiah detested it. After a short stay in New York, Colonel

Samuel returned to his plantation. The colonel wrote in September to Samuel that he had learned that Josiah was in good health but that Elizabeth was "again breeding sick." Then followed a frank comment about the Martin men: "That fellow will kill ye poor Woman with kindness, as I did your good Mother and his. But as old Bishop Burnet sayed upon the like occasion, it is better the wife should go to Heaven, than the husband go to Hell, by deviating from the marriage bed."[33]

Concern for Josiah and his family seemed to be the motivation behind Colonel Samuel's trip to New York. He planed to "purchase a Farm, which may be the basis of a better fortune for my family, when America is ye Seat of British Government." The colonel's faith in the development of Anglo-America was not shared by his children. He sailed to Philadelphia in late October, 1767. While in Philadelphia, the colonel visited several old friends, including Governor John Penn, grandson of William Penn, and several friends of Sir George Thomas, a former governor of Antigua. In New York, the colonel was entertained by the governor, Sir Henry Moore, who was a former Jamaican governor, General Thomas Gage, John Watts, the merchant prince, and other prominent members of the New York establishment.[34]

After the hospitality in the mansions of the elite in Philadelphia and New York, the colonel was disappointed when he arrived at the homes of his son and brother on Long Island. The colonel reported to Samuel that Josiah was "as fat as a hog," and lived in "a poor Country hovel, without accommodation either for me, my Servants, or horses: by which means I am disappointed of spending the winter with him, and for ye same reason with my brother, who is worse situated: so that I resolve to return for Antigua next February. . . . " In all probability the old gentleman was given to exaggeration because he had decided to return to Antigua in February rather than November. Despite his pique, the colonel's generous nature again surfaced. Learning that Josiah's expenses exceeded his income, he wrote to Samuel: "I wish you had interest enough to get him one of the best Governments of these Provinces." The kindly colonel later wrote a codicil to his will, adding a legacy of £1,000 each for Josiah's three daughters to the £3,000 he had already bequeathed to Josiah.[35]

Josiah delayed his return to Antigua when he discovered that the barrackmaster generalship would become vacant if the current occupant was appointed lieutenant governor of Virginia. Josiah asked Samuel to help him secure one of those vacant offices. He admitted that he was in the predicament of a "sinking man catching at every hope of deliverance." Josiah needed his powerful brother's help because Sir Jeffrey Amherst favored a Colonel Robinson for the Virginia office. Moreover, General Gage wanted his brother-in-law, a captain, to have the quartermaster office. Josiah again postponed his trip because a smallpox epidemic swept through New York City and he wanted his children to be innoculated. Samuel continued, unsuccessfully, to search for a preferment for Josiah. Finally Josiah and his family returned to Antigua to visit his father in May, 1769. They were accompanied by Uncle Josiah and his family.[36]

The visit was a short one. Josiah arrived in Antigua in the middle of May, but by mid-June he was in Philadelphia on his way back to New York. Why was the visit cut short? Josiah's "old sickness" returned. He told his brother: "It has extinguished every spark of military ambition in me." His father agreed that Josiah should return to New York to improve his health. The colonel described to Samuel, Jr., Josiah's illness; he was much "indisposed with the pain in his side, his old Complaint, which attacked him as soon as he came into the warm climate, which cannot agree with him either in body or mind." Illness caused Josiah to lose weight, and he could not rest at night. After ten days of ill health, his father advised him to return to New York on a ship that was about to leave. Josiah took his father's advice and rushed to the ship leaving behind his pregnant wife and their three children under the care of his father.[37]

Fourteen days after he left Antigua, Josiah Martin was called to rejoin his regiment. He advised Governor William Woodly of Antigua that he had asked for the king's permission to retire for reasons of ill health and he could not return to his regiment. The desperate Josiah urged his brother to place his army commission in the hands of James Meyrick, a London merchant, for an immediate sale. His brother reported on August 2 that Meyrick would sell it for £3,500. Josiah's financial worries were momentarily lessened by the news that Samuel had deposited with Meyrick a modest inheritance of over £374 from his aunt, Mrs. Henrietta Irish. To alleviate his brother's worries further, the generous Samuel cancelled the £500 debt Josiah owed him for past loans; a gesture that Josiah refused. To reimburse his brother, Josiah wrote a draft on Meyrick for £500 chargeable against the future sale of his commission.[38]

The patient Samuel advised Josiah that he knew of no patent places or preferments that were "sold fairly & by open permission: except a few in the Courts of Justice." The practice of the purchase of an individual civil office was confidential, if not secret, in the eighteenth century. Eventually abuses developed; for example, a deputy might be sent to fulfill the duties of the office while absentee officeholders remained in England. Parliamentary reform later ended those practices. Yet in the eighteenth century there were offices sold to the highest bidder, and Josiah Martin knew that. After drawing bills of credit on Samuel, Josiah sailed for London to consult with him.[39]

Following Samuel's advice, he petitioned the privy council for 20,000 acres of land in northern New York on the basis of his service as a veteran of the Seven Years' War. The privy council referred Martin's petition to the Board of Trade on May 10, 1770; on the same day members of the board agreed to recommend Martin's petition to the king. Before his ship sailed for New York on May 24, Josiah paid all bills except his indebtedness to his brother. He appealed once more to Samuel to persuade their father to help him financially so he could purchase a patent office.[40]

In August, 1770, after a passage of eleven weeks and four days from England via Philadelphia, Josiah was reunited with his family on Long Island. Ordinarily a voyage from England would take no more than four or five weeks in good weather. Josiah's voyage was troubled by heat, storms, and adverse winds that seriously restricted water rations for crew and passengers. Martin believed Providence saved him on that trip. The voyage gravely affected his health and may have shortened his life.[41] Safe in the bosom of his family, Martin learned of the confusion and anxiety of some of his friends who were concerned about the New York merchants' boycott of British manufactures. The nonimportation associations of merchants in the colonies had made the repeal of the Townshend duties a condition for dropping their sanctions against British goods. A house-to-house poll in New York City, July 7-9, revealed that its inhabitants favored resuming imports of all but tea and other articles actually bearing a duty. A fortnight after his return Josiah was exultant when he informed Samuel of the defection of some of the New York merchants from the boycott. Exercising caution, Josiah enclosed his letter to Samuel in a second envelope to conceal his conclusions "concerning the present aspect of men's minds here with respect to Great Britain which being discovered might be attended with inconveniences." As the New York merchants began to drop out of the boycott, their actions antagonized merchants in other colonies. Josiah saw the petty animosities among the provinces reviving in that each colony increasingly distrusted the other.[42]

Josiah's ambition soared to new heights when he learned that his father had agreed to let him use part of his inheritance of £1,500 to pay for a preferment in North America. He wrote on September 22, 1770, to tell Samuel the news, and he also reported that New York's Governor Henry Moore had died. There was a rumor circulating that Lord Dunmore would become the next governor of New York. Josiah's imagination was fired with the possibilities of a civil office and buying some land for speculation. On October 5 he received the long-awaited king's mandamus to buy lands in New York. He sought Samuel's judgment on buying lands in British East Florida because his father had described the opportunities in East Florida which bloomed like "the Garden of Paradise." Moreover, his father had asked Samuel to explore the possibilities of securing a land grant for Josiah and a governorship for him there.[43]

As Josiah made plans for his family's economic future, his faithful brother Samuel was busily working in his behalf. Negotiations with the secretary of state for the colonies, Lord Hillsborough, began to bear fruit. With the death of the governor of New

York, Hillsborough reshuffled three governorships of the thirteen colonies in North America. On December 1 Hillsborough told the Board of Trade that the king approved Lord Dunmore as governor of New York. Eleven days later, with the news of the death of Lord Botetourt, governor of Virginia, Hillsborough again reshuffled the governorships. He advised the Board of Trade that the king had been pleased to appoint Dunmore governor of Virginia. Hillsborough then transferred William Tryon from North Carolina to New York, and he appointed Josiah Martin governor of North Carolina.[44]

Both Hillsborough and Samuel Martin wrote letters to Josiah Martin on December 13, 1770, notifying him of his appointment as governor of North Carolina. The official news of the preferment did not reach Josiah Martin for two and one-half months because of the time and distance required to cross the wintry seas. Unofficially, the news reached him earlier. In February, 1771, an unidentified English newspaper brought from Boston to New York gave an account of Governor Tryon's transfer to New York and the appointment of "Henry Martin" to succeed Tryon in North Carolina. A friend of Martin, a Colonel Maitland in New York to whom the news story was reported, concluded that Josiah, not Henry, was the appointee referred to in the news story. Maitland sent his congratulations to Josiah. When Josiah received this news, his baggage was on board ship. He had been waiting for two days to sail for St. Augustine, Florida, where he hoped to investigate the possibility of a settlement. Still not sure of the authenticity of the report, but persuaded by his friends, Josiah delayed his departure.[45]

Taking advantage of the delay, Josiah consulted a physician. Examination revealed that he was suffering from a fistula believed to have been caused by "my sufferings & bad living at sea, on my tedious voyage from England last summer." His illness proved to be time-consuming and painful; eventually he had to have four operations. For five months Martin was delayed from going to New Bern, where Tryon's legacy of problems awaited him. Martin's suffering was alleviated to some extent by the joy he experienced in receiving on March 1, 1771, from Hillsborough the official notice of his appointment and a letter from Samuel telling him about it. Martin immediately sent Hillsborough a formal acceptance. His letter to his brother was grateful, humble, and affectionate for the "miracle" of his appointment:

I cannot say how much I am obliged to you for this gleam of prosperity; so opportune; so critical; so consoling to my afflicted mind labouring under all the pain, & solicitude that can attend a desperate fortune. Ten thousand thanks to you for this relief; infinitely the more acceptable to me, as I am willing to consider it a proof of the conciliation of your heart towards me, much changed by my misconduct; the circumstance of my life, I solemnly assure you, the most painful to my mind, not unacquainted with distress & anguish.

Although confined by illness, Martin wrote to Governor Tryon for information about North Carolina. Josiah mentioned to Samuel that Mrs. Tryon had suggested that the two governors exchange portraits. Martin agreed to her request.[46]

Martin's illness increased his concern about the finances required for his position as governor. He anticipated that he would have to affect a standard of living very unsuitable to his current resources. He confided to Samuel: "There is however no help for it; and all I can do is not to exceed in pageantry, what may be strictly proper & necessary in my situation." Josiah recalled

. . . that as I walked with you one day in the Park just before I left London; speaking of the possibility of the event which your friendship hath so soon brought to pass, you observed that in such cases I should want all manner of equipment; to which I answered I had been obliged to buy some little furniture which might serve until I could supply myself from England.

When he told Samuel that he would write to a Mr. Ottley, the merchant, for a modest coach, he added a wry comment: "a piece of furniture indispensably necessary I apprehend to my mock state."[47]

His father learned about Josiah's appointment on April 25. Delighted, he promised to send Josiah a mulatto girl and a Negro cook, his post chaise, and all his chinaware. He told Samuel he would have sent Josiah his silver plate except that he had already promised it to him. In addition to the furnishings and slaves, the colonel arranged to send sugar and rum to Philadelphia and New York for Josiah to sell or credit to his account. He believed that these items would bring more than £600 on the open market and the proceeds could help pay for the governor's commission. He had been told that the fee would amount to about £500. In addition Josiah would receive the promised £1,500 sterling and £1,000 for the purchase of a summer retreat that could be used later by him and his family when he retired from the governor's office. All in all these were very generous gifts from a loving and wealthy father who had seen his dream come true for another of his sons. Why was the colonel so generous? Earlier In March the father had written Samuel about the possibility of a civil office for Josiah. He thought Josiah had an advantage over some of his competitors because "His character will I think bear that of good sense, good nature, and probity." While that analysis is a different one from his earlier comments about Josiah's indolence and mulishness, it indicates that the father believed Josiah had matured enough to accept responsibility, and that he would do a good job as governor.[48]

Governor Martin shared a common denominator with other colonial governors who were members of the gentry class, active in politics, and experienced in business and in military service. Martin belonged to that minority group of governors, such as Henry Ellis of Georgia and Thomas Pownall of Massachusetts. Since he was a lad Martin imbibed colonial and imperial politics at his father's table when the colonel entertained visiting and local politicians, business agents, and planters. He shared his father's pride in the experience of his grandfather in the Antiguan government and his elder brother's position in the imperial government in London.

Josiah quoted from Hillsborough's letter when he complimented Samuel: "I have the greatest satisfaction in communicating to you this gracious mark of the King's favour on account of the regard & esteem I have for your brother, & my friend, Mr. Samuel Martin." He mentioned that to Samuel because he would know "in what light to consider it." Josiah was grateful to his brother for the preferment "for unknown, & insignificant in myself, it could never be imagined that I should suppose it the reward of my own merit," but as a favor conferred on Samuel. Aware of the responsibilities of the office of governor, Josiah wanted to prepare himself for that office. He told his brother:

The office of Chancellor is I own to me the most formidable part of a Governor's business. I shall be very thankful to you for instruction on this head, as well as on every other subject. Your studies in the former part of your life may probably have made you acquainted with some books which may tend to guide my judgment.[49]

While Martin was being treated for his illness, he remained in New York City. There he received visitors, listened to political gossip, and tried to sort out the rumors from the facts. He learned that the Virginia government was worth at least £10,000 a year, and Lord Dunmore wanted the appointment. Dunmore told Josiah that he had asked to stay in New York and that Tryon might take his place in Virginia. However, this did not happen; Dunmore went to Virginia and Tryon to New York. Martin received his credentials as governor of North Carolina on May 1, and he wrote to Hillsborough to explain his delay in going to North Carolina.[50]

Underneath the joy of the appointment as governor, there was a foreboding uneasiness that threatened Josiah Martin's well-being. There was trouble and danger in North Carolina for William Tryon and for Josiah Martin. Disturbing accounts of the Regulator rebellion had appeared in the New York newspapers in October and November, 1770. Martin's information about the Regulators was fragmentary. He had not received letters from Tryon or Hillsborough about the rebellion. Martin told his brother Samuel: "Governor Tryon's present situation in No. Carolina promises me no such tranquility as is there to be enjoyed." He recounted how "near one thousand" Carolinians were in arms and open defiance of all law and government, and that Tryon was marching against them. Josiah added:

All I can learn of this commotion is that the Inhabitants of Two Counties, under the influence of & at the instigation of four or five factions, artfull

& designing villains, refuse to comply with the assessments of law upon pocket, that the oppressive exactions of the Public officers are unpunishable & on this ground they oppose the execution of all law;—Thus by violence enjoy an exemption from taxes. The spirit with which the majority of the Province seems disposed to act, under the direction of Governor Tryon cannot fail to restore very soon, the affairs of that Province to good order.[51]

Martin thought that coercive measures should be used with extreme caution on the Regulators. Josiah told his brother, that he "despised such a secession of a tumultous rabble, yet in the delicate situation of a Civil Governor," he thought it might be embarrassing. He decided that "the nice limits & prescription of our constitution, according to modern interpretation, allow little latitude for such vigorous exertion as appears under certain circumstances, necessary to its very being notwithstanding." Josiah speculated that the first appearance of Tryon and his troops would suffice to quell the "present disorders in Carolina," yet he thought the "evil" might break out again. Early in June, Martin received a letter from Tryon in which the governor spoke of military preparations "Against the Insurgents but not whence the disorder has arisen." Near the end of the month, Martin learned that Tryon had defeated the Regulators, "killed, wounded & taken prisoners of upwards of 300." Martin did not envy Tryon's achievement because it was like "a sacrifice—like a slaughter of defenceless, deluded sheep. The history of this peoples discontent I have not however been able to learn & I can therefore form no judgment." Martin expected to learn more about the Regulators when he consulted with Governor Tryon after the latter's arrival in New York City sometime in early July. Martin had been uneasy about his health and "the Commotions in Carolina," but he advised his brother: "I shall be a new man & I hope to find a field for the exercise of mercy & the display of the olive branch."[52]

Hillsborough wrote Martin on May 4 advising him to continue the same measures against the Regulators that Tryon had used so successfully. By emulating Tryon, Hillsborough told Martin "you will have the merit of restoring peace and transquility to the Province." There is no indication that Martin received Hillsborough's dispatch while in New York. Martin arrived at his preliminary conclusions about the Regulators before he received Hillsborough's dispatch or consulted with Tryon.[53]

From North Carolina Governor Tryon reported to Hillsborough on June 29 that he had received his dispatches and circular letters that contained certain instructions. Since he was commanded by His Majesty "to repair without loss of time to the government of New York, I am constrained to leave such things as remain to be done to the discretion of Governor Martin, as I embark tomorrow for my new government." He sent a similar dispatch to the Board of Trade on the same day, advising it that he would leave for Governor Martin the members' requests for amendments to laws.[54]

Martin met with Tryon in New York City on July 9, and the two governors discussed some of the problems of North Carolina. Their discussions were limited because Tryon was occupied "between business, and ceremony, on his arrival in his new Government." Martin declared that he was much indebted to Tryon for the "candor & politeness with which he answered all my inquiries." When Tryon assured him that North Carolina was in a peaceful state Martin postponed his departure. He hoped to secure useful information and "instruction" from Tryon concerning the affairs of North Carolina, "in which I was not dissappointed." Martin advised Hillsborough: "I should be wanting in justice to that Gentleman if I omitted this occasion, to acknowledge my great obligations to him, for his free, & open communication. . . ."[55]

As Martin consulted with Tryon and finished preparations for his departure, Lord Dunmore and Tryon became involved in a controversy over where they would collect their salaries. Dunmore had delayed leaving for his new government in Virginia. He wanted to collect his salary in New York up to July 9. Tryon had arrived on July 8. Tryon wanted his salary to start with the date of his new commission; otherwise, he would collect his North Carolina salary until the date on which he left New Bern. If that happened then Governor Martin would be the loser. The extant records do not reveal the solution to that impasse.[56]

Governor Martin sailed for New Bern, North Carolina, on July

22. In the euphoria of his appointment as governor, he saw himself as a peacemaker who would reconcile the Regulators and bring enlightened government to the good people of North Carolina. He discovered the problems that Tryon and his predecessors had struggled with and had not solved were awaiting him. Instead of people who would be happy with their lot, he found men and women who had a dream of a new kind of life and government; one that would allow for home rule. The young man of thirty-four years had embarked upon a voyage that would carry him into history and the perplexing problems of revolution and republicanism in North Carolina.

II. The Tryon Legacy

After a passage of nineteen days, Governor Martin and his family arrived in New Bern on Sunday, August 11, 1771, a voyage that ordinarily took about four to five days. The ship stopped at several ports on its way to New Bern and it was plagued by adverse winds and becalmed at times, not unlike his career as governor. Anxious to perform his new job, Martin fretted at the additional delays of getting to New Bern. He reviewed in his mind the delays in New York when he had to have medical treatment. He did not want to be suspected of being delinquent in his duties; he was annoyed because he had to stand by while Governor Tryon quelled the Regulator insurrection. It is doubtful that Lord Hillsborough was critical of Martin for being tardy for he, too, spent several weeks away from his office during that period while he visited his estates in Ireland. Time schedules in the eighteenth century often were not important to many people. It should be noted that the specific time schedule for inaugurations in the United States had no precedents in the British Constitution or practice.[1]

It was a typical Carolina summer day as Martin's ship sailed through the Pamlico Sound and up the tidal river Neuse to its junction with the Trent River. Martin admired the wild beauty of the land as it met the water. While the ship approached the dock, Martin stood at the bow shading his eyes from the shimmering sunlight on the water and the trim white houses of New Bern. Through the humid heat he saw to his left the governor's residence, Tryon's Palace, rising above the humbler buildings. He surveyed his promised land and despite the discomfort of the heat and perspiration, he was pleased. The arthritic but kindly old James Hasell, acting governor and president of the council, hurried up the gangplank to greet him.

The following day, on Monday, August 12, 1771, in the handsome council chamber of the governor's palace at New Bern, Josiah Martin presented his commission. It was dated January 19, appointing him "His said Majesty's Captain General Governor and Commander in Chief in and over the Province of North Carolina." The commission was read in the presence of three of the councillors: the Honorable James Hasell, president of the council and acting governor, Martin Howard, the chief justice, and Samuel Cornell, Esq. Then His Excellency Josiah Martin took all the oaths appointed by law and watched while the councillors took their oaths. On the same day Governor Martin issued a proclamation for continuing provincial officers in their respective employments, and he received the seal of the province from the hands of Mr. President Hasell.[2].

James Hasell, the president of the council, was a genial man anxious to cooperate with Martin, and Martin "took early occasion to recommend him for the position of lieutenant governor in place of George Mercer," who was thought to have been appointed to a new government in the Ohio country. The rumor proved false. Mercer, the absentee lieutenant governor, remained in England. Besides Hasell, two other prominent North Carolinians had high expectations for Martin, and in their remarks there was an implication of criticism of Tryon. James Iredell, comptroller of customs in Edenton, told his relative, Henry E. McCulloh of Salisbury, he thought Martin had too much spirit to suffer usurpations of those over whom he had control. Another of Iredell's influential friends, Samuel Johnston, wrote to Thomas Barker:

"We are in daily expectation of Mr. Martin our new Govr. and as we hear a very amiable Character of him are not uneasy at the approaching change most among us thinking Govr. Tryon however well calculated to discharge the duty of a Soldier, that his Talents are not so well adapted to the Station he is now in."

Thus, Governor Martin had the support of several influential North Carolinians at the beginning of his administration. He would need that support and more to help him solve the problems of the Tryon legacy.[3]

The Tryon legacy included problems that William Tryon had

inherited from earlier governors of the province. Those were the result of years of frustration on the part of the governors in trying to solve problems on the provincial level by applying imperial policies. Beginning in the seventeenth century, North Carolina leaders had consistently opposed the Crown and its representatives on the application of imperial policy to the province. That pattern of political behavior was ingrained in North Carolina politics. When the Seven Years' War ended with the Treaty of Paris, 1763, Britain had conquered enormous areas of land in the New World and India. The vast new empire forced the Crown and its planners to rethink their concepts of management and the enforcement of laws in their empire. Moreover, they had to liquidate a huge war debt incurred in their conquests. The burden of the enforcement of the New Imperial Policy and the laws fell largely upon the colonial governors.

Martin inherited five major problems that plagued North Carolina. They were the fiscal and psychological effects of the War of the Regulators; the unsettled and expensive dispute between the Carolinas about their mutual boundary line; the struggle over the court law bills and the judiciary, especially the attachment of property of debtors who had never lived in the province; the old quorum trouble in the House that caused a conflict between the House and the governor; and the conflict over the selection of the chief personnel of the provincial government by the Crown rather than through the assembly.

The conflict between the assembly and the governor exercising the royal prerogative lay at the root of their difficulties. Though the War of the Regulators had temporarily submerged these difficulties they reemerged after the war was over. The struggle was basically economic between the governor and the North Carolina oligarchs. The oligarchs described their local grievances as colonial rights in order to persuade all the colonists to support their program against the Crown and the imperial acts of Parliament.

Governor Martin discovered that Tryon's seven-year administration had added almost £80,000 to the debt of the province. One of the major causes for the increase in the provincial debt was Tryon's urging the assembly to build an official residence for the governor. The magnificent building, Tryon's Palace, saddled the colony with an additional debt of £15,000 that was to be obtained from a poll tax on 51,044 taxables, the majority of whom were poor farmers who had difficulty securing hard money to pay their taxes. Begun on August 26, 1767, the palace was finished in 1770.[4] Many of the taxpayers resented the cost and magnificence of the structure built in New Bern.

As immigration began to move toward the Piedmont in the late 1750s and early 1760s the first villages developed as trading posts in the western part of the province. The most important of these new trading villages were Hillsborough in Orange County and Salisbury in Rowan County. These new trading centers were connected with older trading posts by rudimentary roads which ran eastward to Halifax and Cross Creek on the Roanoke and Cape Fear rivers. These rivers provided water transportation to the seaports of Edenton and Wilmington. Attracted by the commercial development of the piedmont and the possibility of government jobs, merchants and lawyers began to settle about 1760 in the new piedmont villages. As the immigration increased, the economy changed from one that was barter to one that was becoming a money economy. The poor farmers resented how quickly merchants and lawyers acquired wealth and political power and this fueled the Regulation movement.[5]

The War of the Regulation was basically a rebellion of taxpayers living in the North Carolina backcountry. The poor farmers had been exploited by the older settlers and by most of the county officials, particularly the sheriffs and the county clerks. Questionable practices were common, such as, a sheriff appearing unannounced at a farmer's house to demand payment of the poll tax. A farmer often had to borrow hard currency from a neighbor in order to pay his tax.

Sometimes a sheriff would tell a farmer he could be found on a particular road and could pay his tax there; but frequently, the sheriff would take a different route and could not be found. Subsequently, the farmers's property would be sold for taxes. Exploitation also occurred when farmers were charged more than the usual fees for recording deeds and other legal papers at the cour-

thouses. Many of the county officials have been described as colonial carpetbaggers, because they came from the northern colonies and took advantage of the farmers. One of the most notorious
officials was Edmund Fanning, a Yale graduate who was an intimate friend of Tryon. He represented Orange County in the assembly and served as registrar of deeds, judge of superior court,
and colonel of the militia. The system of buying and selling offices,
whose holders were paid by fees, was resented by the populace;
and though both Tryon, and later Martin, issued proclamations to
prevent illegal fees, the prohibitions were often ignored by the
county oligarchs.[6]

The roots of the Regulation rebellion were complex, because
the movement originated in sweeping changes that were taking
place in Carolina society.[7] Eventually the oppressed farmers, who
became known as Regulators, banded together. As early as May,
1768, disturbances occurred in Hillsborough, and outbursts in
other areas followed. A major riot took place in Hillsborough in
September, 1770, when officers and attorneys of the court, including Tryon's friend Edward Fanning, were assaulted by the Regulators. Hermon Husband, one of their leaders, owned large tracts
of land in Orange County, but he sympathized with his neighbors
in their grievances against officials and helped them with their
plans. Initially trying constitutional means, the group elected
their men to the assembly. Husband was elected in 1769 and 1770-
1771, but he was discredited, jailed, and expelled from the assembly. Tryon, after listening to Fanning and other advisers, called out
the militia to suppress the Regulators. The governor and his
troops defeated the Regulators at the Battle of Alamance on May
16, 1771.[8]

The effects of the Battle of Alamance were serious for the future well-being of North Carolina and for the career of Governor
Martin. A result of the Regulator movement was an alliance between the tidewater leaders and the Scotch-Irish Presbyterians in
the backcountry. Tryon had encouraged the alliance by supporting
the passage of laws to permit Presbyterian ministers to perform
marriages (until then only clergymen of the Church of England
could do so) and by supporting the efforts of Presbyterians to ob-

tain a charter for a Presbyterian academy in Mecklenburg County. The tidewater leaders' alliance with the Presbyterians would later become a threat to the Martin administration. It should be noted that many of the Regulators were Baptists; in fact, Herman Husband claimed that Tryon represented the Regulators as "a faction of Quakers and Baptists."[9]

The War of the Regulation also produced bitterness and hatred that disrupted the province of North Carolina, causing hundreds of former Regulators and their sympathizers to move across the mountains into territory that eventually became the states of Tennessee and Kentucky. The economic and demographic loss to the colony of North Carolina is difficult to assess, but the migration westward may have been one of the several factors that kept North Carolina a group of isolated settlements in the coastal plain and in the piedmont until the first decade of the nineteenth century.[10]

As Martin talked to, interviewed, and investigated the former Regulators, he began to realize that the dissidents may have had justifiable cause for their discontent. Martin wrote to Lord Hillsborough, assuring him and "His Majesty that I will vigilantly attend to the disposition of the lately disaffected parts of this country, and take every measure in my power to support the honor of His Majesty's Government, and to secure the peace of this colony." In the same letter he noted that "Husbands, the great promoter of Sedition in this country, finds sanctuary in Pensilvania, but I cannot learn certainly where." With the letter he enclosed copies of six Tryon proclamations extending "Overtures of Mercy to these deluded people." In reply, Lord Hillsborough wrote:

> The Tranquility which you say now reigns in that Country, which has of late exhibited Scenes of so disagreeable a Nature is most pleasing to the King; and it is His Majesty's Command that you should pursue every lenient Measure that may conduce to quiet Peoples Minds, to extinguish the remembrance of such unfortunate Events, and to obviate all just round of future uneasiness & Discontent.[11]

During the summer of 1772 Governor Martin made his summer capital at Hillsborough, away from the hot and humid coastal area of New Bern. While there he had long discussions with for-

mer Regulators living in Orange County. He also took advantage
of his proximity to the Moravian settlements, visiting them and
being entertained by members of that sect whose industry and
settlements he greatly admired.

Martin's friendship with the former Regulators and the industrious Moravians made for persuasive public relations for the governor and contrasted dramatically with Tryon's discriminating attitude toward most dissenters. According to Colonel Saunders, "of
the forty-seven sections of the State Constitution adopted in 1776,
thirteen, more than one fourth, are the embodiment of reforms
sought by the Regulators. . . . The War of Regulation ended, not
with the battle of Alamance in 1771, but with the adoption of the
State Constitution in 1776."[12]

The Moravian leaders, Brn. Marshall and Bonn, met Governor
Martin and his suite at their border on August 10 and were ush-
ered into Salem with the playing of trombones. With the governor
were Colonel Abner Nash, the "lawyer Canon," and Martin's secretary, James Biggleston. The governor invited the six Brethren,
Marshall, Tiersch, Utley, Bagge, Bonn and Muschback, to join
them at meals for all four days, thus taking an opportunity to learn
about Wachovia in general and about the settlement and parish of
Salem in particular. In the late afternoon the governor's party visited the Single Brothers House, the store, apothecary shop, pot-
tery, and blacksmith shop. At 8:00 o'clock each evening the entire
company attended the Singstunde, where the Passion of Jesus was
sung with alternate German and English stanzas interspersed
with choir anthems. On the following day, August 11, His Excellency visited Bethabara and Bethania where they had breakfast
and visited the mill at Bethania. The governor and his suite lodged
at the doctor's house where they dined at 2:00 o'clock with the
Brn. Marshall, Bonn, Bagge, Graff, and van der Merk. The governor's plan to leave Salem on August 13 was thwarted because
one of his horses had strayed. Presumably the horse was found because the governor and his party left the following day.[13]

During his visit to Salem Martin promised to assist the Moravians in their efforts to persuade the assembly to provide new
county boundaries. The Moravians had initially sought Tryon's

help with the county problem, and he had assured the members of his support; but the matter remained unresolved when he left North Carolina. At the time Rowan County covered a large area and many of the inhabitants had to travel a long way to Salisbury where the county court, general muster, and public meetings were held. Those members on the north side of the Ysdkin River had long desired that a part of Rowan should be erected into a new county and from 1769 on earnest attempts were made to induce the assembly to bring that about. The Brethren did what they could to help and in the spring of 1770, they presented to their county representatives a petition in which they gave their views as to how the new county might best be laid out. The assembly of 1770 erected Surry County out of part of Rowan, but the new county's boundaries were such that the northern part of Wachovia fell into Surry and the southern part into Rowan County. The line ran east and west between Salem and Bethabara not far from the Spangenbach and thus divided the Moravians between the jurisdiction of two courts.[14]

The first assembly called by Governor Martin received the Moravian petition asking that Wachovia be placed in one county, but nothing came of this petition except a promise that the matter would be adjusted by the next assembly. At the next assembly in January, 1773, Br. Marshall and Bagge went to New Bern to present their request for an enlarged Surry County. They discovered that every careless or ill-considered word or deed of an individual brother was held against the entire settlement and made an occasion for false accusations. Most of the Moravian affairs, material and spiritual, were painted by many of their critics in the "most unpleasant colors." Gradually more and more colonists began to learn the truth and became more favorable to the Brethren. After a long wait, a bill to enlarge Surry County was introduced to the assembly, read the first time and passed. After another long wait the bill was read and passed for the second time on February 5. The bill passed the council on its second reading and its dedicated enemies laid plans to defeat its third reading. Before its final adoption, the Brethren had to combat another campaign of slander against them and the bill. Stories were circulated that the Brethren were planning to have their own government in Wachovia; that they were a lazy, useless people who ate five times a day; that they harbored runaway negroes, etc. Despite these rumors the bill was passed for the third time without further opposition. Assured of the approval of the council and the governor they happily set out for home with their good news.

Including Wachovia in Surry County proved of great benefit to the Brethren during the Revolution for it took them from under the control of the Presbyterians "who were very strong and hot in Rowan," and in a large measure freed them from the commands of the officers of that county. In Surry county there were officers who did not permit anything to injure the Brethren. Those Brethren who lived across the boundary in Rowan County "had much more to bear."

Although some Highland Scots and others emigrated to North Carolina after the Battle of Alamance, it is possible the newspaper coverage of the War of the Regulators in the northern colonies discouraged colonists from moving to the province. Newspaper reports about the Regulators could have been interpreted as proof of the Crown's oppression of the colonists, particularly in the newspapers of Massachusetts and Pennsylvania where the restless people read of the struggle of the oppressed Regulators. Lurid language was used to describe the Crown officers' treatment of the unfortunate Regulators in such newspapers as the Boston *Gazette*, the *Massachusetts Spy*, and the *Pennsylvania Journal* in Philadelphia. Many of those news reports were reprinted in other colonial newspapers, and thus reached a larger public.[15]

The most urgent problem that Governor Martin inherited was the necessity to pay the troops Tryon had used against the Regulators. The £60,000 cost of the war, coupled with provincial debts already owed, posed a major problem. Many of the officers were also members of the assembly. Both Tryon and council president James Hasell had advised Martin not to call a new assembly as instructed by the Crown but to use the old assembly that had authorized the use of troops. Later, the secretary of state for the colonies, Lord Hillsborough, approved Martin's request to do that. Martin prorogued the assembly to meet on November 19 in New

Bern, and when the assembly met he faced monetary and political problems.[16]

Martin expected the assembly to create a currency to pay for the expenses of the Regulator War, but he was disappointed. A struggle with the assembly developed over its attempts to discontinue a poll tax on rum, wine, and other liquors. The house argued that there was a surplus in the treasury and that those taxes had been used for their original purpose. Martin vetoed the bill when Speaker of the House, Richard Caswell, presented it to him on December 23.[17]

While Martin's move was necessary, the House expected him to prorogue the assembly. Caswell had already sent a request of the assembly to the treasurers ordering that the taxes in question be omitted from the tax lists sent to the counties for collection. The House had reported resolutions discontinuing the tax and indemnifying the sheriffs for noncollection. Martin countered by issuing a proclamation, January 29, 1772 requiring the sheriffs to make collections as usual and reminding them that they could be sued upon their bonds for noncollection.

It was a clever move on the part of the assembly to try to usurp the royal prerogative; but the sheriffs were appointees of the governor, not the assembly. Moreover, the sheriffs were interested in collecting the taxes as well as heeding the serious threat of the governor. The first skirmish with the assembly was a technical victory for Martin, but the conflict continued over the collection of taxes throughout his administration. Martin received support of his council and Hillsborough for continuation of the taxes. The governor gave a full report to Hillsborough and noted that the assembly attempted "a monstrous usurpation of authority that I think proves irrefrageably the propensity of this people to democracy." He added that they were trying "to nourish the flame of discontent which I hoped was expiring."[18]

The experience with the Debenture Bill of 1771, to finance the expenses of the Regulator War, was a more satisfying one for both the governor and the assembly. Nevertheless, much time was spent on disagreement over details. Representatives from the southern district argued for paper currency while a minority of the assemblymen from the northern district opposed them. Martin described to Hillsborough the citizens of the southern district as universally in debt and desirous of paper currency. At first some of the assemblymen tried to force through a bill creating debenture notes on bank paper to the amount of £120,000 proclamation money and to be exchanged for all such debentures and tender bills in circulation in the province. That bill was passed by the assembly but was rejected by Martin. The assembly then reduced the total to £60,000 and the bill passed the assembly and received Martin's assent on December 23.[19]

Two days earlier the assembly had appointed a committee to write an address to the king, lords, and commons of Great Britain to notify them that the debenture vote plan had been formed to finance the expenses of the recent Regulator War. Members of that committee were Robert Howe, Cornelius Harnett, and Maurice Moore. The assembly instructed the committee to make a request to Parliament to repeal the 1764 act against issuing paper currency respecting North Carolina, and still protect the British creditors. Later, Hillsborough approved the debenture bills. He had earlier advised Martin that a paper currency based upon a just foundation of credit without making it a legal tender was permissible provided it was used within the province and that British and foreign traders were not required to accept it as legal tender.[20]

The success of the Debenture Bill of 1771 illustrated how the governor and the assembly could work together to solve the needs of the citizens and the province despite their difficulties over the poll and impost taxes. The expenses of the War of the Regulators were paid and more currency was made available. Yet on the same day, December 23, Martin vetoed the tax bill and gave his assent to the Debenture Bill. The assembly belatedly advised him that orders had been given to the two treasurers to sue the tax collectors to recover the arrearages in the hands of the collectors. Immediately, Martin prorogued the assembly. It had again tried to usurp the governor's powers. Since dissolution was a much used device by his predecessors, the House was not surprised when Martin dismissed it.[21] Under the present American constitutions, a legislature cannot be dismissed by a governor.

At that juncture the Carolinas boundary again became a problem; but it was a problem that could bring a certain relief to a hard pressed governor, because it was one matter upon which he and the assembly could safely agree. Both the governor and the assembly had vested interests in the boundary line. The assembly did not want to lose perhaps a thousand squatter citizens and "a great tract" of valuable, sparsely settled lands; and the governor did not want to lose fees for granting those lands to settlers. The Crown had instructed Martin to cooperate with South Carolina in running a new boundary line; but again he and the assembly came into conflict over the issue as they had over the debenture notes. In 1763 the assembly had appropriated a large sum to run the boundary only to find that the line was proved useless. The 1763 line was carried due west from Yadkin River to the junction of the Charleston and Salisbury roads. The assembly wanted the line run due west of the Charleston road but the Crown, allegedly influenced by Lord Charles Montague, governor of South Carolina, ordered the line to be run substantially like the present-day line. Governor Martin communicated the royal instructions to the assembly on December 17, 1771, and asked for an appropriation to pay the commissioners named to survey the line with the South Carolina commissioner. The line surveyed was to be permanent.[22]

The House protested vigorously. It reminded Martin that the proposed line would deprive North Carolina of "a great many useful inhabitants," "take from us a great tract of Valuable Land," cut off commerce with the western Indians, and "defraud this Province of several thousand pounds laid out in running the Western line, which will be by this plan taken into South Carolina." The assembly added that it did not wish to spend more of its constituents' money to establish a line "highly injurious to the Colony." Moreover, the assembly advised the governor that it would petition the king not to make the proposed line permanent but to permit the line already run to remain the dividing line. Two days later Martin informed the speaker and the House that he would "not fail faithfully to lay before His Majesty your Representations on this subject, at the same time, that I greatly fear it will be displeasing to the King to find that the Customary provision has not been made for carrying into present execution His Majesty's Royal and solemn determination." Though Martin was ill when he received the assembly report, he managed to attend to the business at once. He wrote to Hillsborough, enclosing a copy of the assembly's address to him. The young governor may have considered the proposed address to the king as a personal affront, for it did seem to imply that he lacked influence with the Crown's ministers. Tryon, he knew, had always told the colonists that he had influence with the Crown. Martin, however, was still anxious to further the interests of his colony. He asked Hillsborough for parliamentary relief for the "distressed state of this Country's finances. . . . " In their correspondence about the boundary question both Hillsborough and Martin expressed concern about the assemblymen's growing independence and their refusal to obey the king's instructions regarding the line. Hillsborough denied the allegations of the assembly that the Board of Trade had been influenced by Lord Montague. He emphasized that the board's plan differed essentially from the Montague plan. He declared that the board had been impartial in considering what was best for the interests of the Crown and both colonies. If the province suffered any loss of inhabitants or lands, he argued, that loss would have to be "attributed to their own Indiscretion in forming those settlements and erecting a County in that part of the Country before His Majesty's pleasure respecting the line of Partition could be known." Hillsborough condemned the actions of the assembly when he wrote Martin: " . . . the indecent manner in which they express themselves to you upon that subject has not escaped his Majesty's notice." He advised in his dispatch that the assembly's petition to the Crown would be heard by the Board of Trade and the Privy Council.[23]

Reacting to the independence of the assembly, Martin employed the old tactic of procrastination. He delayed calling the assembly from May 11 to December 10, 1772. With the House in check, he then proceeded with the plans for the boundary line commission. He was uneasy because he had not heard from Lord Montague for two months and the "hot season" was "fast approaching." Martin had notified Montague that the North Carolina commissioners could meet with commissioners he had appointed at Catawba Town on April 20, ready to carry out the king's commands. Meanwhile, it seems probable that Martin had discussed the boundary question with Lord William Campbell, when he and Lady Campbell had visited New Bern on their way from Nova Scotia to Charleston in the late winter of 1772. Soon after Campbell became governor of South Carolina.[24]

With no response from Montague, Martin pursued his plans for the boundary line. At the same time he continued to grant patents to land along the borders of the Carolinas. On June 5 he notified Hillsborough that he had concluded the business of the court of chancery and the granting of lands. He reported that he was chagrined to discover that Montague had ignored his request for the meeting on April 20. One of Martin's commissioners, William Dry, had learned that Montague was on a pleasure trip to the town of Camden. Dry at once went to Camden and called upon Montague. Montague advised Dry that he expected Martin to appoint the commissioners after the South Carolina assembly had agreed to defray the whole expense of the survey. Thus, Montague delayed the meeting of the commissioners until May 20. Finally, the boundary line was run and on July 8 Martin advised Hillsborough that it had been completed although he had not yet received the commissioners' report. Martin investigated the claim of the assembly that a great body of useful citizens would be lost by the boundary partition. He told Hillsborough that he had discovered that the so-called useful citizens of the border were "licentious and lawless Banditti equally useless and troublesome to both the Provinces acknowledging and disclaiming as served their sinister purposes the jurisdiction of each and paying taxes to neither. . . . " With the boundary survey completed, Martin sent to the new assembly on March 3, 1773, "a draft of the line of boundary between this Province and that of South Carolina" together with a list of expenses and a note suggesting that the king was annoyed by their refusal to pay for the boundary survey.[25]

On March 3, the speaker, John Harvey, replied to Martin. Harvey declared that since the assembly had paid for one boundary survey under Tryon there seemed to be no reason for another.

He charged that the province was losing "a great tract" of land to South Carolina along with many citizens who were still in arrears with their taxes. Couched in the clichés of respectful political prose, Harvey added that since the line was advantageous to South Carolina that province should pay the expense incurred in establishing the new line. Harvey noted that the assembly was struggling to pay the enormous debt of £60,000, "incurred by subduing a dangerous insurrection against the peace, safety, honor and dignity of his Majesty's government in the Colony. . . . " The defiant tone of the statement was not lost on Martin or the crown. The house resolved to send instructions to its business agent in Westminster together with a copy of the answer to Martin's message containing the reasons why the survey expense was refused payment. The House added that in case another line should be ordered to be run on the hearing of its petition, it was ready to answer to the whole expense. Thus, the problem of the boundary line stood unresolved in 1773.[26]

Governor Martin inherited two other vexatious problems from his predecessors, "the old quorum trouble" and the selection of the provincial goverment personnel by the Crown rather than through the assembly. The two problems are closely related to those discussed above, but they were not at all unusual. Most British colonial governors experienced them. During the court quarrel, Martin prorogued the assembly on March 6, 1773, to the following Tuesday to let the representatives regain a more objective attitude through sober reflection. On Tuesday, the clerk of the assembly sent word to the governor that there were not enough members in town to "make a House." Martin then sent a note of inquiry to the speaker of the house, John Harvey. Harvey replied that a majority of the members had already left and that others were preparing to leave. Martin reminded Harvey that in the Crown's instructions fifteen members constituted a quorum, that there were still fifteen members in town, and that business should proceed with such a quorum. Harvey replied that members then in town thought they should not "proceed to make a House unless they be a majority of the Representatives of the people to constitute the same." The governor then asked if additional members were expected to arrive, to which Harvey replied that he did not anticipate the return of any of the absentees; neither did he think that those then present in New Bern would remain there. Martin consulted with his council upon hearing Harvey's answer, the members of which determined that the assembly had deserted the business and the interests of their constituents. The council members advised Martin to dissolve the assembly by proclamation and order new writs to call it in session again on May 1. Martin reported to Dartmouth on the situation in a letter dated March 12, 1773. He said the argument that had been advanced—that a majority of the representatives was not present—was based on a direction in the Proprietary Charter. Martin agreed that "Such are the terms of the Charter most certainly, but the principle that the Charter is still binding upon the Crown, and the people is not too well established, and involves questions not for me to answer." He continued by pointing out reasons why the document was not relevant to the quorum question.[27]

There may have been a defiant spirit in the assembly in 1773, but it is likely that there were other practical reasons for interest in adjourning. In early March the assemblymen needed to go home to plant their crops, inventory their warehouses and ships, take care of their law clients, and care for their families. The quorum problem remained, and it was used as a weapon against the governor whenever it suited the assembly's needs, especially when the House was trying to get control of its internal proceedings. The March, 1773, episode was just one of many examples of the controversy over the quorum problem through the royal period in North Carolina.

Closely related to the quorum problem was the House's campaign to secure the right to select provincial personnel. Like the quorum problem the personnel problem plagued the North Carolina governors throughout the royal period. The selection of provincial governmental personnel by the king and his ministers rather than through the assembly encouraged corruption and inefficiency in the administrative offices and caused envy, resentment, and distress among the settlers and their representatives. Many of the offices in the English colonies were filled by men who had secured the favorable opinion of the Crown, the ministers, or their women. The purchase or rental of some offices was practiced in North Carolina. All the chief provincial officers, governor, chief justice, receiver general, attorney general, secretary, and clerk of pleas were directly appointed by the Crown. The governor nominated members of the council, the associate judges, the magistrates, and the sheriffs. The clerk of pleas bought his office in England; he in turn rented the offices of the clerks of the county courts and the registrars of deeds. In 1772 those rents provided £560 a year according to Governor Martin for "an absolutely sinecure office." It was a vested right. "Farming out offices" was done openly and the buying and selling of them was considered respectable, if not honorable.[28]

Like many other governors, Martin had difficulty with his appointments of officers and personnel. Moreover, near the end of his administration, Martin requested approval from the secretary of state for the colonies to make some changes in the membership of the royal council. These council changes will be discussed later. In response to Samuel Johnston's request to investigate the charges of extortion against the collector and the comptroller of the port of Currituck, Messers Pierce and Malcom. Martin appointed James Biggleston as judge of the admiralty to investigate the charges. He also wrote to Johnston on February 6, 1772 asking for more information regarding the alleged extortions by Messers Pierce and Malcom. John Pierce had told the governor's secretary that he was authorized by His Majesty's Customs commissioner at Boston to remove the Customs House at Currituck. The governor also wrote a letter to Pierce inquiring about Malcom's alleged malpractices.

Martin's correspondence regarding the two accused men, Malcom and Pierce, covered a period of over three years, February, 1772 to March, 1775, which was very frustrating for the governor. Speaker of the House, John Harvey thought that Martin should suspend both men since they had not accounted for their receipts nor had they posted a bond to cover them. Martin advised Hillsborough that he had suspended Comptroller Malcom shortly before Hillsborough stepped down from the colonial secretary's office and was succeeded by Dartmouth. Lord Dartmouth approved Martin's removing John Pierce and then had second thoughts on the matter. He told Martin that he would check with Lord North on whether a governor could suspend custom officers. Martin was still waiting for Lord Dartmouth's advice on March 23, 1775. With the imminent revolution on the horizon, the matter of suspension of Malcom and Pierce disappears into history where, no doubt, the patriot leaders solved the problem.[29]

Two other opportunists had used their positions in the assembly to hassle the governor. Tryon's former secretary, Isaac Edwards, was recommended to Martin for the office of deputy auditor of the King's revenues. After he received the appointment, Edwards flattered Martin while he held that office; but after he was elected to the assembly as a representative of the town of New Bern, his attitude changed. He opposed Martin's policies and measures because he wanted the office of treasurer that was granted by the assembly. He did not become treasurer but he served in the third and fourth assemblies, December, 1773, through April, 1775, and later he served in the first provincial congress, again representing New Bern. Martin was able to replace Edwards as deputy auditor by putting his friend, the merchant Archibald Neilson, in the office. Edwards' ally in the assembly was Robert How (later he spelled it Howe), who had been reprimanded by Martin for holding a judgeship and the command of Ft. Johnston at the same time. Howe was made second in command when Martin appointed the Swiss Captain John Collet to serve as commander of Ft. Johnston near Wilmington. Howe had a personality that seemed to attract criticism about his morality. He was a plantation owner near Wilmington and a widower. He was thought to be a womanizer by the gossips. There were whispers that Howe profited from the expense money allowed the soldiers at Ft. Johnston but apparently this could not be proven. Nevertheless, the governor was irked by the story about the soldiers expense profit to Howe and that he also worked with Edwards to irritate the governor in the assembly. Edwards married the daughter of a rich merchant; Howe became a general in the patriot army and was later court-martialed.[30]

The assembly came into conflict with the Crown on the question of tenure for the chief justice and judges of the superior court. The House had long contended that judges should hold office during good behavior rather than at the pleasure of the Crown. The desire to control the courts and judges goes back to the struggles of Englishmen with the Stuart kings who manipulated them with two legal institutions, the notorious Star Chamber court and the High Commission. Both institutions were used against the alleged enemies of the king through the use of the "Corporal Oath" by which a defendant might be forced to testify against himself and the levying of extortionate fines that benefited the Crown, particularly Charles I. As far back as 1761 a North Carolina legislative provision for tenure during good behavior for superior court judges had been disallowed at the request of the Board of Trade. The board found the law obnoxious because it violated instructions, and more importantly it made associate justices more independent than the chief justice, who was appointed from England and held office during pleasure. In 1768 Governor Tryon was able to get an act passed providing the judges' salaries for five years and agreeing to the royal position on tenure. When the act expired the struggle began anew. Governor Martin reported to Dartmouth that it was the principle of the House to withhold a permanent salary from the chief justice until such time as the Crown had appointed him for service during good behavior. Under the system in North Carolina, the chief justice was subject to salary fluctuation at the whim of the assembly, and Martin urged Dartmouth "to move His Majesty to grant him a salary adequate to the dignity and importance of his station, out of some certain fund." The tenure question remained unsettled at the outbreak of the revolution because it had been submerged in the fight over the foreign attachment controversy.[31]

Of all the southern royal colonies, North Carolina was the most successful in gaining complete control over the nomination, appointment, and salary of its clerk. The struggle began in North Carolina with the first royal legislature in 1731 when Governor George Barrington issued a commission for Ayliffe Williams to be clerk of the House. The House refused to recognize Williams' commission. The Board of Trade in London noticed the deviation and advised Governor Burrington that he was not to allow the House superior advantages to the British House of Commons. Burrington, they ordered, was to appoint the clerk. Burrington then decided he should appoint all the House's officials. The House referred the problem to a special committee and it found that it had been "a constant practice of the House to name and appoint all their Officers. . . . " The committee added that the "Lords proprietors or their Governours ever attempted to Name or appoint those officers." The House waited until the Board of Trade forgot what they had done and then quietly slipped their own candidate as clerk to Governor Gabriel Johnston in 1739 who did not object to the candidate. The House also paid the salary of the clerk which meant that they had gained complete control over the nomination, appointment, and salary of its clerk.[32]

The struggle between the governors and their assemblies helped prepare the way for the American Revolution; but in North Carolina it was the struggle over the Tryon court laws and judiciary that acted as a lever to launch the province into the Revolution. It should be noted that the widespread discontent over the royal policy of tenure of judicial office was reflected in the Declaration of Independence, which charged the king with "the establishment of an absolute Tyranny" in that "He has made Judges dependent on his will alone, for the tenure of their offices, and the amount and payment of their salaries."

III. The Foreign Attachment Law

Although all the problems inherited by Martin from his predecessors were important and intimately related, the most crucial problem was that of the struggle over the renewal of the Tryon court law. The assembly had insisted that the law should include provision for the attachment of property belonging to debtors who had never been in the province. Forbidden by the Crown's ministers to include the attachment clause in the new court law, Martin faced accelerated antagonism in his relationship to the assembly. Without law and order, the colony drifted toward psychological and political anarchy providing a fertile field for the patriots to exploit.

The dispute about the court laws had been developing since the administration of Governor Arthur Dobbs, 1754-1765. Under Dobbs the assembly's efforts were directed toward securing the independence of the judiciary, it also wanted the right to proceed by attachment against the property of debtors who had never been in the province. The right to attach the property of debtors who had absconded was never questioned or objected to from the earliest days of the colony. The first appearance of the foreign attachment clause in North Carolina statutes was in the court law that was passed in 1746.[1]

Historical precedence for the attachment law was established earlier when London, Bristol, and York received that right in their royal charters. The purpose of the law was to enable a creditor to attach money, credits, or goods belonging to his debtor in the hands of a third person. The owner would be deprived of all control until he satisfied the debt or appeared in court.[2]

As consumer markets began to expand in North Carolina, some British merchants appointed agents to represent them in the colony but they themselves never lived there. Moreover, British absentee landowners possessed large tracts of land within the province. In time both of those practices resulted in great hardships for North Carolina creditors who were forced to go to England to initiate proceedings for the collection of their debts. Hoping to solve that problem the assembly under Governor Tryon, in 1768, established a system of courts that made it possible for creditors to proceed by attachment against debtors who had never lived in the colony. Richard Jackson, legal adviser to the Board of Trade, in November, 1770, noted that the court act of 1768 had flaws but did not recommend disallowance of the act because it would lapse in three years. The board, concerned that the foreign attachment clause might be misapplied to other citizens in Britain, permitted the act to continue although it urged Tryon to persuade the assembly to change the attachment clause or omit it entirely when the act was renewed.[3]

When Martin became governor, the Tryon court law was about to expire. Martin had been listening to complaints of creditors and studying the judicial system. Early in February, 1772, circular royal instructions were issued expressly forbidding most colonial governors in North America from giving their assent to any foreign attachment bills that did not include clauses suspending their operation until Crown approval was obtained. Martin asked Hillsborough for advice on the Tryon court law. The colonial secretary agreed that the inferior courts of common pleas should be reorganized when the law expired in 1773; and he advised Martin to refuse assent to any court law that contained clauses obnoxious to the Crown.[4]

Martin continued to study the North Carolina judiciary system and soon had specific recommendations for serious reform. He suggested that the governor with advice of the royal council select seven magistrates out of each division to serve as a commission of the peace and that the seven would have power to hold courts of pleas and quarter sessions in their counties. Three would constitute a quorum for court business. Martin believed that the governor should share in the nomination of the sheriffs with the local inspectors and thus prevent naming men who would automatically decline the office and make it possible for the favored candidate to secure the office of sheriff. In the past the favored candidate did not always cooperate with the governor. The governor proposed that not less than five of the magistrates should constitute a quorum to "settle the public Accounts with the Sheriffs," and thus gain better control over the sheriffs' accounts than was then possible.[5]

What Martin did not know was that Hillsborough was considering resigning from both his offices. According to Walpole, Hillsborough could not reconcile himself to a plan of settlement on the Ohio River that "all the world approved." There probably was another reason for Hillsborough's resignation, but the comfortable working relationship for Martin with Hillsborough was gone. Martin believed that Hillsborough's resignation would hurt his chances to advance himself in other colonial offices.[6]

William Legge, second earl of Dartmouth and a favorite of George III, in August, 1772, succeeded Lord Hillsborough as secretary of state for the colonies and president of the Board of Trade and Foreign Plantations in Lord North's administration. Dartmouth counselled Martin early in November, 1772, to be cautious in his proposals for court reforms and urged him to get the cooperation of the "upper house," his royal council. Dartmouth advised that the legislature "should be left entirely to their own free choice and that any positive Instructions from the King of the nature you suggest would not only be questionable in point of Propriety but would be the most likely means to defeat the Object."[7]

Later in November, Martin reported to Dartmouth his concern for law and order in the Granville Grant. The Granville Grant had become an asylum for outcasts and fugitives. He suggested that the Crown should purchase the grant to control the vice and corruption, but if the Crown would not purchase it, Martin hoped to be Lord Granville's agent. Martin argued that the grant could produce in the future quitrents that could be applied to the North Carolina provincial civil list. Later Martin became Granville's agent.[8]

To dispel doubts in the minds of opposition members, Martin, in January, 1773, formally laid before the House a copy of the Crown's written instructions relating to attachments. The assembly still insisted on incorporating the attachment provision into the new court law drafted to replace the 1768 law that was soon to expire. The House reacted by passing its version of the bill which Martin vetoed. The House then passed the bill with a provision that it be effective for only six months, but that bill was rejected by the royal council. The next court bill, passed by both houses contained a clause suspending operation until the pleasure of the Crown should be known. Martin approved this bill. In his dispatch to Dartmouth, Martin explained his reason for giving his assent that it would have no effect until the bill was approved by the Crown. He had advised the Board of Trade earlier that "there was a temperate but firm resolution in the majority of the House, rather to be without Courts of Justice, than conform to the direction of that Instruction." The bill was rejected by the Crown. North Carolina was now without courts because the 1768 court act expired at the end of the assembly's session in March, 1773.[9]

Near the end of February, Martin reported to his brother that he was busily "watching over the little Politicks of the Provincial Assembly now sitting." He complained to Samuel that the people of North Carolina regarded their governor "as a being set over them by the Sovereign to steal away their liberties & properties." He added that when he tried to get the assembly to accept the Crown's ideas it always resulted in a quarrel with the assembly. Martin confessed to Samuel that he expected trouble from the coming assembly and that he would try to avoid the assembly and still do "his duty to the King." The controversial nature of the assembly was probably the main reason why Martin prorogued the legislature as often as he did. The struggle with the assembly increased Martin's anxiety about his relationship with Dartmouth. Martin's fears gnawed at his self-confidence. He told his brother that in the past he had seen himself as "a pygmy Governor of Ld. Hillsborough's" and admitted that he had some fears about Lord Dartmouth, probably stemming from his criticism of Martin's suggested court reforms.[10]

Martin was in a dilemma because he agreed that the province should have equal rights on the attachment process but he had to obey the Crown's directions. The assembly continued its strategy of pressuring the governor. It refused to pay for the boundary line expense and encouraged the citizens of the province not to pay the poll and impost taxes. Then it appealed to the colony's business agent in Westminster, Henry E. McCulloh, for help in persuading the Board of Trade to keep the foreign attachment law. McCulloh was asked to describe to the board the anarchy that would occur in the colony without courts. It instructed McCulloh to argue for the approval of the law because the assembly would not give up the controversial clause.[11]

Martin analyzed for Dartmouth and the Board of Trade the reasons why the assembly refused to surrender the attachment clause. He believed that the assembly had deliberately included the inferior and superior court bills in one bill so that the board would accept the attachment clause. In the past, the Crown's ministers had often deferred to colonial wishes to maintain harmony. Martin declared "that the Expediency of a regular Administration of Justice, and the many salutary provisions of that part of it which relates to the Constitution of Superior Courts," will prevail "against the innovation, and extension of Jurisdiction aimed at" in the establishment of inferior courts "and gain acceptance to the whole."[12]

The court issue worried Martin more than any of his problems. In a long letter to Dartmouth he made a very careful analysis. He summarized the arguments of the assembly regarding the attachment law. Martin advised Dartmouth that he thought the assembly was right in expecting the attachment process practiced in Great Britain and the other colonies should be practiced in North Carolina. The governor emphasized that the capital defect of the attachment process was the possible injury to the property of the debtor whose effects were attached by not allowing sufficient time for remote debtors to appear, plead, and give bail and replevy. It was not compulsory on the garnishee to give notice to the owner. This practice had been much abused in the past, especially for absentee defendants who discovered that their property had been taken through collusion or ignorance. Some debtors, Martin noted, converted their estates into "Negroes, and other moveable shapes," and carried them out of the colony. The governor believed that the colonial creditors should be put on the same equal footing as with those of Britain so that equal justice would be done for all.[13]

Martin asked Dartmouth for advice and instruction and advised him that he would postpone the meeting of the new assembly until he received instructions. He was convinced that frequent dissolution of the assembly tended "to excite opposition and resistance. . . . " If after receiving the Crown's instructions the assembly did not concur in passing court laws agreeable to the Crown, Martin would exercise his royal commission to erect courts of civil jurisdiction.

Many individuals in the colony shared Martin's concern about the lack of courts. Litigation ceased, large debts could not be collected, and criminals escaped arrest and punishment. Without law and order, anarchy could sweep across the colony. A New England visitor expressed concern over the lack of courts in North Carolina, but there was a purpose behind his concern: he wished to discover and meet the Whig leaders in the south because he carried letters of introduction to them. The visitor was a famous Massachusetts lawyer and Whig, Josiah Quincy, Jr., who was touring the south because he was tubercular and needed a milder climate to strengthen him. The young Whig dined with and talked to prominent southern leaders in the colonies of Maryland, Virginia, North and South Carolina. When he visited North Carolina in March and April, 1773, he talked to several leaders. He soon discovered that Colonel William Dry, a collector of customs and a member of the council, was sympathetic to the Regulators and was critical of British and continental administration. In Wilmington, Quincy was the guest of Dr. Thomas Cobham, William Hooper, and Cornelius Harnett. He thought Harnett to be in the "Whig interest" and supported by the Whigs in his election. The Boston born Quincy described Harnett as "the Samuel Adams of North Carolina (except in point of fortune)." It was at Harnett's house that Quincy discussed with his host and Robert Howe the plan for continental committees of correspondence. Perhaps this meeting can be considered the origin of North Carolina committee of correspondence, although it was not organized until much later.[14]

Meanwhile, the Board of Trade had asked Richard Jackson to analyze the North Carolina Court Act of 1773. He advised that the board should not approve the act because it contained the prohibited attachment clause. The board decided not to recommend the disallowance of the act until it discovered what kind of a compromise Martin could bring about in negotiating with the assembly.[15]

Dartmouth had written Martin in August, 1773, advising him that the king had grave questions about the absence of courts in North Carolina and that he wanted a compromise. He advised Martin that the attachment clause would be allowed where the action arose "within the colony, and due proof has been made upon oath, before such attachment issues, whether original or Judicial, that the Defendant . . . has absconded to avoid Payment of his Debt and that the ordinary process of Law cannot be served upon. . . . " The secretary argued that the regulations with regard to attachments in the commercial cities of England do not go beyond "what is here suggested. . . . " He was confident that the assembly would accept this compromise to replace the extreme form of attachment in North Carolina. He concluded that if the assembly refused to accept that compromise, Martin was expected "to exert the Authority vested in you by your commission" and create with the advice of the council as many courts as were necessary for civil and criminal cases.[16]

In the event that the assembly should not wish to accept the compromise offered by the board, Martin was prepared to use his royal commission and create prerogative courts for the summer. On March 16, 1773, in preparation for the summer, he issued commissions of oyer and terminer. The canny governor appointed two opposition leaders, Maurice Moore and Richard Caswell, to hold those courts with Chief Justice Martin Howard. The pragmatic chief justice asked James Iredell to keep his attachment for safekeeping until the court dispute was settled. While Iredell was friendly to Howard, he was critical of Martin's handling of the court dispute.[17]

In the summer of 1773, the prerogative courts were held in several counties. Although his commission gave Martin the right to create those courts, some of the colonial leaders insisted that only the assembly had a right to create courts. A letter from James Iredell was printed in the *North Carolina Gazette* for September 10, in which he reviewed the colonial concept of the legal foundations of the provincial government. Iredell denied that "the Governor's commission and instructions are the foundation of our political constitution." His commission and instructions were simply regulations for the governor's conduct. Iredell saw the provincial charter as a contract between the Crown and the inhabitants, and that the governor's commission and instructions were similar to a special letter of attorney that empowered the governor to execute the contract for the Crown. For Iredell, the royal prerogative was a vital part of North Carolina's government, but it was as limited as any other part of the constitution. The Crown and its ministers could not supply "any defect which they may imagine in the constitution; this can only be done with the consent of the inhabitants, signified either by themselves or their deputies in some public act."[18]

Iredell's interpretation of the constitution of the colony was the opposite of the one upheld by the Crown and its ministers. More and more business and political leaders throughout the colonies began to view the Crown's exercise of the prerogative as a threat to their provincial governments and their rights. Dartmouth and his governors were increasingly aware of the growing prerogative question in all of the American colonies and they sought ways to solve it. In their correspondence Dartmouth and Martin discussed the thorny problems of the court laws, the proroguing of the assembly, and the proper handling of assemblymen, the customs and other royally appointed provincial officers. On October 6 Martin finally prorogued the assembly to November 29, thinking that a new assembly might be easier to work with, although he told Dartmouth that the assembly probably would be selected from the former members.[19]

Grassroots discontent over imperial policies in a county may be seen in the special set of instructions that the leaders of Orange County sent to their representatives, Thomas Hart and Ralph Macnair, in the House in December, 1773. The Orange County leaders resolved that when anyone not residing in North Carolina was indebted to someone in the colony that his effects "within our reach should be made liable." Because those effects would be in the hands of a third person, acting as an agent or factor, that person should notify the principal debtor of the action. Failure to do so should place liability on the agent. The instructions made it clear that there was a need for courts of justice to provide redress for men who were injured, but the late law of attachment had been abused and used against the people. Problems stemming from the distance from and the time needed to travel to court were cited. The Orange leaders did not object to the principle of the Tryon attachment law so much as the lack of proper safeguards against its improper use. Hart and Macnair were warned that should the courts of oyer again become a subject of debate, they should insist that courts be erected only by the assembly.[20]

When the assembly convened on December 4 at New Bern, Martin presented his legislative program in a speech in which he announced that the Crown was willing for the province to have the attachment clause as long as it applied within the province. He stated that the limitations of the original jurisdiction of the superior courts and the extension of that of the inferior courts in the act of the last session are deemed totally inadmissible by the Crown. He added that Inferior courts would be allowed power to "Judge and determine in all cases to the amount of twenty pounds proclamation money." Their judgments were to be final and without appeal as far as five pounds proclamation money, and where titles to land, or the rights of the Crown shall not be involved in the question.[21]

Martin advised the assembly that he was obliged to exercise the power vested in his commission to appoint courts of oyer and terminer and jail delivery for the immediate dispensation of justice. He said he was satisfied that the courts had maintained the public peace and security, and he commended the judges. The governor then asked for an appropriation to defray expenses of the courts of oyer and terminer.

A part of Martin's legislative program was designed to encourage reconciliation of former Regulators. The governor asked the house to pass an act of pardon and oblivion for the men involved in the Regulator insurrection with such exceptions as deemed proper. Martin's humanitarian gesture was not always appreciated by some of the Whigs for they thought he was trying to build support for his program among the former rebels.[22]

The assembly replied to the governor's legislative program on December 9. In a speech prepared by Samuel Johnston and signed by the speaker, John Harvey, the house rejected Martin's program. The assemblymen were concerned for the "present disordered state of this province." They argued that security for their properties was essential to their commercial interests as a trading people and the suggested change by the Crown for domestic attachments was not an adequate remedy. They could not in duty to themselves and their constituents adopt Martin's program. In the speech to Martin, the assemblymen declared that commissions of oyer and terminer and general jail delivery, delegated by the Crown to Martin, "cannot be legally carried into execution without the aid of the legislature." The assembly could not consistent with "the justice due to our constituents make provisions for defraying the expences attending a measure which we do not approve." After making their protest, the aroused assembly proceeded to pass legislation that had been previously rejected. The legislation included the court bill with the usual attachment clause in it. This bill was rejected by the council. Martin accused the house of leaving the province defenseless in the last session, and he defended his policies. He advised them to consult with their constituents. The council expressed its approval and support of the governor's actions.[23]

On December 16 Martin wrote to Dartmouth, and criticized the assembly for being "gulled into any absurdities by a few artfull and designing men, influenced by selfish and interested motives. . . . " He saw them as demagogues. Martin was reacting to the rejection of his program by the assembly and its leaders, but what he did not know was the action taken by the house. The missing piece of the jigsaw puzzle for Martin was the meeting ten days earlier when the speaker of the house, John Harvey, laid before the House letters from various committees of correspondence in the other colonies inviting the North Carolina assembly to create a committee of inter-colonial correspondence. The House ordered that Samuel Johnston, Robert Howe, and Cornelius Harnett be a committee to draw up answers to the letters, and report the same to the house for approbation. Several historians have stated that the committee of correspondence in North Carolina began after February 1774 but this does not seem to be correct. It could be argued that December 6, 1773, was the date of the origin of the committee of correspondence in North Carolina, although the earlier visit of Josiah Quincy may have helped lay the groundwork for the creation of the committee. Meanwhile, on the same day that Martin wrote to Dartmouth, December 16, Samuel Adams sent a disciplined group of men disguised as Indians to seize and destroy the tea in Boston harbor. The news of this demonstration, the Boston Tea Party, would take several days to get to New Bern.[24]

Robert Howe reported to the House on December 8 that the committee had prepared answers to the earlier letters. A letter from the House of Burgesses was read referring to Virginia's resolution of March 12, 1773, when an eleven man standing committee for intercolonial correspondence was appointed. Virginia asked North Carolina to appoint a similar committee to correspond with them. The assembly resolved that a standing committee of correspondence and enquiry be appointed to consist of nine men: John Harvey, Robert Howe, Cornelius Harnett, William Hooper, Richard Caswell, Edward Vail, John Ashe, Joseph Hewes, and Samuel Johnston. Five members of the committee were to serve as another committee to gather information about acts and resolutions of the British Parliament, or proceedings of administration as may relate to or affect the British colonies in America and to keep up and maintain a correspondence with the other colonies. From Martin's point of view, he was correct when he told Dartmouth that there were "artfull and designing men" who led the assembly in December, 1773.

The governor, on December 21, sent an oral message by his secretary to the House requiring the members immediate attendance at the palace. Suspecting that Martin was going to prorogue the assembly, the house delayed waiting on the governor and prepared a surprise and an insult for him. The House formally resolved that an appeal be made to the king asking him to withdraw the instruction regarding the foreign attachment clause. It then proposed asking Governor William Tryon of New York to forward the address to the king, supporting it with his interest and influence. The House asked Tryon to accept "this important Trust as testimony of the great affection this Colony bears him, and the entire confidence they repose in him." The resolution was recorded in their journal as a matter of public record. It is doubtful that the House had great affection for Tryon, but it is clear that the members intended the resolution as an indication of their dislike for Governor Martin. A committee composed of John Harvey, Robert Howe, Samuel Johnston, William Hooper, Isaac Edwards, John Ashe, Cornelius Harnett, and Joseph Hewes was appointed "to carry into Execution the purposes of the . . . Resolves."[25]

It is interesting to note that six of the committee were members of the new committee of correspondence, and that Howe and Edwards personally detested Martin for blocking their earlier appointments to provincial offices. The House succeeded in offending Martin because he interpreted it as such to Dartmouth. Martin considered Howe and Edwards as authors of the petition to the Crown, and he was probably correct in this assumption. Tryon told Martin that he was amazed to learn of his difficulties with the assembly.[26]

Martin described to his brother Samuel his problem with the assembly and how he had voted the court law. His remarks to Samuel echo informally his explanation to the council why he prorogued the assembly until March 1, 1774. The governor reported to Samuel that "the heated imagination of the Patriots had now wrought up that House to consider, and to contend for, as a Constitutional right and Privilege." He informed his council that he had discovered in the House "a temper throughout their Session from whence more violent and offensive steps might be apprehended, if that House continued sitting. . . ."[27]

Anticipating "violent and offensive steps," Martin had proposed to the secretary of war, Lord Barrington, that in case of war he should organize a battalion in the province provided that his old army rank could be restored. He told his brother that restoration of his old rank "might be good . . . for me, when Civil Governments should be no longer tenable: a case that I own, the late frantic proceedings in the Northern Colonies, have at times, brought me to think possible." He was referring to the terrorizing of the tea consignees in the North and his concern that the disturbances might spread to North Carolina.[28]

Besides concern about the assembly and the worry about the possibility of war, Martin was beset with personal financial problems. He wrote letters telling his brother and Dartmouth about them. He had lost £1,000 of "my little income" when the Orders in Council forbade the granting of Crown lands. Martin asked Dartmouth to request the king to grant some equivalent support. Thus, the governor's problems with the assembly were compounded by the decline in his income. Martin suspected that his problems would soon worsen. He was right.[29]

The House had moved against the governor when it proposed the petition to the king and had insulted him by asking Tryon to forward it to the Crown. The House had also ordered its version of the proceedings of the assembly published in the North Carolina Gazette in New Bern. It was published on December 24, 1773. Despite those moves by the House, Martin continued to regard the foreign attachment clause as a discriminating burden on the citizens of North Carolina. He wrote to the Board of Trade on December 24 in an effort to persuade the board to reconsider its interpretation of the attachment clause relating to North Carolina. He explained the attitude of the assembly, and he listed the reasons why no court law could be passed. He reported that the assembly was determined to maintain the foreign attachment law and every method for the recovery of debts that Englishmen might use against them. With the foreign attachment right, Martin argued, "a citizen of London, Bristol, &c., can attach the effects of an American found within their Jurisdictions, for a debt contracted here or there; and whether the American has, or has not been there, or may or cannot (according to the common acceptation of the word) be said to abscond." Martin declared that the assembly of North Carolina should be allowed to pass the foreign attachment law because New York, Pennsylvania, and Virginia had it.[30]

Martin, in January, 1774, sent to the board abstracts of the attachment laws of New York and Pennsylvania and copies of two Virginia laws regarding attachments. The governor tried to demonstrate to the board why the North Carolina assembly feared that without its own foreign attachment law its citizens would be blocked from recovering debts from individuals and firms in the other colonies.[31]

To persuade Dartmouth to support the assembly, Martin analyzed for him the confusion over the words "abscond" and "conceal" when related to the foreign attachment clause. He reported that members of the assembly interpreted that a debtor could escape his creditor by staying in his house (a man's home is his castle), and block his creditors. He could thus keep his goods "from Attachment under the restrictions of that process, intended by my instructions" because the creditors could not "make any due proof that he absconded &c, but only, that the ordinary process of Law could not be served upon him." Martin argued further that in England the statutes of bankruptcy allowed the creditor to seize a debtor's goods in similar cases. Unfortunately, the bankruptcy statutes did not apply to the colonies, and the only way for relief in North Carolina, was through the foreign attachment law when the debtor concealed himself. Martin suggested that the word abscond encompassed the idea in the word conceal. In North Carolina a man could "abscond from his dealings with the world, and to the detriment of his creditors, in his own house . . . as much as if he removed to Japan." In his conclusion, Martin suggested to Dartmouth that his offer of August 4, 1773, to the assembly was not adequate for the needs of the people.[32]

The governor changed his strategy when he addressed the joint session of the assembly on March 2, 1774. He urged that a regular system of courts be established without delay and that the court law exclude the attachment clause because in the other colonies it was in a separate act. He encouraged the assembly to try to resolve the court law quarrel to prevent anarchy. The council readily agreed to the governor's proposition. The House members responded on March 5, telling the governor that they had again consulted with their constituents and had received from them "their warmest approbation of our past proceedings." The House stated that it had been given "positive instructions to persist in our endeavors to obtain the process of foreign Attachments upon the most liberal and ample footing."[33]

The governor urged in a calm and objective manner that the assembly trust the king's justice and create the much needed courts without providing for an attachment law. Martin argued calmly that the other colonies enjoyed the attachment clause in separate laws was proof of the king's approval of an attachment law, but separate from the court law. If the House continued in its determination, Martin hoped that they would at least cooperate in establishing courts to handle criminal matters, and thus providing for law and order.[34]

The council, acting as an intermediary, proposed that there be two bills: the court bill and the attachment clause would be divided with a suspending clause in the attachment bill. "The assembly rejected that proposal by a vote of 49 to 16 . . . " and entered in its journal " . . . the names and votes of the members of the assembly." The recorded votes reveal that the house members differed in their interpretations. The difference seemed to be sectional with only three members from the east voting against the council's proposal. The Orange County members split their vote: Ralph Macnair voting for and Thomas Hart against.[35]

The council continued to try to find compromise measures to solve the impasse over the foreign attachment clause. No solution could be found that was acceptable to either the House or the governor. With the collapse of negotiations, the assembly passed a court bill with the usual provisions, which was presented to the governor along with twenty-six other bills. Martin gave his assent to all of them except the superior court bill.[36]

Frustrated by the defeat of its superior court bill with the attachment clause, the House entered in its journal a resolution declaring that the power of foreign attachments was "founded upon principles of the strictest equity." The principle of the foreign attachment "was so essential to the commercial Interest of this Colony, that we think it a duty we owe our constituents, and posterity to retain it unimpaired. . . . '' Moreover, it declared that the lack of a foreign attachment law was the source for the distress of the colony.[37]

The House began work on a bill to establish inferior courts and the differences between the council and the House were easily solved. The county courts were limited to cases involving less than £20 proclamation money. The assembly also prepared a bill establishing courts of oyer and terminer and general jail delivery. Both bills were accepted by the governor. The governor's assent was a modest victory for the House's principle that it had a right to create courts.[38]

During the last days while the assembly was sitting, the House resolved to ask Thomas Barker and Alexander Elmsly, former members of that body and presently merchants in London, to be its agents in petitioning the Board of Trade to accept the attachment clause as modified in the 1774 superior court bill. The House advised the governor of its action and asked for his support. Members argued that Martin's instructions from the Crown that prohibited foreign attachments "arose from the abuses to which the mode of attaching the effects of Foreigners by our former Laws were liable to . . . [but the revised clause] is so framed as not in any manner to be injurious to the interest of foreign debtors. . . . ''[39]

Besides the frustrating struggles over the attachment question, Martin was worried about the threat of Indian violence in the west. John Stuart, the southern superintendent for Indian affairs, had warned him about the encroachment of the Watauga settlements on the Cherokee hunting grounds. A militia bill was passed and Martin on March 28 prorogued the assembly, announcing that it would meet again on May 26.[40]

Martin, on April 2, wrote Dartmouth that he had sent a letter to the Board of Trade explaining and defending his veto of the superior court bill. His reasons for vetoing the bill, he explained, were that it limited the original jurisdiction of the superior courts to bases involving more than £20, where both plaintiff and defendant lived in the same district, and to matters over £10 value when both lived in different districts. He elaborated on problems that would result from the restrictions, adding that the alleged compromise of the House had no benefits at all. Martin thought that the justices of peace were too ignorant to determine "what is the due proof of such circumstances that should entitle a Plaintiff to a Writ of Attachment. . . . " The governor argued that in other colonies except for Virginia that only the justices of the supreme courts could issue original attachments, but his vetoed bill allowed justices of the peace to issue attachments for any sum whatsoever. He added: "and it is notorious, that they have heretofore granted them without any proof of debt, and without any Oath whatsoever."[41]

Martin further argued that he vetoed the bill because the assembly's amendment that no attachment would issue unless the cause of the action arose in North Carolina. This amendment was "destroyed by the . . . Clause, which directs that before the Defendant be suffered to plead, he, or his Attorney, shall give bail to a new suit or action, if the Plaintiff judges . . . " it necessary. Martin's interpretation was that if the defendant had no attorney and no bail was offered, the attachment would still be good, even though the cause of action clearly arose outside North Carolina. If the defendant had an attorney, the plaintiff could hold a person to bail by the 1774 superior court law in all cases deemed to be special "upon his own suggestion of Damage, without affidavit, as Writs are in all other Actions obtainable here. . . . " Martin thought that this might put the damages so high that the attorney of the defendant would not be able to procure bail.

Most administrators expect their advisors to support them when they make an important decision. Martin was no exception to the rule. He was very annoyed when the council passed the superior court bill and advised him to accept it, although they had received a copy of the royal instructions prohibiting the attachment clause. Martin requested that the council members who had advised him to pass the bill to give him in writing their reasons for approving the bill. These councillors were Samuel Cornell, Lewis H. DeRosset, William Dry, and John Rutherford. The councillors who voted against the bill were James Hasell, Alexander McCulloch, Samuel Strudwick, and Chief Justice Martin Howard. The governor sent copies of their letters to the board of trade.[42]

The five councillors who advised Martin to accept the superior court bill may have met together or corresponded with each other in writing their explanatory letters, for they seem to be almost identical. They stated as their main reason for advising the acceptance of the bill that the province was without either civil or criminal courts. The councillors believed that the remedy for the threat of anarchy in North Carolina was to accept the bill as passed by the assembly. Moreover, the bill included Dartmouth's suggestions that the attachments should not issue unless the cause of action arose in the province. They advised that acceptance by Martin would have had "a tendency to quiet the minds of the Inhabitants of this Country" and "His Majesty's service would have been more effectually promoted by your Assent to the Bill then to suffer the Country to remain longer in anarchy and confusion."[43]

Martin explained to Dartmouth his trouble with the assembly and particularly the councillors who did not support him. He reported to Dartmouth that he had seen in the last two sessions of the assembly, a tendency in the council to side with the House. He added that: "These Members seem to have . . . studied to throw the odium of resisting the Assembly's wishes off their own shoulders upon the King's Governor . . . becoming thus an embarrassment rather than a bulwark & defence to Government. . . . " Martin considered removing them from the council.[44]

Earlier in June, 1772, Martin had apparently considered a reshuffling of the royal council because he had written to his brother Samuel for advice and support in talking to John Pownall, secretary of the board of trade, about changing the membership of the council. Martin, in April, 1774, asked Dartmouth to replace the five maverick councillors with Lancelot Graves Berry, Hugh Finlay, Thomas Markwright, Robert Munford, and Robert Schard. The fifth councillor to be replaced was John Sampson who was not present because of illness when the council voted on the court bill, but he did submit a letter explaining why he supported the bill. Alexander McCulloch was listed as voting against the bill and yet Martin wanted him replaced on the council. Perhaps McCulloch was too friendly with the dissident councillors because later he would join the patriots. Moreover, Martin had a poor opinion of McCulloch too. In his dispatch to Dartmouth, Martin mentioned Thomas McGuire and Willie Jones as new council members, but it was still too soon for news to arrive of their appointment in New Bern. In the past, Martin's attitude toward his councillors had been friendly and supportive, particularly those who cooperated with him. He tried to get James Hasell nominated lieutenant governor, but failed. Pointing out that the councillors were not wealthy men, Martin asked Dartmouth to consider granting each council member a regular salary to attend council meetings three or four times a year. The governor thought the salaries could be paid out of the revenue of the Crown's quit rents once it became a competent fund. Apparently, Dartmouth did not consider Martin's suggestion seriously.[45]

While the foreign attachment law was causing trouble for Martin and the assembly, across the sea the Board of Trade was beginning to look more favorably upon some of the complaints of North Carolina. The board, on April 22, asked Richard Jackson to analyze the superior court bill and to advise it if any instruction could be suggested to approve the attachment without prejudicing the principles of the laws of England, and still remove the objections stated by the assembly.[46]

Early in May, Dartmouth advised Martin that the assembly's amendments to the attachment clause in the court bill had some merit. He said that the oath required before an attachment could issue in which the plaintiff swore that the defendant in the suit had "according to the best of his belief and information" absconded to avoid payment of his debts so that the law process could not be served upon him, that the Crown would certainly consent to the oath in that form. Dartmouth concluded that Martin could accept any law by which the mode of attachment adopted in other colonies could be enacted with regard to defendants resident in either Virginia or South Carolina. Dartmouth believed that this explanation of the Crown's wishes would be acceptable to the assembly and it might permit the establishment of the much needed court system in the province.[47]

Martin was not as confident and hopeful as Dartmouth. He was not sure that the assembly would accept Dartmouth's proposal until they knew the result of their own application to the Board of Trade upon the subject. The governor thought that the assembly would object to the restriction of using the attachments only in the adjoining colonies "while the Inhabitants of other Provinces are at liberty to employ that process against Debtors in all parts of His Majesty's Dominions." Martin knew that the colony's trade with the neighboring colonies was modest compared to the larger trade with Massachusetts, New York, and England. Trade with the northern colonies and England was greater and thus the need for the foreign attachment clause was more compelling in these areas.[48]

While the assembly and board were trying to solve the problem of foreign attachments, two other men were trying to find a solution. The two agents appointed by the house to prepare a memorial to the board were Alexander Elmsly and Thomas Barker, Carolina merchants in London. They were searching the area of attachments in preparation for their memorial. Elmsly was experienced in the practice of foreign attachments in England. He informed Samuel Johnston that foreign attachments were available only in London, Bristol, and York. He explained that

" . . . no attachment takes place except where the cause of the action arises within the city, and that if the affidavit of the debt is not made by the plaintiff upon suing out the attachment, it may be set aside on entering common bail and in no case can the garnishee be compelled to answer, unless he voluntarily . . . comes into Court and discloses the amount of the effects in his hands; but if the plaintiff can prove that at the time of laying the attachment, the garnishee was either indebted to the defendant or had effects of his in his possession, he is admitted to do it, and such proof is as good as the garnishee's confession."[49]

Elmsly told Johnston that the assembly was wrong in trying to retain the old attachment law. He believed that justice required the creditors in England and North Carolina to be equal. Elmsly advised "that if one of our merchants fails, his English and American creditors should receive the same dividend; whereas, as things stood under the late law, the American creditor who could find effects in that country has his whole debt, when the English creditor often got little or nothing."

Elmsly argued that there were no provisions in the provincial law that would "warrant an attachment against the estate of a person who had never resided in the colony because that person neither conceals, absconds nor absents himself, which the form of your attachment makes a *sine qua non*." He further advised that the province needed an act similar to a Virginia act "respecting persons never resident in the Colony, which . . . puts all creditors on a footing."

Samuel Johnston's reply of September 23 is interesting not only for the difference in opinions but for Johnston's reason for the necessity of an attachment law, social mobility. Johnston explained that he had always believed that it was only fair that contracts should be enforced under the laws of the country where they were entered into. If the defendant withdrew from that country then his creditor should have the option to follow "the person of his Debtor or have recourse against the property he left behind him." He thought attachments were necessary to regulate trade especially in countries where men were "continually rambling."[50]

Elmsly reported to Johnston on the status of the attachment memorial. He reported that Governor Tryon was visiting in London and had told him that he would speak to Richard Jackson about the province's attachment law. Tryon thought that certain persons (he did not identify them) wanted to block extension of bankruptcy proceedings to the colonies because "some Gents in England held large tracts of Land in America which they would wish exempted from attachments."[51]

Dartmouth advised Martin on March 3, 1775:

"The difficulties which have accompanied the establishment of proper Courts of Justice from the obstinate adherence of the Assembly to their erroneous opinions respecting the Laws of Attachment will I hope be soon removed as their Agents here in that Business Mr. Barker and Mr. Elmsly have desired to be heard and have presented a Memorial in which they have stated the matter in a way that I think will lead to Accommodation."[52]

The memorial to the Board of Trade traced the history of the dispute to the current crisis. It stated that the instructions to Martin allowing the process to extend to persons residing in Virginia and South Carolina was useless because trade between North Carolina and her neighbors was not important compared to the trade with Massachusetts and New York. The memorialists urged the necessity of the attachment law because of the "unsettled state of the Colonies," a reference to the Boston Tea Party and the subsequent disorders. That reference may have been used to spur the board into agreeing to the attachment law. The memorial further argued that the attachment was used in all the other colonies and had never been complained about, "either here or there, except in the single case of their taking place in favour of American creditors, of Commissions of Bankrupts sued out in England." The memorial concluded that the assembly could remedy this inequity "if permitted to put their Court Laws on the same Footing, in other respects as formerly."[53]

The memorial was read to the Board of Trade on May 8. It was forwarded to Richard Jackson to give them his judgment within the next ten days. He replied on May 17. It was Jackson's opinion that regulations governing attachments against debtors who lived in a neighboring colony could be easily written for the purpose of preventing such a legal action without notifying "the defendant of its commencement." Jackson pointed out that action described was inconsistent with the common law and with the rules of justice as practiced by most European states. The wise Jackson cautioned that personal actions always required "witnesses who are probably to be found where the cause of action arises, and not where the effects of the defendant happed to lye." Thus according to Jackson "a personal suit should be prosecuted only in that country where the Defendant resides unless he had absconded." Jackson reasoned that if more freedom of action were permitted in North Carolina "it would answer every end of Justice to permit such Attachments in cases where the Plaintiff shall swear that the Defendant conceals himself, or absconds from" his residence. He argued that injustices would result besides the use of gaining preferences to other creditors "who have proved Debts under a Commission of Bankruptcy," but if colonial creditors did not use such attachments they would "frequently lose their whole debts for want of being able to prove them in time."[54]

The Board of Trade finally moved on May 18, 1775, but it did little. It decided to draft instructions for Martin based on the following:

That it would not be advisable to allow Attachments of the effects of persons not residing within the Province or within the adjoining Provinces of South Carolina & Virginia . . . except only when proof should be made that the Defendant in any action the cause of which arose in Great Britain, Ireland or any other of the Plantations, had removed from his usual place of abode in order to avoid payment of his debt, and that in allowing Attachments in cases of Defendants residing in the adjoining Colonies of South Carolina & Virginia, due provision should be made by Law for giving such persons timely notice of the process.[55]

Three years before, the board's decision might possibly have been accepted by the assembly; however, time, ideas, and actions had made acceptance of such a decision in the colony almost impossible. The board had fallen into a trap of its own making: procrastination had defeated its purpose. The compromise was not worth the paper on which it was written.

The crisis of 1773 over the attachment clause revived the old quarrel over the courts between the governor and the assembly, and it became one of the major reasons for the Revolution in North Carolina. Although Martin had made a concession to the assembly to let it create the inferior courts in 1774, the assembly pressed forward for the attachment law. In all probability the attachment question did not affect financially most North Carolinians, but the resulting lack of courts did frighten many citizens and caused them to question the intentions of the Crown and the governor. The canny leaders of the tidewater played upon the fears of the Mecklenburg leaders and other colonists about the lack of courts and the problem of law and order. According to one historian, "It was the attachment question that kept the revolutionary pot boiling ever higher." Once the Whigs saw that they could manipulate most of the Carolinians through the propaganda that the king and governor were intent upon bending them to their will, the radicals embarked upon a program for revolution.[56]

IV. The Governor and the Whigs

Throughout the long quarrel over the court system, the Whig leaders in the House used the lack of a foreign attachment law as a means to dramatize to everyone in North Carolina how the Crown and Parliament were trying to destroy the constitution and deprive the colonists of their rights. The radical leaders purposely combined the superior court and inferior court bills into one which included the prohibited foreign attachment law and a suspending clause. The Whigs knew that Governor Martin had to obey the Crown's instructions and veto it. Thus, at the end of the assembly's session in 1773, the province had no courts. This gave the Whigs an opportunity to blame the Crown and the royal governor for the hardships and to warn of the imminent anarchy that would result from the loss of the courts.

As in many revolutions the American was a conservative one as suggested by Carl Lotus Becker in his famous set of questions: who shall rule? and who shall rule at home? This thesis has been further developed by many American historians, for example, Elisha P. Douglass, who described the revolution as the struggle for equal political rights and majority rule during the American Revolution. The struggle suggests difference of opinions that become polarized around the conservative and radical ideas, but basically the American Revolution was conservative with the exception of the desire for the abolition of political privilege on the part of groups outside the politically active classes who felt that in the past they had not received the power they should. Yet when it came to writing the state constitutions many of these incipient radicals became conservatives because they feared that unchecked majorities of constituents or representatives could produce tyranny as any unchecked dictator.[1]

For years many readers of North Carolina history and even

some of the historians accepted the myth that the October election of 1776 was a radical victory. This was an invention by Joseph Seawell Jones in his *Defence of the Revolutionary History of the State of North Carolina from the Aspersions of Mr. Jefferson* (Boston, 1834). Later in 1857-58, Griffith McRee, an early biographer of James Iredell, accepted and embellished Jones' rabid Federalist-Whig account. Jones hated Thomas Jefferson and his party as well as Andrew Jackson and the Democratic Party because he feared and distrusted the rising democracy of the period. Robert L. Ganyard returned to the documents and checked Jones' work and discovered that he had deliberately set up the myth that the October election of 1776 in North Carolina was a radical victory when in reality it was a conservative one. Jones "glorifies the conservatives and their cause and is notoriously prejudiced against the radicals." He was guilty of misrepresentation of historical fact and even of the invention of historical situations in other instances. He was a notorious "hoaxer who delighted in the creation of historical myths to feed to a credulous public." Unfortunately Jones' misrepresentations have influenced many historians, including Robert D. W. Connor. Samuel A'Court Ashe was one of the few who was not beguiled for he too went back to the original sources.[2]

R. Don Higginbotham has recently questioned the use of the conservative and radical labels during the early days of the Republic. For example, a conflict historian describes staid dignified Samuel Johnston, brother-in-law of the young Iredell, being opposed by "the radical chieftain, Willie Jones of Halifax, who though a wealthy eastern planter, was a liberal idealist, a champion of the common people." Higginbotham also challenged the myth of Willie Jones as a radical chieftain.[3]

Many of the southern leaders were moved "by an intense desire for personal independence or freedom that was in their society a mark of honor," and they wanted to pass on to their children the gains of earlier generations. Moreover, many of the Whigs were concerned about upward and downward social mobility. All of them were to a great extent "outsiders, opponents, as they saw it, of an inner clique of powerful men, whether Crown appointees" or men of wealth and position who supported the Crown and were later called loyalists. There were North Carolina leaders such as James Iredell and William Hooper who were Whigs not because they were incendiaries but because they were committed to a moral interpretation of politics and history. There were other men such as Cornelius Harnett, a pragmatic politician like Samuel Adams to the north, who was committed to the idea of independence and if necessary he would use incendiary ideas. Other men seem to be more interested in personal gain through political power and who would hesitate to use incendiary ideas; such as Robert Howe. The North Carolina Whigs shared with their southern and northern colleagues the ideas of freedom, frugality, independence, and power.[4]

When Parliament reacted to the Boston Tea Party and disciplined Massachusetts with the Coercive Acts this gave the radical leaders in all the colonies further proof that the Crown and Parliament were determined to destroy the constitutional basis of the American governments and their liberties. Specific proof of Britain's intention to keep the colonies in slavery was indicated in a series of letters written in the later 1760's by native-born Massachusetts governor Thomas Hutchinson and his lieutenant, Andrew Oliver, to Thomas Whately, an influential treasury official in George Grenville's government. Massachusetts' colonial agent, Benjamin Franklin, and a friend to Thomas Whately, secured these letters after Whately's death. Franklin sent the letters to his friend, Thomas Cushing, Speaker of the Massachusetts House of Representatives, stipulating that the letters were not to be copied. These letters shocked the patriot leaders for their criticism of the Americans' reaction to the stamp and tea taxes. Particularly shocking to the Americans was Hutchinson's statement that he doubted if it was possible "to project a system of government in which a colony 3,000 miles distant shall enjoy all the liberty of the parent state." When Samuel Adams saw these letters he knew that the American public should see them. He had them published in the *Boston Gazette* under the heading "Born and educated among us!" The other colonial newspapers reprinted them. Immediately the Massachusetts legislature sent a petition to the king for the removal of Hutchinson and Oliver. Once the London newspapers learned of the petition there was an uproar among the public. Franklin publicly admitted that he alone was responsible for exposing the letters because he hoped to effect a closer understanding between the Crown and America. Franklin's overture to the British leaders did not satisfy them because the Privy Council summoned him to their chamber known as "The Cockpit" where Solicitor Alexander Wedderburn humiliated Franklin, the Citizen of the World and transformed him into a dedicated patriot of the American cause when he stripped him of his royal office of Deputy-Postmaster of North America and charged him with stealing the letters. In America Franklin became a hero. During the furor in London Alexander Elmsly wrote to Samuel Johnston on March 24, 1774 a brief letter commenting about his illness and relaying London political gossip. He said that when the Privy Council had received the Massachusetts legislature's petition the Hutchinson-Oliver letters affair became a scandal. Elmsly also reported the second reading of a bill in Parliament that became the first Coercive or Intolerable Act, the Boston Port Bill.[5]

Johnston lost no time in sharing this information with William Hooper. Hooper and James Iredell agreed with Johnston's concern for the colony. Hooper wrote Iredell on April 26 in which he predicted America's political future: "with you I anticipate the important share which the Colonies must soon have in regulating the political balance. They are striding fast to independence, and ere long will build an empire upon the ruins of Great Britain. . . . Be it our endeavour to guard against every measure that may have a tendency to prevent so desirable an object."[6]

Meanwhile, John Harvey, speaker of the house, was moving towards the idea of independence. He laid before the assembly a letter from his counterpart in Maryland. The house resolved that Harvey should answer the letter thanking the assembly of Maryland for having "adopted the Patriotic Resolutions and measures of the truly Respectable House of Burgesses of Virginia." A few nights later Harvey and two other leaders sat late discussing continental and provincial affairs. They were Colonel Edward Buncombe and Samuel Johnston. Harvey said that Martin's secretary, James Biggleston, had told him that the governor did not intend to convene another assembly unless he saw some chance of a better one than the last. Harvey then replied to the secretary "then the people would convene one themselves." Johnston thought Harvey was "in a very violent mood, and declared he was for assemblying a convention independent of the Governor, and urged upon us to cooperate with him." Harvey promised he would lead the way and that he would issue handbills under his own name. He thought the committee of correspondence ought to go to work at once. Harvey added that he had only mentioned the matter to Willie Jones of Halifax the day before, and he approved it. Johnston confided to William Hooper: "As for my own part I do not know what better can be done. Without Courts to sustain the property and to exercise the talents of the Country, and the people alarmed and dissatisfied, we must do something to save ourselves." He asked for Hooper's counsel and advice on the subject and urged him to discuss it with Harnett and Colonel Ashe "or any other such men."[7]

Martin had not yet received from Dartmouth the latest instructions of the crown regarding the quarrel over the courts. He told Dartmouth that the discontent manifested and declared by a great part of the "Inhabitants of this Country at the Proceedings of the Assembly with regard to the Court-laws, at the three last Sessions incline me to hope that as soon as answers are received to the representations made by the late assembly, a better system for the administration of Justice will be adopted." Until then, the governor thought it "fruitless to make further attempts."[8]

Of all of the groups that suffered the most from the lack of courts was probably the clergy of the Church of England. The cause for their distress was that the church depended upon provincial taxes. With no courts, no taxes could be collected to pay their salaries and expenses. Many of the priests were critical of the radical disturbances in the north and their stand antagonized many of the members of their churches. The colonists would consider the priests as supporters of the crown rather than serving their needs in the parishes. Discrimination was not just limited to the Church of England clergy for during the revolution other preachers were subjected to abuse and expulsion from their churches. During the revolution, Martin could not help these abused ministers, but before the revolution he tried to help them. Governor Martin corresponded with the Bishop of London to gain his support to secure the salaries for the local priests of the Church of England, but he failed. Martin's parish priest, the Reverend James Reed, reported to his superior in London: "All America is in a most violent flame and every good man would forbear as much as possible adding the least Fuel to the Fire."[9]

Meanwhile, the *North Carolina Gazette* in New Bern was adding "Fuel to the Fire" when it devoted its July 15, 1774 issue to the problem caused by the famous tea party in Boston. An account described the difficulties between the people of Massachusetts and the Crown and Parliament. At the same time, William Hooper and his friends in Wilmington were adding "Fuel to the Fire" when they planned for a general meeting to call the first provincial congress on July 21, 1774. A committee was named to prepare a circular letter to the counties of the province inviting them to send deputies to attend a general meeting at Johnston Courthouse on the 20th of August. At this meeting they were to elect delegates to an American Congress to be held in Philadelphia on the 20th of September or at a convenient time for the other colonies. In both meetings the delegates were to consider ways and means to avert the British evils threatening the American colonies, and in particular to come to the aid and support of their sister colony, Massachusetts, for having exerted itself in defense of the constitutional rights of America.[10]

The committee members that prepared the circular letter were Colonel James Moore, John Ancrum, Fred Jones, Samuel Ashe, Robert Howe, Robert Hogg, Francis Clayton, and Archibald Maclaine. The Wilmington meeting further resolved to support the other colonies "with Purses and Persons," and to send a supply of provisions to Salem to alleviate the distress of the citizens of Boston. In response to this circular letter, freeholders meetings were held in many of the counties and handbills were issued calling upon the people to elect delegates. The time and place for the provincial convention were changed to August 25 at New Bern.[11]

Martin had blocked a challenge to the royal prerogative by Isaac Edwards, a personal enemy, in the Beaufort inferior court in

July when Edwards had questioned Martin's authority to appoint a local county clerk. Edwards tried to clear his client by pleading in abatement that the clerk was not qualified. A council meeting investigated Edwards' challenge and upheld Martin. Andrew Miller told Thomas Burke that he thought Edwards "blameable." Successful in defeating Edwards' challenge to his authority, Martin believed he had control of the dissidents when he refused to call a new assembly until he could get a more amenable one. In the past, the regular way to select delegates to a continental congress, such as the Stamp Tax Congress, had been by election of the assemblies. Since Martin had dissolved the March assembly, he thought he had gained control of the situation as Tryon had done in 1765 in the Stamp Tax crisis, but the radicals had outmaneuvered him by calling a convention based on a popular will. Martin told his council that he had read newspapers and handbills of the invitation of the people in the province to meet to discuss the problems with England.[12]

On August 13 Martin issued a proclamation warning the people of the province to forbear attending any such illegal meetings as the one appointed for New Bern on August 25. On the morning of the twenty fifth Martin asked his council for advice on whether he could take further measures. Because Martin refused to call an assembly, it has been argued that the people of North Carolina should be grateful to Martin because the provincial convention became the first representative assembly of North Carolina and in all of America based on popular authority rather than royal.[13]

The provincial convention met in New Bern on August 25, 1774. With this meeting the American Revolution began in North Carolina. John Harvey was unanimously chosen moderator and Andrew Knox clerk. Seventy one members were present on the first day, representing twenty nine of the thirty five counties of the province. There were no representatives from the counties of Edgecombe, Guilford, Hertford, Surry or Wake and none from the towns of Brunswick, Campbellton or Hillsborough. Eight counties had only one representative each on the opening day.[14]

The merchant Andrew Miller criticized the patriots to Thomas Burke because some of the western counties were not represented and others had only one or two members while the southern and lower counties had six votes each. Since the western counties had no share in the nominations of Hooper and the other delegates to Philadelphia, Miller expressed the hope that they would not pay any share of the delegates' expense. Miller wrote: "It is not in character, to dispute the power of Parliament when we say we are not represented, and yet quickly Submit to so unequal a Representation in a body formed by ourselves." Nevertheless, the representation was better than could be expected considering that only a month intervened between the date of the Wilmington circular letter and the first day of the meeting. Besides their duties at home, the members had to travel great distances over poor roads.[15]

On the second day, the convention members listened to Joseph Hewes of Edenton report on the activities of their committee of correspondence. He read selected letters from other colonies which presumably gave them a more detailed report of the patriots' activities in their colonies and a fuller picture of Boston's struggle with the Crown. After Hewes' reading, the convention resolved that three delegates be appointed to attend the "General Congress to be held at Philadelphia sometime in September next." They adjourned until the next morning.[16]

The next day, Saturday, August 27, 1774, the convention came to grips with basic problems. After the flowery rhetoric declaring love and loyalty for the House of Hanover, the convention launched a torrent of denunciation and declaration. It denounced the claim of Parliament to tax the province, the tax on tea consumed in America, the Boston Port Act, and the act of Parliament regulating the police of Massachusetts. It declared the cause of Boston the cause of all, and that it was the duty of the province to contribute in proportion to its ability to ease the burden imposed upon that town, and to enable it to persist in a prudent and manly opposition to the schemes of Parliament.[17]

The convention members declared that after September 10, 1774, their families would not use East India tea and that all users would be considered enemies of their country. After January 1, 1775, they would not import from Britain any merchandise, except medicines, nor purchase articles so imported. After October 1, 1775, they would not export to Britain any articles whatsoever. They asserted that a continental congress ought to be held in Philadelphia on September 20, 1774, to define with certainty the rights of Americans, and for guarding them from future violations under the sanction of public authority. They declared non-intercourse with any colony that failed to abide by a general plan that might be adopted in the Continental Congress. They warned abut inflation of prices by stating that vendors of merchandise ought not to take advantage of their resolutions relating to non-importation, but sell their goods at the same rates they had been accustomed to selling them within the last three months.

The convention members then paused and caught their breath. They elected Richard Caswell, Joseph Hewes, and William Hooper delegates to the Continental Congress with authority to bind the people by their action. Moreover, the convention levied an assessment of twenty pounds proclamation money on each county to pay the expenses of the delegates.

The convention ordered that a committee of five be chosen in each county to see that the resolutions of the convention were obeyed, and to correspond with the provincial committee of correspondence. It then ordered that the moderator, John Harvey, or in case of his death, Samuel Johnston, be empowered on any future occasion to call another convention whenever the future might require. After three strenuous days, the delegates signed the journal of their proceedings and returned home. They had laid the foundation of a new government for the State of North Carolina.

Martin had been watching and listening for any reliable information about the convention proceedings before he reported to Dartmouth on September 1, 1774. He believed the reasons for the convention were to be found in the disappointment of two candidates for the Treasurer's office and the struggle that ensued. He thought the fuss over the attachment proposed by the government was a specious argument that served for a color and pretense for the struggle over the Treasurer's office. Moreover, Martin believed that Richard Caswell had accepted the election as a delegate to Philadelphia because he wanted to remain popular so that gate to Philadelphia because he wanted to remain popular so that he could continue in his office as Treasurer. Martin respected Caswell but he saw the other two delegates, Hewes and Hooper, as "professed champions of all popular measures." Martin was blinded by his attitudes which made him a loyal governor when he believed his difficulties were motivated by the struggle for a provincial office by two "professed champions." His training had not prepared him to comprehend, let alone accept, the idea of democracy for the masses. He was an honorable man but his observations and experience in the struggle for place and profit caused him to interpret some of the Carolina leaders' activities as a desire for power and profit. However, he had good reason to interpret the struggle for office and profit if one remembers his experience with Isaac Edwards and Robert Howe who sought office and profit and then turned against him.[18]

Despite his misunderstanding about Caswell, Martin did see clearly when he recommended to Dartmouth that the northern counties' representation be reduced from five each to two to make their influence more equitable to the western and southern counties. Later under the Constitution of 1776, each county had only two representatives. Martin was correct when he reported the activities of the committee of correspondence and its "cabals" with other colonies' committees.

Concerned about the loyalty of the members of the council, Martin told Dartmouth that some of them were fraternizing with the convention members. He had invited the council members to stay at the palace during the convention sessions, but only James Hasell had accepted. Martin complained about the hypocrisy of the council in supporting his proclamation and declaring the convention to be illegal when he was present but behind his back they were meeting with the members of the convention. Martin believed that the assembly would not change until they received an answer to their petition about the attachment instructions from the board of trade, and after the appointment of the treasurers in March 1775.

Once the convention adjourned (Martin called it the "end of the cabals here"), the province was quiet until the congress in

The governor sought to take advantage of the lull in the storm for he advised Dartmouth that he had to go to New York for a short time to see his doctor. The governor's health had been declining all summer, and "by a late severe return of illness is exceedingly impaired." Martin's illness was probably the recurrence of his fistula. He told Dartmouth he would "leave the Government in the hands of Mr. Hasell, president of the Council, until my return, which will be as soon as possible and before anything material can happen."

Conscious of the opposition of the house and aware of the desertion of his councillors, it is doubtful if Martin knew the extent to which his enemies were going to discredit him in the eyes of the people. Replying to Thomas Burke about Isaac Edwards' challenge to the governor's authority at Beaufort, Andrew Miller wrote on September 4 that Burke should have no doubt that Mr. Hamilton had the story from Edwards' friends, who, "like him, are not disposed to give the most favorable representations of the governor's conduct. I don't know how it happens but I believe no governor ever deserved a better character," and yet his enemies, "who are more numerous then one could expect, Stop not to utter any falsehood to make him appear Odious to the people in general, but however their Story may gain Credit at present, in the end they themselves must be despised. . . . " Miller concluded: "I doubt not to see him so generally esteemed, as any Governor on the Continent, tho' until the present disturbances are settled, I have no hopes of any of them being Treated with the respect that is due to them."[19]

Martin believed he had left the government in the secure and sensible control of the elderly James Hasell, but a new government was slowly emerging in the various committees of safety which were being established by the counties upon the recommendation of the provincial convention. Everyday these committees usurped some new authority, executive, judicial or legislative, and their power soon became all inclusive throughout the province.

The Rowan committee resolved that the people of the county "will break off all Trade, Commerce and Dealing" and they would not maintain trade with any resident in the county "who shall refuse, decline or neglect to carry into Execution the Resolves made at a general Meeting of Deputies of the Province at New Bern the 25th of August last." The committee declared that those who did offend should be deemed enemies to their country and treated accordingly. The committee singled out for contempt the merchants John Dunn and Benjamin B. Boots because they were the authors of a protest about the price of gunpowder. Their written protest was ordered to be placed on the two posts of the gallows and whipping post to demonstrate the contempt of the committee for these men. At their next meeting the Rowan committee accused William Spurgin of having signed the protest, but he denied this charge. The committee members were not satisfied with Spurgin's denial and they declared that he was an enemy of the people for supporting the illegal British taxes.[20]. . The Wilmington committee investigated merchants who were intending to sponsor horse racing for the Wilmington subscription purse. The committee directed the attention of the offenders to the order of the Continental Congress to discourage every form of extravagance, "especially all horse-racing." Because Wilmington was the most important port in the province, the committee was particularly busy investigating the illegal importation of slaves and the rising prices of rum, both of which had been forbidden by the provincial convention. Other merchants cooperated with their colleagues in the committees in getting their approval to sell goods recently received, but ordered before the convention met. Slaves recently shipped to Wilmington were ordered returned to the West Indies. The merchants selling rum and gunpowder were allowed to raise their prices.[21]

The Halifax committee placed Andrew Miller on a blacklist for refusing to sign the association because he argued that his creditors in Britain could not change Parliament's attitudes and his creditors would suffer if he withheld goods that rightly belonged to them. Miller swore he was a patriot, but the committee urged all Halifax citizens not to trade with Miller. Writing to his friend Thomas Burke on December 12, Miller told of his interview with the committee. Although he refused to sign the association he still did business with some of the patriots, such as Willie Jones. Miller claimed he was a patriot but he did not approve of the way the others were going about getting their rights. He told Burke that he had not received a letter from Britain dated later than July, except for one of August from Colonel Edmund Fanning. Miller noted that Lord Granville's commission making the governor his agent had arrived. Two copies had been sent by Charleston and New York. Both were "open'd and read by every Storekeeper on the Way. It's the freedom of the times," Miller concluded.[22]

By comparison to Andrew Miller, the conservative Samuel Johnston was quite radical in his attitude toward Parliament. For Johnston, the freedom of the times meant self-determination. Johnston wrote Elmsly in September that he had lived so long in America (he was an immigrant) that he considered it his home. He saw the Crown from the time of the Stamp act crisis to the present as using "every opportunity of teizing and fretting the people here as if on purpose to draw them into Rebellion or some violent opposition to Government." Johnston believed that "once the Sword is drawn all nice distinctions fall to the Ground; the difference between internal and external taxation will be little attended to, and it will hereafter be considered of no consequence whether the Act be to regulate Trade or raise a fund to support a majority in the House of Commons." Johnston argued: "By this desperate push the Ministry will either confirm their power of making Laws to bind the Colonies in all cases whatsoever or give up the right of making Laws to bind them in any Case." A right, Johnston concluded, "which they might have exercised in most cases to the mutual advantage of Great Britain and the Colonies for ages to come, had they exercised it with discretion."[23]

In New York City for medical treatment, Martin warned Dartmouth in a perceptive private letter of November 4, that "The crisis my Lord is come in my humble opinion and perhaps in the best time when Britain must assert and establish her just Rights and authority in the Colonies whatsoever they may be or give up forever all pretensions to dominion over them." Martin enclosed a newspaper which reported on the late Continental Congress. He described the delegates as an assembly of "the most inflammatory Spirits selected out of the several colonies for their democratical principles," and their known opposition to the government. The governor thought that the spirit of loyalty to the Crown was greater in New York than in any of the other twelve colonies but he feared that the friends of government in that city were awed by the "mob." He suggested that the Crown should send troops to over-awe the radicals and their followers. The governor reported that many of the friends of government wanted the tea duty removed because they, too, saw it as an internal tax. The loyalists thought that with the removal of the tax a reconciliation could be made. Furthermore, Martin thought that if the tea tax was removed it would destroy the monopoly of the Dutch tea smugglers and their support of the radicals. He said the Dutch tea smugglers were de-liberately encouraging the radicals in opposing the tea tax so that they could enjoy greater profits.[24]

The governor saw another threat in the democratic spirit of the Presbyterians. Based on his observations in New York and North Carolina, Martin said that the Presbyterians "are not of the prin-ciples of the Church of Scotland, but like the people of New Eng-land, more of the leaven of the Independents, who according to the English Story have been ever unfriendly to Monarchial Gov-ernment." Did Martin consider that Dartmouth was a devout Methodist and called "a Psalm Singer" when he urged him to give "greater encouragement to the establishment of the Church of England in a political view with respect to religion" because it was more congenial to the monarchial form of government? Martin particularly wanted to strengthen the Church of England in North Carolina; an idea that was not popular among most of the colonists in that province or for the other twelve colonies.

Early in November Martin sent, to an unknown correspond-ent, a detail of the proceedings of the Continental Congress. He remarked that his health had improved and he hoped to return to New Bern. He said that among all the embarrassments and diffi-culties of his administration, nothing had so mortified him or made him "so sensible of the weakness of my hands to carry on the Public Service in Carolina, as the undutiful and inconsistent be-haviour of the Council."[25]

Waiting for Martin to return, the faithful acting governor, James Hasell, with the advice and consent of the council once more postponed the assembly. It was to meet in New Bern on November 24. Hasell and the council thought the assembly "would precipitately adopt and give sanction and approbation to the measures of the Philadelphia Congress." When Martin returned to New Bern he approved the council's action, and he further prorogued the assembly to March 27, 1775.[26]

Eight days after the Martin family returned to New Bern on December 23 the governor's oldest son, Samuel, died and the family was plunged into a season of grief. Archibald Neilson, a close friend of the Martin family, told Andrew Miller: "Governor Martin has . . . lost his charming little boy Sam, the darling not only of his parents but of all who knew him." Martin advised Dartmouth: "This my Lord is the third of my dear children which this most baneful climate has brought untimely to the grave within the space of three years."[27]

When Neilson reported Martin's sorrow to Miller, he was outspoken in his denunciation of the "violences to the Northward" and he declared them to be folly and wickedness. He also commented rhetorically about Judge Richard Henderson's attempt to create an illegal proprietary colony across the Appalachians: "Pray is Dick Henderson out of his head?" Meanwhile, Martin had sent Dartmouth a copy of the proceedings of the safety committee of Halifax against Andrew Miller. He was ashamed to see at the head of the committee Willie Jones, whom he had formerly recommended to a vacant seat on the council.

Martin's concern for dissident leaders like Jones can be seen in his report to Dartmouth on his observations of the northern colonies on his recent trip to New York. He repeated again the necessity of sending additional troops to New York to restrain the patriots, but in New Jersey Martin considered the Sons of Liberty as more numerous and diligent, although they had gone no further than preaching sedition from the pulpits. In Philadelphia, Congress was paramount; it had little criticism except from the peaceable Quakers. While the gentry in Annapolis adhered to the government, they were against the parliamentary right of taxation. The general public in Maryland was wrought up to a high pitch of extravagance, and Martin believed his "old acquaintance and brother Officer" of Annapolis, Colonel Charles Lee was responsible for the frenzy because he found Lee drilling troops and "exciting contempt" for the power of Great Britain. In Virginia, Martin discovered the patriot leaders more violent and the committees appointed under Congress had proceeded in some places to the most arbitrary and unwarrantable exertions of power. He added: "The ferment there I perceive has in no sort abated as I think the advertisement of Mr. Washington and others that your Lordship will find in a News Paper of that colony enclosed plainly discovers."[28]

Martin advised Dartmouth that he wished he could "justly represent the temper" of the North Carolinians "to be generally more conformable to their duty to Govt. and their Country's Welfare than I have found it." He enclosed an advertisement of the Safety committee of New Bern "that may serve as a specimen of their atrocious falsehoods which are reported to stimulate the people to revolt." The advertisement was published in response to Martin's proclamation, which he enclosed, supporting the Crown's policy and warning the people not to choose delegates to the second illegal provincial convention. Martin thought the advertisement was the composition of Abner Nash, "an eminent lawyer but a most unprincipled character of this Country." The governor noted that there were rumors that the counties of New Brunswick and New Hanover had chosen field officers for a regiment, and that Robert Howe was reported to be training men in New Hanover. He thought there was little danger from Howe as a "military character" for he had formed a low opinion of Howe's ability as commander of Ft. Johnston. Howe became his enemy when he was replaced with Captain Collett. On a happier note, the governor told Dartmouth that the people of the western counties withstood for the most part all efforts to seduce them from their duty to the government. To support his statement, he enclosed some addresses from the counties of Dobbs, Rowan, Surry, and Guilford which declared loyalty to the Crown.

The committees of safety in the counties continued to usurp the royal governor's powers and put into effect the resolutions of the first Continental Congress. Wilmington had a very active committee with Cornelius Harnett as chairman. Harnett had previous political experience in the assembly; in 1773 he was chairman of the powerful standing committee of privileges and elections. The Wilmington committee was supported by most of the merchants but those men who tried to raise prices or engaged in public entertainments, and the sale of British goods were reprimanded, fined, and sometimes ostracized. The committee was particularly effective in enforcing the congressional articles of association by requiring all citizens of Wilmington to sign a copy of them. Despite congressional resolves against importing slaves, the committee permitted Harnett to import a slave from Rhode Island. Harnett and the committee had influence on other committees of safety, especially those in Brunswick, Chowan, Duplin, and Edenton. Perhaps the most effective influence besides control of commerce was the committee's decision on January 30, 1775, to finance a propaganda organ, Adam Boyd's *The Cape Fear Mercury*.[29]

The activities of other safety committees were reported by Andrew Miller of Halifax, to Thomas Burke in Hillsborough in March 1775. Miller commented on one committee summoning its chairman before them "as a Culprit" but it could not prove the charge. He noted that Parson Agnew was "advertised as a Violator" because he refused to appear before the committee regarding his renting a "flatt" to a merchant. The merchant had to give up the flat. Parson Agnew was much criticized for preaching obedience to the "King and the Laws of the Country, and admonishing his Congregation against Riots, &c." The perceptive Miller reported to Burke that "The Govr. is now very unwell, which fancy is in a great measure occasioned by the present plan of Politicks in this Country."[30]

Martin might have felt better if he had known that James Iredell had received a letter from his uncle, Thomas Iredell, in St. Dorothy's, Jamaica, in which he urged James, who was "so full of Politics," to remain neutral in the struggle of the patriots with the Crown. Thomas Iredell saw the struggle as "mercenary Men in Trade, who were trying to destroy the commerce of the mother country." A few days later James received a teasing letter from his sophisticated brother Arthur in London: "Pray are you become Patriotic? I see by the News Papers the Edenton Ladies have signalized themselves by their protest agst. Tea Drinking."[31]

Janet Schaw, a Scottish lady of Tory persuasion visiting her brother Robert, a Wilmington merchant, recorded in her journal that she had not had a "dish of tea" during her month's stay at Brunswick in the winter of 1775. Early in April while visiting Wilmington, Miss Schaw tartly observed that "The Ladies have burnt their tea in a solemn procession, but they had delayed however till the sacrifice was not very considerable, as I do not think any one offered above a quarter of a pound." This little known event (apparently Miss Schaw was the only person to record it) probably does not refer to the Edenton ladies since they did not burn their tea, but in all likelihood refers to a demonstration sometimes called the Wilmington Tea Party.[32]

Dartmouth was concerned that it took so much time to receive Martin's dispatches. He regretted that there was not a more direct channel of communication with North Carolina. He told Martin in his dispatch of February 1, 1775, that he had not received Martin's dispatch of September 1, 1774, until January 27. This letter described the activities of the assembly in the court quarrel and the cabals of the committee of correspondence with the other colonies. Dartmouth reported that the king and his ministers were alarmed about the activities of the correspondence committees as well as the recalcitrant members of the council. He was concerned because the long delay in delivering Martin's dispatch had kept the king and his ministers ignorant of the extraordinary proceedings of the people of North Carolina.[33]

Martin was advised that the board of trade would consider replacing the council members guilty of duplicity and Dartmouth requested him to name replacements. Moreover, Dartmouth told Martin he could replace Samuel Johnston as deputy naval officer, but since the governor had written to the Reverend Robert Cholmondley, the auditor general, Dartmouth wanted to see him before replacing Isaac Edwards, the deputy auditor of the province. In March Dartmouth removed Edwards.

With the assurance of support from Dartmouth, Martin, on

February 10, issued a proclamation declaring Richard Henderson and his associates in direct violation of the Royal Proclamation of 1763 which prohibited buying Indian lands except with permission of the Crown through the Royal Superintendent of Indian Affairs. The proclamation was made in the king's name as well as the Earl of Granville. Part of Henderson's proposed colony was in the Granville District, the last of the lords proprietors, the original English owners of the Carolinas. As Granville's agent, Martin forbade Henderson and his confederates on the pain of the Crown's displeasure and rigorous penalties of the law to prosecute this unlawful undertaking. The proclamation for apprehending Judge Henderson was published in the *North Carolina Gazette* on February 24, 1775.[34]

Martin reported his actions to Dartmouth on March 10 while Governor Dunmore of Virginia on March 21 also issued a proclamation against Henderson and warned the public to ignore his pretensions to owning Indian lands that belonged to Virginia. John Stuart, the superintendent for Indian affairs of the southern department, reported to Dartmouth on March 28 and enclosed letters from a Mr. Cameron complaining about Henderson and from Martin advising he had issued a proclamation.[35]

While Judge Henderson was defying royal authority, John Harvey was planning to take over the royal government in the province. On February 11, John Harvey issued handbills and circular letters in Perquimans County requesting the counties and towns in the colony to elect representatives to a convention that would meet in New Bern on Monday, April 3. The purpose of this convention was to elect deputies to attend a general congress at Philadelphia on the tenth of May. April 3 was the day before the assembly was to convene in New Bern. Harvey's bold announcement must have electrified the patriots and horrified Martin and the friends of government when they saw these handbills and their publication in the newspapers. Many of the patriots proceeded to announce county elections for their representatives.[36]

Martin, on March 1, issued a proclamation warning the citizens not to subject themselves to the "Restraints of tyrannical and arbitrary Committees." He declared that the assembly was the only lawful representative body of the people. Martin called on the good people to forbear to meet to choose persons to represent them in the convention and to renounce and discourage all such meetings as cabals and illegal proceedings in which "artful and designing Men" would lead the province into anarchy, and the destruction of the real interest and happiness of the people.[37]

Meanwhile, across the Atlantic in Westminster the petitions and declarations of the first Continental Congress were laid before Parliament on January 19, 1775. Lord Chatham's request that the king remove the troops from Boston was defeated as was his later plan of reconciliation introduced on February 1. Parliament, on February 9, declared Massachusetts to be in rebellion. On February 20 Lord North presented the ministerial plan for reconciliation to which George III gave a reluctant consent. By its terms Parliament, with royal approval, would forbear to lay any but regulating taxes upon any American colony which, through its own assembly, taxed itself to provide for the common defense and for the support of civil government and judiciary within its own province. The Commons endorsed the plan on February 27. Dartmouth, on March 3, sent a circular letter to all the American governors advising them of the Crown's "gracious concession" to them. On the same day the Commons endorsed Lord North's conciliation plan, February 27, a bill was introduced forbidding the New England colonies to trade with any nation but Britain and the British West Indies after July 1 and banning New Englanders from the North Atlantic fisheries after July 20. Despite a brilliant speech by Edmund Burke on March 22 the bill was passed and received the royal assent on March 30. Within a fortnight, on April 13, the provisions of this restraining act were made to apply to New Jersey, Pennsylvania, Maryland, Virginia, and South Carolina because of news of their ratification of the Continental Association had reached London. The restraining act was transmitted by the board of trade in a circular to all governors in America dated April 5, but presumably received by them after the Lexington Alarm. This act provided sensational material for the patriots' propaganda agencies, and it was generally known by the colonists long before the governors received the official documents. At the second Continental Congress, delegates were maintaining the strict secrecy placed on them, but William Hooper sent word to Samuel Johnston that a resolution had passed Congress that no ships could supply the British vessels along the coast of America.[38]

Alexander Elmsly reported to Samuel Johnston on April 7 that William Tryon had proven to be a friend of North Carolina because his advice had made the province exempt from the restraining law. Elmsly advised that the proffered Olive Branch to the colonies from Parliament was similar to one proposed by Lord Chatham and approved by Benjamin Franklin. He noted that transports had sailed from Cork and in the following week Generals Howe, Burgoyne, and Clinton were to follow in a man-of-war. Some of the troops were destined for New York and two companies and a sloop were to be sent to Georgia. He added that America's seaports were to be turned into garrison towns and the people left at liberty to form any establishment they think proper.[39]

In late March, Martin had written his brother Samuel and asked him to send his letters via South Carolina rather than New York since he could not trust the New York postal service. He regretted that Samuel was no longer in the Commons because he thought "your counsel is wanting in that Grand Assembly of the nation at this time of high frenzy & dissension. I take most kindly your friendly caution to be steadfast in my political duty." Martin immediately began to consider how to strengthen Ft. Johnston and recruit loyal troops to support his government. A year before, Captain John Collet, commander of the fort, had expended £1500 to repair the fortifications. The assembly at first refused to pay for the repairs arguing that Captain Collet acted without authority. Martin excused Collet's oversight by explaining that the expense was necessary for the defense of the colony. On March 24, 1774, the assembly and council approved the appropriation, but apparently delayed in giving the money to Collet because Martin had to ask Dartmouth for help in reimbursing him. The assembly resolved that Ft. Johnston be abandoned at the end of the next session of the assembly.[40]

With Britain's preparations for war in the spring of 1775, Martin wrote on March 16 to the British commander of the army in

America, General Thomas Gage, for arms and ammunition, "of which last we are totally destitute." He advised Gage that he thought the western counties would unite to support the government with the aid of a considerable body of "Highlanders in the midland counties who have given the best proofs of their attachment to Govt." Martin was convinced that he would have to maintain "the Sovereignty of this Country to his Majesty if the present spirit of resistance which runs high in Virginia and has infested many parts of this Colony should urge matters to the extremity that the People of New England seem to be meditating."[41]

Martin on March 23 had written to Dartmouth asking him to secure from the king his old army rank should trouble break out. He told Dartmouth that he thought he could distribute arms and ammunition among the king's loyal subjects, and he could form a useful and serviceable corps out of the Highlanders in the province.[42]

Meanwhile, the Whig leaders were planning their strategy against Martin. The speaker of the house, John Harvey, wrote to Governor Martin and suggested that an attachment law be designed not to harm foreigners and submit it to the board of trade. He hoped that the king would grant approval on this proposed law. Harvey believed that the manner of attaching effects of foreigners was the chief reason why the previous court law was not approved; an interpretation Martin had reached earlier. The speaker declared that an extension of the jurisdiction of inferior courts would aid the traders in the colony. He hoped that the governor would support the house's efforts and approve the act for the good of the colony. Harvey's appeal to the governor was a strange mixture of a desire to help the colony and at the same time an attack upon the governor. He told Martin that his refusal to give assent to the establishment of superior and inferior courts was one of the main causes of trouble in the province. He must have known that the governor could not give his assent to a law the Crown had forbidden and the board of trade would veto.[43]

Considering the activities of the correspondence and safety committees to usurp the government and the temper of the Carolina Whigs just before the assembly was to meet, was Harvey a peacemaker or was he trying to throw Martin off balance by drawing a red herring across the governor's path?

V. The Constitutional Crisis
and the Road to Cape Fear

While John Harvey, the speaker of the house, called the second provincial convention, the radical leaders of North Carolina had begun to see the possibility of a new order in government. Without courts, the system of law and order had crumbled and left the province defenseless. Governor Martin was committed to the system of royal government by oath, principles, and philosophy. He valiantly tried to block the radicals with the weapons he had at his command: the royal prerogative, proclamations, moral persuasion, and the veto. The provincial royal government was frustrated by the activities of the radical committees. All that remained was to clear away the debris of the royal government and erect a new state government that in principle was created to respond to the needs of the Carolinians.

The day before the convention was to meet in New Bern, on April 2, 1775, Governor Martin met with his council. He advised that he had received the king's commands to use all his endeavors to prevent appointment of delegates to the second Continental Congress in Philadelphia. Martin asked for advice on measures to block the meeting of the unlawful provincial convention. The council was unanimous in its opinion that His Excellency had no other means than to issue a proclamation forbidding the convention, and to declare that such proceedings would be highly offensive to His Majesty. The proclamation was dated and issued on April 3, the first day of the convention; the day before the assembly was to convene.[1]

Defying Governor Martin's proclamation, the second provincial convention of North Carolina convened in New Bern on April 3 with John Harvey as moderator. The convention resolved that

His Majesty's subjects had a right to petition the throne for redress of grievances, and that such rights included a further right of appointing delegates for such purposes. Therefore, the governor's proclamation issued to forbid the meeting was an infringement on their just rights, and it should be disregarded as wanton and "Arbitrary Exertions of power." The delegates prudently planned that in case of the death of the moderator that Samuel Johnston, once more, be empowered on any future occasion that may require it to direct delegates to be chosen to meet in convention in the town of Hillsborough at such time as he should think necessary. John Harvey died less than two months after this convention.[2]

Although there are two separate and distinct sets of journals for the convention and the assembly in the *Colonial Records of North Carolina*, there was only one body of men meeting in New Bern from April 3 to April 8. At times this body was called the convention and at other times it was called the assembly, depending on what the members were discussing. Both the convention and the assembly had the same man presiding, John Harvey. For the convention Harvey acted as moderator, and for the assembly he was the speaker of the house. The clerk for the convention was Andrew Knox, and the clerk for the assembly was James Green, Jr.; an arrangement probably necessary to keep the journals separate. In the assembly there were 52 members who answered the roll call, and the convention had 67 members. Every member of the assembly was a member of the convention except Ralph McNair of Orange County who later became a Tory. It is believed that some of the members of both the convention and the assembly are shown on the records to be members of the convention only. This omission from the assembly records could have been done by accident or design. Another reason there were more members listed for the convention than the assembly was that there were delegates appointed in some counties for special reasons. For example, John Harvey from Perquimans County had a fellow convention delegate who was Benjamin Harvey, possibly an illustration of patriotic nepotism or pride. Still another difference in the two meetings were the dates convened and adjourned. The convention convened on April 3 and adjourned on April 7, whereas the assembly convened on April 4, and it was dissolved by Martin on April 8.[3]

The Whigs stood firm on constitutional rights and defied the royal prerogative by outmaneuvering Governor Martin in the game they were playing. When the convention was sitting with John Harvey in the chair as moderator and the governor's secretary was announced at the door, the convention automatically became the assembly with Harvey as speaker of the house waiting to receive the governor's secretary with all the dignity of his office. It is tempting to imagine that Harvey must have exchanged a wink with the members or a slight bemused smile or a tense twitching of a facial muscle occurred, depending on his mood, just before the governor's messenger entered the room.

Governor Martin, on April 4, appealed to the representatives' sense of loyalty to king and empire and the sad state of affairs of the province when he addressed them in a joint session of the assembly and the council at the palace. He reminded them that they were "the only legal and proper channel" through which to lead the people away from sedition and insurrection, and he wanted them to take the great opportunity now offered them to serve king and country. He directed their attention to the necessity of solving the problems of finance and taxation, to relieve the exhausted state of the public treasury, and then asked that they establish a permanent court system. Furthermore, he asked that they appropriate funds to strengthen Ft. Johnston.[4]

Despite the gravity of the situation (Martin knew the high stakes he was playing for, the willing cooperation of the assembly), the governor may have seen the irony of the situation when he called upon the gentlemen of the assembly to oppose the illegal meeting of the convention "appointed to assemble at this very time and place in the face of the Legislature." Martin declared that he had counteracted the illegal meeting and that he would continue to resist it by every means in his power. This appeal failed because most of these men were either Whigs or sympathized with them in the convention.

In a conciliatory mood, Martin concluded that "I am sensible that the advanced season of the year requires your attendance on your domestic affairs;" and "I shall be therefore glad to find, that your unanimity in the conduct of the very important business you are now met upon, affords me opportunity to conclude your Session, speedily, and happily." The assembly members must have immediately recognized that beneath the conciliation was irony and a threat for the next day Martin issued a proclamation forbidding all meetings for electing delegates to the second Continental Congress.

The assemblymen prepared an answer to the governor's speech in which they attested to their loyalty to the king but added that loyalty was a reciprocal duty that became incumbent upon both sovereign and subject. They argued that His Majesty's subjects had an undoubted right to petition for a redress of grievances either in a separate or collective capacity and that they could not deem the convention an illegal meeting. Although they said the assembly was the legal representative body, yet the frequent prorogations "gave the people no reason to expect that the Assembly would be permitted to meet 'til it was too late to send Delegates to the Continental Congress at Philadelphia." The steps they had taken in the convention "resulted from a full conviction that the Parliament of Great Britain" had made the measures they pursue absolutely necessary. The house argued that the committees appointed by the people in the colony in consequence of the resolutions of the Continental Congress were the result of necessity, not choice, as the only means left them to prevent the operation of those oppressive and unconstitutional acts of Parliament imposed upon America. Moreover, the assemblymen believed that the loyalty addresses, recently published in the *North Carolina Gazette* were not "signal proofs His Excellency speaks of " but a minority in the province "who could be found weak enough to be seduced from their duty" by the "base acts of wicked and designing men" to adopt measures contrary to the sense of all Americans and destructive of their just rights and privileges it was their duty to support.[5]

The house members resolved to investigate the deficiency of public funds, but they could not provide money for the repairs for Ft. Johnston. The members expressed willingness to adopt a plan for the establishment of courts of justice. They concluded that the "advanced season" would induce them to forward the public business with all possible expedition. It should be noted that the assembly used Martin's rhetoric against him in their reply.

The house on April 7 approved the proceedings of the Continental Congress, including the Continental Association of October 18, 1774, which had been previously approved by the convention. This association was an economic weapon pledged by the delegates that their provinces would cease all importation from Britain and totally discontinue the slave trade as of December 1, 1774; institute nonconsumption of British products and various foreign luxuries on March 1, 1775; and place an embargo on all exports to Britain, Ireland, and the West Indies effective September 1, 1775. In the association document provisions were made for establishing extralegal machinery for enforcement. A committee was to be elected in each county, town, and city to enforce the association. Violators were to be punished by publicity and boycott.[6]

All the House members signed the association except for Thomas McKnight from Currituck, who refused. McKnight had been nominated earlier by Governor Martin as a council member. The convention resolved that McKnight's intentions were "inimical to the Cause of American Liberty, and we do hold him up as a proper object of Contempt to this Continent, and recomend that every person break off all connection, and have no further Commercial Intercourse or Dealings with him." The convention resolved that its statement about McKnight should be published in the newspapers of this and neighboring colonies. It appeared in the *North Carolina Gazette* on April 7, 1775. The house was determined to adhere to congressional resolutions, and they would try to induce every individual in the colony to do so.

On April 7 the House approved the appointments by the convention of William Hooper, Joseph Hewes, and Richard Caswell as delegates to the Congress. The house members voted to thank these men for their faithful and judicious discharge of the important trust imposed on them during the late Congress. The house adjourned until ten o'clock the next morning, April 8, when the angry Governor Martin dissolved the assembly by proclamation.

Thus, ended the last assembly that sat in North Carolina under royal rule.[7]

Meanwhile, Governor Martin reported to Lord Dartmouth the activities of the convention and the assembly. The assembly was to have met on March 27, but Martin had to prorogue it from day to day until April 4 when a sufficient number of members arrived to make a house. Martin traced Harvey's activities of calling and convening the convention and his own two proclamations declaring the convention to be illegal. The council advised Martin to accept Harvey as a speaker so that it would not give the assembly a new cause for discontent. Martin reluctantly agreed although he considered Harvey's "guilt of too conspicuous a nature to be passed over with neglect." The governor added: "the manner however of my admitting him I believe sufficiently testified my disapprobation of his conduct while it marked my respect to the election of the House."[8]

When the house resolved itself into the convention on April 5, Martin had sent his second proclamation by the High Sheriff to read it to them but not a man obeyed the request for dismissal. James Coor of Craven County told the sheriff that he had read the proclamation and he could carry it back to the governor. The governor then laid this problem before the council and they advised that since the assembly had not under its name done anything offensive to let it sit until it should offend its own name and character. To this Martin grudgingly agreed, "and the Assembly still sits transforming itself from time to time into a Convention or an Assembly."

Martin discovered that the assembly had omitted his speech from their journal, leaving a blank space. When he questioned the clerk about the omission, Martin learned that a committee was working on a reply to his speech and presumably were referring to the copy of his address to them. Martin's speech had been written before he received Dartmouth's circular letter of January 4, but he was happy to note that he had followed the king's commands to resist "the growth of a most daring Spirit of Sedition." He declared to Dartmouth that "it is a matter for great reproach and censure of me among the Members of the Assembly that I have taken so many steps against the Convention while the Governors of other Provinces have omitted them." He noted that "their reflections are of little account to me . . . while I have the approbation of the King and that of my own conscience in the discharge of my duty to his Majesty and the State."

The governor believed the convention had been "inflamed by the Communication of the Proceedings of a like monstrous Body lately assembled in Virginia that had allegedly arranged for a company of 68 men in each County." The convention at New Bern had considered a similar proposition, but it was overruled the day before. Martin concluded that "Government is here as absolutely prostrate and impotent, and that nothing but the shadow of it is left, similar to the rest of the colonies, except for New York." Martin predicted that unless effectual measures were speedily taken "there will not long remain a trace of Britain's dominion over these colonies."

Martin's friend in Halifax, the thoughtful Andrew Miller, was equally concerned about the lack of courts, the threat of a Virginia army and an "illegally Constituted" congress. He analyzed the activities of the radicals for his friend, Thomas Burke. He believed that the Virginia leaders in raising an army were trying to widen the breach and prevent reconciliation. Miller speculated that the Crown's ministers might repeal some of the laws if the provincial assemblies applied to them, but they would never repeal them while the colonists applied through an illegal congress. He argued that the "Infant State" of the colonies could not exist without protection from a maritime power, such as Britain, and therefore the colonies should submit to Parliament except for taxation and even then "I would submit to for awhile" until America had built up its manufactures, increased its population, and emancipated the slaves. He saw British taxation as extending only "to Superfluitys or Luxurys or Life." Miller concluded: "We are not in a Condition to combat with Britain, nor do I believe she intends to make war on us. — I rather think she wished to give up the power of Taxation, but will not be threatened out of it by a Congress or a Virginia Army." He was convinced that the conduct of Virginia would antagonize even their best friends in England against them.[9]

Across the Atlantic in London, Alexander Elmsly wrote to his friend, Samuel Johnston, and discussed recent developments in the American crisis and then turned to matters concerning North Carolina. Elmsly and Thomas Barker were still working for the assembly by petitioning the Crown's ministers to resolve the province's court law quarrel. He noted that Governor Tryon was about to leave for New York. He believed that Tryon had influenced Lord North to exempt North Carolina and New York from the restraining act.[10]

Elmsly was suspicious of the unsavory influence of two of the Crown's ministers and their alleged impact on the court laws of North Carolina. His suspicions echoed his earlier reported quote from Tryon about the gentlemen who owned large tracts of land in North Carolina who had not favored the foreign attachment law in the provinces. Elmsly reminded Samuel Johnston: "You asked Mr. Barker to let you know who it was that first moved here, against your Court laws. Neither he nor I know certainly;" but when Mr. McCulloh, the provincial agent, first received a report of "your Court Bill miscarrying, an account of an instruction to your Governor [Tryon] against attachments; he hinted that Lord Hillsborough, then Secretary of State for America, and Lord Hertford, then and now Lord Chamberlain, and both members of the Privy Council," and friends and neighbors of "your Dobbs's, might probably, at their solicitation, have been the means of sending out the instruction." Elmsly said that "Nash had an attachment depending against their estate." He added that this is only conjecture, but "I think it probable, because had the measure originated amongst the merchants, we certainly should have heard of it long ago." Elmsly concluded: "it is not of much consequence now, as the new laws have taken place, whether old ones are restored or not."

If Elmsly was correct then the motivation for excluding North Carolina from the foreign attachment clause was the desire of Lords Hillsborough and Hertford who wanted to protect themselves and their friends from Carolina creditors. The Dobbs referred to by Elmsly was Governor Arthur Dobbs that Tryon succeeded in North Carolina. He too was a North of Ireland man like

Hillsborough. Nash was probably the influential attorney from Craven County, Abner Nash. Hillsborough's office, as secretary of state for the colonies, made it easier for him to block North Carolina from securing the advantages of the foreign attachment law. After he resigned from his office, Hillsborough became more anti-American, especially as the American crisis accelerated. He continued to use his influence with the King's Friends in Parliament in a determined opposition to any concessions to America.[11]

Although the assembly was dissolved, Governor Martin continued to meet with his council. The council advised him to delay issuing writs for a new assembly until the end of June. Martin laid before the council the proceedings of the convention signed by John Harvey. After some discussion about the subversive proceedings, the council approved Martin's suggestion that they revoke Harvey's commission as justice of the peace in Perquimans County. Martin then secured the council's approval to issue warrants on the treasurers for expenses for Ft. Johnston.[12]

General Gage advised Martin that he could not supply him with the arms he had requested, but he would arrange to send gun powder from New York for use at Ft. Johnston and to be distributed among the loyal men of the western counties. Massachusetts was still in a state of sedition and license stirred up by their leaders, but Gage was happy to learn that many of the people in North Carolina were still loyal to the Crown. Martin again assured Gage on April 20 of the loyalty of the western counties.[13]

Dartmouth urged the governor to encourage the loyal citizens of Guilford, Dobbs, Rowan, and Surry Counties to support the Crown against the patriots. Perhaps as an additional incentive for loyal support in the colony, Dartmouth advised Martin that all the insurgents from the Regulator War would receive a general pardon except for Hermon Husbands. If war came, Dartmouth suggested that Martin should consider organizing an armed resistance made up of leading loyal men. He advised Martin that he had written General Gage to send him a "discreet officer" to encourage loyalty, and, if necessary, to lead the people against any rebellious attempts to disturb the public peace.[14]

News of the battles of Lexington and Concord of April 19 was forwarded southward from Massachusetts by relays from one committee to another. The news arrived in New Bern on May 6. Henry Montfort of Halifax reported to Thomas Burke the news of the Lexington Alarm on May 9: "We have just recd. some very shocking accounts from Boston. The Regulars and the Bostonians Have Had an Engagement, the former were Intirely defeated with the loss of 1200 men and 800 taken prisoners." Despite his assurance to Burke that he could rely on the figures as facts, Montfort was mistaken as to the figures. British casualties were 73 killed, 174 wounded, and 26 missing.[15]

Martin quickly saw the effects of the news of the patriot victory for he described for Dartmouth the inhabitants of the sea coast of the province "for the most part infected with ill spirit that prevails in the adjacent Provinces of Virginia and South Carolina" by arming men and electing officers. In New Bern, they were "actually endeavoring to form what they call independent Companies under my nose, & Civil Government becomes more and more prostrate every day." He added the people "fartherest away from Virginia and South Carolina" were still loyal to the government.[16]

Events began to accelerate for Governor Martin on Tuesday, May 23. He reported to Dartmouth that "Without any previous notice of their purpose, A motley mob appeared before the governor's palace." Martin did not see them until they were near the door. He directed his secretary, if they announced themselves as a committee, to tell them he could not see them. The secretary returned to him a few minutes later and said the people were citizens of the town. They asked permission to speak with him. Martin directed them to be shown into an apartment below stairs. He immediately went down to them.[17]

Abner Nash, the "oracle of the Committee" for New Bern (Martin later described Nash to Dartmouth as a "principal promoter of sedition here"), came forward out of the crowd and presented himself as the leader of those present to find out why Governor Martin had dismounted the ritual cannon behind the palace that morning. These people had become alarmed because they knew that Lord Dunmore had recently deprived the Virginians of their gunpowder. They requested that the governor order the guns to be remounted. Martin thought that it was a pretext to insult him. He replied that it was an extraordinary request since the guns belonged to the king, and that they were used to celebrate the king's birthday. To quiet their fears, Martin told them that the wooden gun carriages were rotten and he had ordered the guns dismounted so that they could be repaired for the celebration of the king's birthday early in June. Nash accepted Martin's answer and "bowing retired with his mob."

Martin later admitted to Dartmouth that the reason he gave the mob was correct, but not the whole answer because he had been advised some weeks before that the committee had planned to seize the guns. While it was necessary to repair the gun carriages, it was also convenient to make their removal more difficult for the committee to seize by force.

A day or two after "this studied insult," probably May 24, an "old soldier" arrived from New York. He had an interview with Martin. He may have been the "Discreet officer" Dartmouth asked Gage to send to Martin. Evidence suggests that the "old soldier" was to give Governor Martin intelligence on the arms and ammunition aboard the king's sloop of war, *Fisher*, at New York City. These military stores were to be sent to Martin at the direction of General Gage by Cadwallader Colden, lieutenant governor of New York. Colden had learned that the New York Safety Committee had violated letters sent through the regular postal system. It was possible, Colden thought, that the patriots had learned about the shipment of arms and ammunition to Governor Martin. The committees of safety forwarded intelligence and news to each other, especially if it was pertinent to a particular colony. Martin feared that his correspondence with Gage had been "betrayed." He was correct. The other governors still holding office had their correspondence stolen and published too. The only other royal governors who were still in office were Tryon of New York, Eden of Maryland, and Lord Dunmore of Virginia.[18]

The old soldier had told Martin he was not sure whether the military stores would be sent by a man-of-war or a merchant vessel. If the expected stores came to New Bern in a merchant vessel, Martin later wrote, he "had not a man to protect them." They would fall "into the hands of the mob, which was continually watching every movement about my house." Martin was concerned for the safety of his family and himself. The mob might use the military supplies as "a pretext for seizing my person and detaining me," according to the plan of all the colonies of making themselves "Masters of the King's Servants among them." Moreover, the Whigs had been circulating "a most infamous report" among the people that Martin planned to arm the Negroes and give them freedom if they supported the king's standard. This was not true. Martin had a grandfather murdered by his rebellious slaves and it is doubtful that he would have considered arming the slaves.[19]

The governor was growing deeply concerned for the safety of his family. Mrs. Martin was pregnant and her children were young. The governor discussed his problem with a close friend, Archibald Neilson, formerly of Dundee, Scotland, who often stayed in the palace when he visited New Bern. Martin had appointed Neilson to several offices in the province, but none of them seems to have given the young Scot any financial return. In January, 1775, on the death of Isaac Edwards, the deputy auditor, Martin appointed Neilson in his place. At the time of the mob's visit to the governor, Neilson was Martin's house guest. With the threat of the mob, the governor decided to send his family to New York and the safety of his father-in-law's estate on Long Island. Neilson made arrangements for a ship to take Mrs. Martin and the children to New York City.[20]

On Monday, May 29, Martin hastily wrote a message to General Gage about the needed arms and ammunition. Presumably this and other letters were carried on the person of Mrs. Martin to escape the vigilant committee's detection. The committee members did stop Mrs. Martin and her party. One of her servants persuaded the committee members not to search their baggage. Mrs. Martin had time only to pack the personal clothing of her family and the family silver. She left behind all of their furniture, furnishings, and two coaches. These were later sold by the patriots at an auction. Mrs. Martin and her family were allowed to board the ship.[21]

In another precautionary move, Martin sent his secretary, James Biggleston, to Ocracoke Inlet, the first entrance to the port of New Bern, to direct any vessel that should arrive there with the military stores to go to the sloop of war, *Cruizer*, in the mouth of the Cape Fear River, near Ft. Johnston. Meanwhile, the governor had to warn some of his friends he had invited to help him celebrate the birthday of the king on June 6. Some of the guests were to be the families of John Rutherford and Robert Schaw, merchants and planters of the lower Cape Fear River. Archibald Neilson sent an express rider to Wilmington to his friends, the Rutherfords and the Schaws, warning them not to come to New Bern. Near Wilmington, Janet Schaw wrote in her journal that they had received the message from Neilson and that the governor's house had been attacked. She noted that the governor's family had escaped in a small vessel, and that the governor had gone to a man-of-war in the Cape Fear River. As it sometimes happens, messages are garbled. Mrs. Martin and the children did escape by boat, but Abner Nash and the mob did not attack the palace until much later.[22]

Under cover of darkness, Governor Martin and Archibald Neilson easily escaped the vigilance of the committee's watchful eyes. Martin left the lighted palace in the care of his butler and servants. In his coach, Martin and Neilson rode openly through the country from New Bern to Cross Creek and down the Cape Fear River to Fort Johnston, where several English war ships lay at anchor. Both men found refuge at Ft. Johnston, near Wilmington on June 2.[23]

The patriot communication network began to spread the news that Governor Martin had "fled" to Ft. Johnston; Robert Salter advised Colonel Richard Caswell on June 3; Richard Cogdell, chairman of the safety committee in New Bern, had written Samuel Johnston on June 8; and a "Letter to a Gentleman in New York," dated North Carolina, June 7, 1775, was printed as an extract in a New York newspaper. This letter described how Governor Martin "has sent his family to New York, and being greatly disgusted with the people of New Bern, has taken up his residence in Fort Johnston, at the mouth of the Cape Fear River, which he has chosen as a place of retreat from popular complaints."[24]

It has been believed that there were three attempts by the rebels to capture Governor Martin, and the first attempt was thought to have been at New Bern. Martin's decisive actions may have thwarted the alleged attempt at New Bern. Josiah Martin was one of the few royal governors to outwit and escape the physical abuse of the patriots. While he had retreated temporarily as any intelligent officer might do, Martin had just begun to fight for what he sincerely believed in: the empire, the king, and himself. The rebels of North Carolina were not rid of him yet. Secure in his temporary capital at Ft. Johnston, Governor Martin began his search for "A Rod of Chastisement for the Rhetoric of Revolution."

VI. A Rod of Chastisement for the Rhetoric of Revolution

At Ft. Johnston, Governor Martin reassessed the position of the rebels, royal government in America, and himself. He tried to counter the rebel propaganda by creating propaganda to support the Crown. He soon realized that the rebels had transformed his refuge at the fort into a prison; he was isolated from the citizens of North Carolina. Martin regretfully concluded that "reason and argument can never restore the just power and authority of Government in America." He advised Dartmouth that there should be a "rod of chastisement to correct the rhetoric of revolution" so that he could restore royal government to North Carolina. He believed the Crown should begin chastisement without a moment's delay.[1]

On June 2, the day Martin arrived at Ft. Johnston, he requested help from the commander of the war sloop *Cruizer* then anchored in the Cape Fear opposite the fort. The commander, Captain Francis Parry, R.N., sent a boat with an officer who returned with Governor Martin. Parry saluted the governor with thirteen guns on coming aboard and when he returned to shore. At the conference on board the ship, Captain Parry agreed to the governor's request "with the utmost alacrity" to send immediately an officer and a party of men in a schooner to Ocracoke Inlet to direct the expected munitions ship to Ft. Johnston. That same day Parry wrote to Captain Edward Thornbrough, R.N., stationed at Charleston, South Carolina, and inquired if the frigate that brought the governor of South Carolina, Lord William Campbell, was to go northward or to England. If so, Governor Martin would be obliged to have him order her to sail here." Parry added that he was "laying off Fort Johnston where the governor is." A copy of this letter was sent by the South Carolina Committee of Intelligence to the Committee at Wilmington on June 6.[2]

The South Carolina committee also intercepted Gage's letter to Martin dated April 12 and sent it to the Wilmington committee. Gage had forced the Bostonians to surrender their arms, about five thousand stands, before they were "suffered to leave that City." The South Carolina committee thought that Gage would send these guns to Martin. The committee advised Wilmington that they had written to New York to stop the powder "if it is not too late," and "if it should have been sent from thence we hope you will secure it."

On June 13, Cornelius Harnett, chairman of the North Carolina Committee of Safety, sent two letters to the New Bern committee. He advised them that Martin had arrived at Ft. Johnston "where he will No Doubt Collect Arms & Ammunition perhaps to put into the Hands of our Domesticks and the Wretched deluded People to the Westward should they be weak enough to accept them." He added that the committee intended to "Disconcert such Diabolical Schemes."[3]

The second communication by Harnett dated June 13 reported that Captain Parry's men with the schooner had sailed northward, and the committee thought it may be going to collect arms either from General Gage in Boston or from New York. Martin was aware of the scurrilous Harnett message to New Bern about his plan to place arms in the hands of the Negro slaves. He was also aware of Lord Dunmore's attempts to lure the Negroes away from their Virginia masters by promising them their freedom if they joined his Negro regiment. Martin described Harnett's charges to Dartmouth on June 20 as "a most infamous report" that "had lately been propagated among the People, that I had formed a design of Arming the Negroes, and proclaiming freedom to all such as should resort to the King's Standard." This radical propaganda would have been easily believed in "two or three counties" in the coastal part of the province because of the large number of slaves in that region. Martin estimated that the colony had no more than ten thousand Negroes. There seems to be no evidence to support Harnett's charge.[4]

Governor Martin, on June 16, issued a proclamation at Ft.

Johnston to the people of the province. He called on them not to heed "the incendiaries who spread these false and seditious reports" and who try "to seduce His Majesty's loyal and faithful subjects to join in their licentious and criminal combinations." He told the people of North Carolina that the House of Commons had agreed that the Americans should tax themselves in their respective general assemblies. The tax would be used for their share of the expense for the "general defence of the British Empire" and for their own civil government.[5]

Ordinarily James Biggleston, Martin's secretary, would have written the proclamation, but he was still at Ocracoke Inlet waiting for Gage's ammunition ship. A Highland officer on half pay, Lieutenant Alexander Maclean, was serving as Martin's temporary secretary. The patriots may have interpreted Maclean's position as an indication that Martin planned to rely upon the Highlanders for support. The committee at nearby Wilmington watched Martin's activities closely. They searched everyone entering or leaving the fort. The patriots prevented publication of Martin's proclamation, and then they published a reply to it. With the people ignorant of what Martin said in his proclamation, the rebels' reply was quite effective propaganda.

The rebels at Wilmington, under the leadership of Harnett, had organized the counties of New Hanover, Brunswick, Bladen, Duplin, and the community of Cross Creek (Fayetteville) into the District of Wilmington. It was the organization of the District of Wilmington that used the reply to Martin's proclamation as a personal attack on the governor, Crown and Parliament as well as a justification for the patriot cause. Martin's proclamation was read on June 16 to the safety committees of the District of Wilmington. Robert Howe, Archibald McLaine, and Samuel Ashe were appointed to a committee to answer the proclamation. Three days later, the patriots published their reply, and ordered it printed in the public newspapers and in handbills as the "Association, Unanimously agreed to, by the inhabitants of New Hanover County, in North Carolina, 19th June, 1775."[6]

The committee members countered Martin's charges by accusing him of trying "to persuade, seduce, and intimidate the good people of the province" and taking measures to preserve their rights and liberties. Martin, they said, had tried to weaken and prejudice the characters of the various committees by representing them "as ill-disposed people, propagating false and scandalous reports, derogatory to the honor and justice of the King." They declared Governor Martin "to be an enemy to the happiness of this colony in particular, and to the freedom, rights, and privileges of America in general." They asserted that Martin was in error when he accused them of compelling citizens to sign association statements. They concluded that Martin and the other governors were "Tools of Government" who tried to divide "this Country" and enslave it, and that no confidence ought to be given them. The committee earnestly commended the "Association" to other committees of the province. The District of Wilmington approved the association statement on June 21, and other committees signed the statement in the following weeks.

Governor Martin held a council meeting at Ft. Johnston on June 25 to discuss the revolutionary activities of the patriots and how to curb them. Members who attended were James Hasell, John Rutherford, Lewis De Rosset, William Dry, and Thomas McGuire. Martin addressed the council and condemned the patriot committees for usurping authority and making various combinations of sedition. He denounced the violent measures used by the committees in compelling "His Majesty's Subjects" to subscribe to associations, for obliging people to frequent meetings in arms, and particularly for the recent meeting at Wilmington when armed men were used to awe the citizens into submitting to "an illegal and tyrannical tribunal created there." Martin denounced as treasonous the publication of the committee in Mecklenburg County for "explicitly renouncing obedience to His Majesty's Government and all lawful authority." He was referring to the Mecklenburg County Resolutions of May 31 which were sent to the North Carolina delegation in Philadelphia, but never presented to Congress. The Mecklenburg Resolves declared all laws and commissions deriving their authority from the king or Parliament to be annulled and the royal government of the provinces "wholly suspended" for the present. Therefore, all legislative and executive power within each colony would devolve upon the provincial congress. Within Mecklenburg County anyone accepting a royal commission was branded an enemy and ordered to be apprehended.[7]

The council replied that Martin had done all he could to suppress the disturbances and that the situation in the province rendered it impossible to take any other steps. The governor, nonetheless, believed he could do even more by using his military powers of his royal commission. The council approved Martin's suggestion to issue the full complement of militia commissions to the counties at large. Then the governor described for the council the defenseless condition of Ft. Johnston. Captain Collet, the commander of the fort, had advised Martin that the garrison of twenty five men had been reduced by desertions to less than half that number. The fort had no gun powder and it could not protect the artillery belonging to the Crown in case of an attack. It was the unanimous opinion of the council that Martin should apply to General Gage or to the Lords of Treasury for money to repair the fort and raise and maintain a garrison to protect the commerce of the river.

By June 30 Martin had a copy of the Association of the District of Wilmington printed in the *Cape Fear Mercury* which he enclosed in his dispatch to Dartmouth. Martin said that the association statement was an illustration of the "same spirit that gave cause to the Restraining Act, and it proved that people embarked on a bad cause, scruple not to avail themselves of the basest falsehoods and calumnies to support it." Martin noted that he and the other governors had to expect being branded as enemies of the people. The governor presented to Dartmouth a proposal for regaining the royal authority in the province. He argued that if he could secure military supplies from General Gage, he could arm the loyal Highlanders, about 3000 men, and maintain the government in the province. The governor thought that eventually he would be able to enlist many of the estimated 30,000 fighting men of the loyal interior counties. If he were permitted to enlist an effective army, Martin said he could restore order in the province and in South Carolina, "and hold Virginia in such awe as to prevent that Province sending any succour to the Northward." Martin

121

requested Dartmouth to present his proposal to the king. Should it be approved, he promised to raise a battalion of a thousand Highlanders. Martin had found the "rod of chastisement." Again the governor requested restoration of his old rank of lieutenant colonel because he thought it was "necessary to exercise military power in support of the high civil office in which His Majesty has been pleased to place me in this country." If the king approved of his proposal, Martin recommended Allan Macdonald of Kingsborough (husband of the famous Scottish heroine, Flora) to be a major and Alexander McLeod of the Marines, now on half pay, to be first captain. Besides their great worth and character, Martin argued, these men had a "most extensive influence over the Highlanders here." He also nominated as subalterns several worthy young Highland gentlemen to help recruit the battalion. Martin suggested three or four men with the surname of McDonald, and Lieutenant Alexander Maclean, now on half pay, and his temporary secretary.[8]

In his lengthy dispatch Martin discussed the usurping activities of the committees. He attributed the impotence of the council to their fear of personal injury and insult from the radicals. Martin admitted that the situation he found himself in was "most despicable and mortifying in any man of greater feelings than a Stoic." He promised that the authors and abettors of the Mecklenburg Resolves would not escape his due notice whenever his hands were sufficiently strengthened "to attempt the recovery of the lost authority of Government." He enclosed for Dartmouth's information a copy of an unidentified newspaper that had printed the resolves.

Martin then discussed the role that John Ashe played in the revolutionary activities in the province. Ashe had declined Martin's renewal of his commission as colonel of the militia of Hanover County giving as his reasons his age and the demands of his business. Yet, Ashe appeared at Wilmington a fortnight later at the head of about five hundred men threatening the Scottish merchants with military execution if they did not subscribe to the association dictated by the committee. They signed, but Martin believed the Scottish merchants were united more firmly in opposition to the radicals because they had since formed themselves into a company for the purpose of mutual protection and defense.

The South Carolina Congress had sent parties into the province to recruit men, but Martin hoped they would be disappointed because he intended to defeat their purpose. He thought that Charleston, the head and heart of the province, might be destroyed by a single frigate and the province reduced to the last distress. Martin regretted to have to say it, he informed Dartmouth, but he was of the opinion that "reason and argument can never restore the just power and authority of Government in America." He argued for the rod of chastisement to correct the rhetoric of revolution, and that the Crown should wield the rod without a moment's delay.

Like the other governors, Martin called the assembly to discuss Lord North's reconciliation plan. The council advised him to prorogue the new elected assembly to September 12, but he expected to have a good reason to prorogue it further. He would accept all the council members, Martin advised Dartmouth, except William Dry, collector of customs at Wilmington.

The rhetoric of revolution can be seen again in "A Circular Letter to the Committee of South Carolina, Charles Town, June 30, 1775" when two versions of the battles of Lexington and Concord were presented for the reader: allegedly General Gage on the one side, and the "Voice of America" on the other. This letter criticized Martin for his proclamation of June 16 and for his glossing over the new tax measures of Lord North, particularly the contingent proportion of the taxes to be paid to the Crown and Parliament for defense and civil government's expenses. While this essay probably had wide circulation in Georgia and South Carolina after June 30, it was not published in North Carolina until it appeared in the *Cape Fear Mercury* on July 28.[9]

The rhetoric of the North Carolina delegates to the Continental Congress was used effectively in their address to the colony's committees which they issued at Philadelphia June 16. It probably took a fortnight to get to the northeastern towns of the province, and so it is probable that most of the colonists had not heard the stirring words urging them to arm themselves and form militia units nor had Governor Martin when he wrote his lengthy dispatch of June 30 to Dartmouth. The delegates signed the document that described the petitions to the throne as buried under a "mass of useless papers" on the table of the House of Commons. This was the usual fate of American remonstrances, to be rejected and forgotten. The delegates added to the catalog of ministerial tyranny the Restraining act and the troops that still poured into Boston. The delegates saw Boston as the first victim to ministerial tyranny and they warned that if the Crown's ministers were successful in Massachusetts the inhabitants of the southern colonies would soon feel the weight of ministerial vengeance. Although the provinces to the northward dreaded "a civil War as the most awful scourge of Heaven," they were determined to suffer the excess of human misery "rather than be brought to the feet of an insulting Minister." The delegates chided their fellow citizens when they reminded them that North Carolina alone remained an inactive spectator of this general defensive armament. She seemed to have forgotten the duty she owed to her own local circumstances and situation. The delegates used Governor Martin as a scapegoat when they asked: "Have you not Fellow Citizens a dangerous Enemy in your own Bosom and after Measures which the Ministry has condescended to in order to carry into Execution his darling Schemes, do you think he would hesitate to raise the hand of the servant against the master?"[10]

With a pointed reference to the Restraining Act, the delegates wrote: "Can you think that your Province is the singular subject of ministerial favour and that in the common crush it will stand secure? Be assured it will not." They asked their constituents to withhold their naval stores to "strengthen the hands of America in the glorious contention for her liberty." One of the reasons given for the province's exemption from the Restraining Act was the British need for naval stores. The delegates admonished their fellow citizens: "You have the Example of New York to animate you, she spurns the proffered Boon and views the exemption" as treachery. The delegates concluded by urging the colonists to form militia and follow the example of their sister colonies: "Study the

Art of Military with the utmost attention, view it as the science upon which your future security depends." They cautioned that the "Crisis of America is not at a great distance."

Actually the crisis was near at hand for many rumors were inflaming North Carolinians against the royal governor. As most thinking people realize, many rumors are based on falsehoods, but sometimes there are a few that have a kernel of truth. Whether false or true, rumors circulating in a revolutionary environment have value for the radicals as propaganda, and, thus, they become part of the rhetoric. The loyalists also made use of the same practice throughout the thirteen colonies. The radicals in North Carolina were not loathe to make use of the rumors about Governor Martin if they would help organize resistance to the Crown and Parliament. Of the three major rumors discussed so far, it has been shown that the stories about Martin's attempt to organize the Highlanders and former Regulators were based on truth. The other two rumors of Martin's organizing slave revolts and the inciting of the Indians to ravage the frontiers were baseless. Martin refrained from the use of slaves and Indians against the colonists, although Governor Dunmore in Virginia did try to organize the slaves to revolt against their masters. Nevertheless, the rumor about the Negroes prompted the patriot committees to establish rules and organize patrols regulating the movement of slaves, particularly in the eastern counties that had numerous slaves.

On July 1 the safety committee of Pitt County resolved to appoint "Patrolers to search all suspected places" and "finding any Negro Slave or Slaves from their Masters Lands without a pass from his Master Mistress or Coroner to take the said slave or slaves" and "give them Thirty nine Lashes or Less if they think proper." Furthermore, "if any Negro Slave be *found with any fire arms* or ammunition in his or her possession that the said Patrolers may seize and take away any such arms." The patrolers had the right to sell these arms at public sale, after "first being advertised ten days." the money from the sales would be paid to the churchwardens of St. Michael's parish for the use of the parish. The committee also organized ten companies as patrols and each company would elect their officers. An advantage of these slave patrol companies was that they could be easily converted into a militia unit in a comparatively short time.[11]

The influence of the three delegates to the Continental Congress should not be underestimated because they were the direct channels of communication of the congress with the patriot leaders in the province. On July 8, when Joseph Hewes wrote to Samuel Johnston, the moderator of the provincial convention, he again referred to the Crown's plans to let loose the Indians and foment rebellion among the patriots' slaves. It would seem then that the threat of the Indians and slaves was part of the psychological fear that influenced most southern colonists' attitudes toward the Crown's servants in the colonies. It is not surprising that with all the talk about slave rebellions that there were some attempts to incite slave insurrections and blame them on Governor Martin.[12]

An account of an intended Negro revolt in Beaufort County was related on July 15, 1775, by Colonel John Simpson, chairman of the safety committee in Pitt County, to Colonel Richard Cogdell, chairman of the Craven committee. Beaufort County is adjacent to Craven and Pitt Counties. The plans for the revolt were discovered by Captain Thomas Respess when one of his Negro men revealed it to him. The conspirators were thought to be a ship's captain, "Johnson of White Haven," who had just loaded his brig with naval stores, and a negro male slave named Merrick owned by Captain Nathaniel Blinn of Bath. The citizens were alerted and patrols set foot in the county. By nightfall they had forty Negroes in jail. Five Negroes were whipped and on the following day punishment was meted out to several slaves. They received eighty lashes each and had both ears cropped.[13]

That same day arrived an express rider from Colonel Jacob Blount telling of a slave revolt on the Craven and Pitt County line. Blount requested assistance of men and ammunition which was granted by the Pitt Safety Committee. Two days later John Simpson discovered the author of the rumor of the rebellion. She was a "negro wench of William Taylor's in Clayroot, with design to kill her master and mistress and lay it upon those Negroes. She has received severe correction." Colonel Simpson reported that every slave they picked up, examined and scourged, confessed nearly the same thing, that is, on the night of July 8 they were to fall in and destroy the family where they were to be received and armed by the royal government and rewarded with free movement of their own. Captain Johnson was alleged to have his choice of the plantations on the river.

With these rumors of alleged Negro revolts in the air, it is understandable that the people of Beaufort, Craven and Pitt Counties were frightened. It is possible that Captain Johnson and the two slaves, Merrick and the unnamed wench, were trying to promote insurrections so that they could profit from them. As the slaves were submitted to scourging, they may have discovered their captors stopped beating them when they told the same story of the royal governor's participation. However, Colonel Simpson did report that when they disarmed the slaves they found "considerable ammunition." It is doubtful that the slaves got the ammunition from Governor Martin or his staff because Martin was still anxiously awaiting the arrival of Gage's munition supply ship. Because of his own family's experience with slave revolts and for humanitarian reasons, the use of slaves against the settlers would be repugnant to him. One historian's thesis is that the Revolution generated powerful internal tensions that racially destabilized society, especially in North Carolina. Another historian could find no slave revolts in the Chesapeake and South Carolina areas during the Revolution.

While Martin had nothing to do with the alleged slave revolts, he did continue his plan to organize a Highlander battalion, but he was moving cautiously for he wanted approval from the king and Dartmouth. Martin agreed with Alexander McLeod that the Highlanders should forbear any open declaration until it was necessary. He advised McLeod that he had written to one of his nominees for the officers in the battalion, Farquhard Campbell. The governor suggested that McLeod work with Allan MacDonald of Kingsborough in Cumberland County. Cornelius Harnett ordered an investigation of MacDonald. Later, on July 7, Harnett's committee branded a young Scot, James Hepburn of Cumberland as subversive and a supporter of Governor Martin.[14]

The unexpected arrival in the Cape Fear on July 5 of the *Scorpion*, Captain Tollemache commanding, bringing mail from Charleston, gave the governor an opportunity to breach the patriot network that had been drawn around him. Tollemach was on his way to Boston, but he agreed to wait forty eight hours while Martin wrote letters to Dartmouth, Gage, and Samuel Martin. Another fortunate coincidence was the presence of Alexander Schaw, a customs officer on leave from the island of St. Kitts, who had been visiting with his sister Janet and their brother Robert in Wilmington. Schaw agreed to be Martin's emissary to Dartmouth and to carry Martin's dispatches on board the *Scorpion*.[15]

Along with his letters to his superiors, Martin wrote his brother Samuel. He advised him that he had sent his family to New York and how he had gone to the fort for security while he continued to support the royal government. He described the fort as a "little wretched place, under the protection of a Sloop of War stationed here," but he added there were potential resources for the defense of the government. With "a motion of his finger," he could call forth 3,000 Highlanders and "a vast body of People who were concerned in the late insurrection, that together with their adherents & connexions" would "make up two thirds of the whole strength of the province." These former Regulators would "gladly resort to the King's Standard" because of their loyalty to the government and their "long nourished resentment" against the colonists on the seacoast who helped Tryon defeat them.[16]

Martin confessed to Samuel: "I am under the feelings . . . of a willing servant seeing himself impotent, & unable to redress His Sovereign's wrongs." He stressed the theme of the necessity of military power "to the support of my Civil authority." He was still waiting for replies to his letters to General Gage and Lord Dartmouth. He asked Samuel to talk to Lord Dartmouth to whom he made the military proposal, and to "my Ld. Barrington as Secretary for War to whom, I think I have told you I made a similar proposition about two years ago." He told Samuel that if he could get military aid he "could engraft a Power that would be highly respectable & sufficiently effectual to crush the Spirit of Rebellion far around me, that is now extending itself most rapidly." This letter would be handed to him by "Mr. Schaw, a gentleman of good understanding and character, who goes to England charged with my public dispatches, & to lay before the King's Ministers the State of this Country which his accurate observations enables him to do . . . better than I can possibly by letter." Schaw, moreover, would be able to resolve doubts, "and to satisfy inquiries that it is impossible for me to forsee." Martin urged Samuel "the expediency of giving me some immediate & effectual support that may qualify me to employ for the national advantage the materials that this Country furnishes."

In his dispatch to Dartmouth of July 6, Martin noted that no communication by sea had been established by Admiral Thomas Graves or General Gage, and "all intercourse by land is cut off by the vigilance of the Committees" which no messenger or letter could escape. He had sent his servant three days before to the postoffice at Wilmington and the man was stopped by the committee of Brunswick who made him swear he had no letters for the governor before they would let him proceed. Moreover, Martin was indignant that Dartmouth's dispatches had been "violated" by the mob at Charleston. To avoid the harassment and disruption of his mail, Martin was sending his personal emissary, Alexander Schaw, to deliver his mail. He referred Dartmouth to Schaw for more detailed information about the situation in North Carolina.[17]

Dartmouth had dictated a dispatch on July 5 telling Martin of some of the latest developments in the American crisis. He was sending his dispatch by the Carolina Packet, and promised to send a fuller reply to Martin's last four dispatches by a store ship that would sail for Virginia a few days later. According to Dartmouth, not only were the four New England governments in arms, but almost every other colony had caught the flame, "and a spirit of Rebellion has gone forth that menaces the subversion of the Constitution." He declared that it was the king's firm resolution that the most vigorous efforts should be made, both by sea and land, "to reduce his Rebellious Subjects to obedience." Measures were now being pursued to build up the army under General Gage, and also for "adding to our Naval strength in North America, so that Admiral Graves could have separate squadrons off New England and

New York, in the Chesapeake Bay, and on the coast of Carolina.[18]

There was still hope in Whitehall, according to Dartmouth, that the colonies to the southward would not proceed to the same lengths as those of New England. It was, nonetheless, "His Majesty's Intention" that the commanders of the separate squadrons blockade the commerce of all the colonies, excepting vessels that belonged to the loyal supporters of the Crown. The squadron commanders were instructed to "give protection to any officers of the Crown, who may be compelled by the violence of the People, to seek for such an Asylum." The commanders were also ordered to proceed against any rebellious seaport towns that offer violence to the king's officers, troops, or ammunition depots. Dartmouth concluded: "I have only to add, that it is His Majesty's express Command that you do exert every Endeavour" to aid and support General Gage and Admiral Graves "in all such operations as they may think proper to undertake."

While Dartmouth was counselling Martin to aid and support Gage and Graves, the safety committees were busily screening and controlling the correspondence of the king's servants and all others suspected of adhering to the Crown. The vigilance of the committees to control correspondence was a major annoyance to Archibald Neilson. Neilson declared to James Iredell on July 8 that he was a friend to liberty and just authority, but that he was also an enemy to anarchy. He was annoyed with the committees for stopping his mail; he had not received some letters from Martin. Neilson added that he suspected the patriots of intercepting his letters. In a postscript to his letter to Iredell he addressed the patriot censors: "If the *gentlemen of the Committee at Bath stop this letter* they will *please forward* it *after perusal.*"[19]

Letters were forwarded after they were copied by the committees. Joseph Hewes wrote Iredell on July 8 and advised him that he had received copies of Martin's letters from the Provincial Convention of New York and the committee at Philadelphia. He had sent Gage's letter of April 12 to the committee at Edenton which was forwarded to the committee at New Bern. On July 17 the committee published the letter because "We thought it would open the Eyes of the People." This letter, the committee thought, seemed to offer conclusive proof of Martin's hostility to the people of the province when he requested guns and ammunition from Gage. Thus, this letter was useful for patriot propaganda. Hewes also received a copy of Martin's letter to Henry White, the New York merchant, requesting a colonel's tent and furniture. Hewes thought a perusal of both Martin letters would indicate "what part our Governor intends to take in the present unhappy dispute." He confided to Iredell: "Strange that we should be deemed Rebels for an article of faith, —after all this they add insult to injury and tell us we are all poltroons and Cowards." This is a strange remark to be made by a man who was a delegate to Congress and had certainly become aware of the uses of propaganda and the foibles of human nature.[20]

Henry White convinced the New York Provincial Congress that his relationship to Martin was that of a merchant only. He knew nothing of his governmental plans and considered Martin "a gentleman with whom he had transacted much business." President Peter Livingston of the New York congress reported to Charles Thomson, secretary to the Continental Congress, that White had been cleared by the patriots. Hooper and Hewes signed a letter of July 8 to the New York congress certifying that White had been cleared by the patriots and at the same time they requested the New York congress for advice on securing the schooner-cutter sent by Martin to receive a supply of gun powder either from the "Asia, or the other man-of-war lying in your harbor."

Hewes, on July 8, wrote Samuel Johnston about the work of the Congress. He cataloged again all the injuries, alleged and real, that the royal government had done to the Americans. He advised Johnston that the royal government must soon be superseded and taken into the hands of the people. Hewes added that "if the Governor attempts to do anything he ought to be seized, and sent out of the Colony;" moreover he thought the same treatment should be accorded to Chief Justice Martin Howard. Later Colonel Robert Howe would try to put Hewes' wishes into action when he attempted to capture Martin at Ft. Johnston.[21]

Freed from the restraint of Martin's presence, New Bern committee men were able to work openly for their cause. During the general election in June, a drunken mob, according to Martin, was rebuffed by the palace servants when it attempted to enter the building. The mob then seized the cannon behind the palace, only to find that the guns had been spiked. According to Richard Cogdell of the New Bern committee, he advised the Wilmington Committee that the spiked cannon at the governor's palace had been taken to the courthouse. Cogdell informed the Wilmington group that "we have joined you in a Letter to Mr. Johnston to Call a Convention at Hillsborough."[22]

When the Wilmington committee requested Samuel Johnston on July 13 to call a convention they gave as their reason Governor Martin's past and present activities. The Wilmington men were alarmed because Martin was recruiting troops, collecting "warlike stores," "spiriting up" the back counties, and "perhaps the Slaves," and finally strengthening the fort with new works so as to make the capture of it extremely difficult. The Wilmington leaders were continually clamoring for a convention: "They hope every thing from its Immediate Session, fear everything from its delay." The committee added that they had a number of enterprising young fellows who would attempt to take the fort but they were afraid of having their conduct "disavowed by the convention." Furthermore, it was necessary for a convention to recruit and pay for the men who would defend the country. Chafing at the delay, some of the Wilmington men led by Colonel Robert Howe were unwilling to wait any longer for the convention to be called. They marched toward Ft. Johnston as the Wilmington committee hurriedly met on Saturday, July 15. It promptly called for volunteers to support Howe's men.

Information about the strength of Ft. Johnston given by the Wilmington committee does not agree with the description of the fort by Martin or Captain Collet. When Martin requested additional naval support from Vice Admiral Samuel Graves, he described the fort "which is to the last degree contemptible, is nevertheless a necessary Door of communication with the Country" and thus would depend upon "the aid it may receive from the King's Ships" which cannot be supplied by the *Cruizer*. Captain

John Collet, the young Swiss born commander of the fort, wrote General Thomas Gage and gave him a description of the fort's condition which was like Martin's earlier report to Gage: "Reduced by desertion to 12 men; with 2 half barrels gun powder, I am left to defend a Fort much too large for that number." He was trying to keep and "save 14 eighteen Pounders, 16 nine do. and 20 swivels." He advised that the loss of this artillery would be "attended with too bad Consequences." Collet saw the fort as a place to "keep up a Communication & correspondence with the Head-Quarters, or any other parts." The captain argued that if he had "fifty good hands, Arms & powder enough" he could hold the fort against the patriots. Collet hoped that the patriots would give him enough time for Gage to send men and ammunition. He promised that "If anything happens before, I'll make the most of a bad game" and that nothing would be wanting in his conduct.[23]

As close as Wilmington was to the fort, the committee could only observe the fortress from the outside. They did not know how weak the fort was. Martin learned from reports received by the river transports that the patriots intended to make themselves masters of the fort. Captain Collet assessed the situation and advised Martin that he could "not pretend to hold the place, with only three or four men that he could depend upon, against a multitude said to be collecting to attack it." Martin decided to dismount the valuable artillery, and lay it under the cover of the *Cruizer's* guns. He ordered the withdrawal of the garrison with the shot and moveable stores placed on board a merchant vessel lately arrived from Boston. The merchant vessel was chartered to load naval supplies, but the patriot merchants of Wilmington refused to load their naval stores in a ship that was engaged in the king's service. Martin reported to Dartmouth on July 16 the decisions he had made for abandonment of the fort and the disposition of the men and artillery. He thought that the only good thing about the fort was the king's artillery which could be protected on the shore under the cove of the *Cruizer* and her guns. Still another reason for disarming the fort, offered by Martin, was that the heavy artillery in the hands of a mob could be turned against the *Cruizer* and force her "to quit her present station which is most convenient in all respects." The governor believed that if he could have garrisoned the fort with Highlanders he might have been able to hold it. Still he did not wish to call on the Highlanders because it would have turned the resentment of the whole country against them before they were provided with a means of defense. With the disarming of Ft. Johnston, Governor Martin frustrated the plans of the patriots to get a cheap victory in capturing the fort and himself. Martin foiled the second attempt to capture him by transferring his headquarters to the *Cruizer* on July 13.[24]

Secure on the *Cruizer*, Martin was elated over the British victory at Bunker Hill telling Dartmouth that he thought the complete reduction of New England, "and the utter extinction of Rebellion in America" would soon be put into effect. Martin noted that the king had proscribed John Hancock and Samuel Adams by proclamation, and he thought further proscriptions would be necessary before the government settled again upon sure foundations in America. Martin had some nominees of his own for proscription: "I hold it my indispensable duty to mention to your Lordship, Cornelius Harnett, John Ashe, Robert Howe and Abner Nash, as persons who have marked themselves out as proper objects for such distinction in this Colony" because of "their unremitted labours to promote sedition and rebellion here from the beginning of the discontents in America, to this time." Martin wrote that they "stand foremost among the patrons of revolt and anarchy."

The governor explained that Robert Howe had "impudently assumed the noble family name of Howe for some years past" but he was too limited to imitate the least eminent virtues of that noble family. Howe in the past had spelled his name as How. His reputation and character vary according to the political sympathies and personal views of people who wrote about him. Both General Washington and Josiah Quincy spoke well of him. Martin saw him as a political opportunist who misapplied public money when in command of Ft. Johnston. The governor removed Howe from his command and thus made him a mortal enemy. Howe's reputation suffers from his allegedly libertine activities and his later court martial (though he was acquitted unanimously) seems to point to flaws in his character that have never been fully explained. While Martin could wish for proscription of some of the rebel leaders, especially Robert Howe, he was still concerned about the lack of a court system for the good people of North Carolina. He told the colonial secretary that he had "long impatiently expected with the poor people here" the royal disallowance of "the present wretched system of Courts here, which I hope will be accompanied with the King's Disallowance of the Sheriffs Law also."

Frustrated in their attempt to capture Ft. Johnston and Governor Josiah Martin, the rebel leaders looked for someone else to attack. Their logical candidate would have to be someone close to Governor Martin where the radical leaders could play upon the prejudices and complaints of the colonists of the lower Cape Fear valley. They decided to attack Captain John Collet in print. Collet was an ideal subject for his control of the river traffic had outraged William Dry, collector of the customs at Brunswick. Martin had removed Dry from his seat in the council because of his friendship with the radical leaders and a series of affronts to the royal government that climaxed at a dinner in his house on July 9. Some of Dry's dinner guests were men from South Carolina who were believed to be recruiting men in North Carolina for the patriot armies there. Another guest was William Todd, commander of the ship *Duke of York*. Todd testified later that William Dry gave a toast three times: "success to the American Arms, adding that he wished ardently from his soul they might conquer." Martin told Dartmouth that this "last unpardonable and traitorous display" of Dry's attitude determined him to suspend Dry from the council. Later the *Cape Fear Mercury* was critical of Martin for suspending Dry and not allowing him to defend himself.[25]

Still smarting from their failure to capture Ft. Johnston and the governor, some Wilmington patriots were busily preparing for an expedition against the fort. They hoped to capture the artillery, the fort, the *Cruizer*, a transport, and Captain Collet, his garrison and stores. Merchant captains signed depositions swearing they heard Colonel John Ashe and his men "gasconading and boasting" of their intended expedition. On the evening of July 16, Captain Samuel Cooper of the merchant vessel *Unity* gave his boatswain

135

and carpenter leave to visit an old shipmate in another merchant vessel at Brunswick. On their return they were fired on twice by a schooner with armed men because they had ignored a request to "bring to." When the two men reprimanded them for firing on an unarmed boat, the rebels excused themselves by saying they had no intention of hurting them. They only wanted to frighten them because they knew they were English, "and would be frightened at a flash in the pan." The rebels then forced Cooper's men to land the armed men with their boat.[26]

The next evening, July 17, two merchant marine captains, Samuel Cooper of the *Unity* and Edward Cheeseman of the *Success*, were in a boat going from Wilmington to the flats in the Cape Fear River when they overtook "roger's Sloop" that had been commandeered for carrying Colonel John Ashe and a number of armed men to Brunswick. They were hailed by Ashe's boat and they were told that the colonel desired them to come alongside and drink some toddy, to which they agreed. While on board Roger's sloop they heard several men, who appeared "to be officers and part of the armed men" then on board, avow that their expedition intended to take Ft. Johnston. "A certain Mr. Robinson" requested Cooper's party of four to hold themselves in readiness to assist in the enterprise. Cooper's men replied that they had fought for the king on board a man-of-war and when they chose to fight it should be there again. Robinson proposed a toast: "Damnation to Tories and that Tory the Governor, meaning the Governor of Fort Johnston, Captain Collet...." About midnight of the 17th "a certain Captain Smith came on board Cooper's ship and getting a light he read to Cooper a letter from Colonel Ashe requesting the masters and commanders of the ships at the flats to assist him with what boats, men, and swivel guns they could spare "in the glorious cause of liberty." Captain Smith also presented similar requests for assistance to two merchant marine captains, William Todd and John Martin. In their depositions both men testified that Ashe's letter said they were preparing fire rafts and they wanted the ships' boats and hands to tow them down the river so that they could burn the transport that carried the garrison and military stores transferred from Ft. Johnston.

About nine o'clock on the night of July 18, Nathan Adams, a river pilot, delivered to Governor Martin a letter from the Brunswick committee signed "The People." Adams said he had received it personally from Colonel John Ashe. "The People" letter was dated July 16. It was critical of Captain Collet, and cataloged grievances and complaints, real and alleged, against him. The radicals assured Martin that they could have overlooked these grievances if Captain Collet had not dismantled the fort, that had been paid for by their tax money, and thrown the cannon over the walls in a place "which must entirely ruin them." So that their conduct would not be misunderstood by Martin, they would proceed to the fort and recover the cannon for the safety of the colony. Under the guise of criticizing Captain Collet, the committeemen were really defying Governor Martin. He did not miss their intent. Martin answered immediately "The People" letter by acknowledging that in all cases of Captain Collet's indiscretions known to him that he had interposed his advice and authority and he had persuaded Collet to correct his errors. Nevertheless, many of the accusations against Captain Collet were groundless, particularly the charge of encouraging Negroes to leave their masters and excite them to insurrection. Martin assured "The People" that the dismounting of the king's artillery at the fort was done by his authority and by virtue of the powers vested in him by His Majesty. Martin told them he hoped that in their mistaken belief they would not remove the cannon as their act would do violence against lawful authority. Moreover, he could not permit it.[27]

About two or three o'clock in the morning of July 19, Martin was awakened by an officer of the *Cruizer*. He was told that Captain Collet's house at the fort was on fire. Captain Parry secured the *Cruizer* and personnel and covered the artillery on shore in case "the People should attempt to possess themselves of it." On the shore, no one was to be seen. All of the wooden buildings of the fort were entirely burnt. By eight o'clock of the same morning, parties of men were observed about and around the fort. Soon a few men entered the fort and set fire to a sentry box and some of the parapet that had escaped the flames of the night before. Martin reported to Dartmouth that about two or three o'clock in the afternoon, "this rabble which amounted as nearly as I can learn to about 300 men" set fire to a large barn, stable, coach house, and a small dwelling house together with several outhouses that Captain Collet had built. Having taken vengeance upon Captain Collet, the incendiaries left the area.

Martin advised Dartmouth on July 20 that he did not think the patriots' arson a sufficient reason to justify "commencing hostilities against the People so long as they forebare to touch the King's Artillery." He noted that he had no men to land and "all the material damage that the Fort could sustain had been affected in the night by persons yet undiscovered." Obviously, Martin did not know that Robert Howe had led the attack on the fort for he told Dartmouth he believed John Ashe and Cornelius Harnett were the "ring leaders of this savage and audacious Mob." The governor thought that "the pretence for these shameful and extravagant outrages" was the animosity to Collet whose zeal for the king's service, and "natural vehemence and impetuosity of temper I fear have transported him to some great indiscretions." Nevertheless, he did not think Collet's actions could justify the "barbarian vengeance" of the radicals.

Cornelius Harnett presided at a meeting of the Wilmington committee on July 20-21. The committee justified their actions because they believed, they said, that Collet was preparing to receive reinforcements at the fort. When the committee discovered that Collet had abandoned the fort they decided to march a band of about 500 volunteers to burn the fort so that it would be useless for receiving reinforcements. In a formal resolution, the committee thanked the officers and soldiers for burning the fort because this act was "of so much real importance to the public." The New Bern committee on August 5 published a short paragaph justifying the burning of Ft. Johnston because of Collet's alleged inciting of the slaves to insurrection. By destroying the fort the patriots had blocked its usage for reinforcements by Governor Martin, who, the committee declared, intended to erect the king's standard and commence hostilities against the people of the province. The committee resolved that "no person or persons whatsoever have any correspondence with him, either by personal communication or letter, on pain of being deemed enemies to the liberties of America, and dealt with accordingly.[28]

The radicals had forced Martin to retreat from his capital, and had then tightened the net around Ft. Johnston until he had to remove to the British warship in the Cape Fear. Twice the radicals had tried to capture Martin, and twice they failed. The fortress was burned so that Martin would not have a land base for his expected reinforcement. All the colonists were forbidden to communicate with Martin on pain of being declared traitors to American rights. Patriot propaganda seemed to decline in the summer of 1775. In North Carolina the decline of propaganda activity may have been because the radicals had isolated Martin on the *Cruizer*. It would appear that the radicals had the rod of chastisement rather than Martin. Nevertheless, Martin would persevere in his search for a means to quell the revolution—"that great game depending between Britain and her colonies."[29]

VII. The Great Game Between Britain
and Her Colonies

Isolated by the radicals, the embattled Governor Martin laid plans for recovering the royal government of North Carolina. He had hopes for eventual success because of the recent victory of the king's troops on Bunker Hill. Unknown to Martin, Lord Dunmore was on board a store ship headed for North Carolina. The ship was carrying 3000 stand of arms and other military stores, a part of which Dunmore was to deliver to Martin. Moreover Dunmore was carrying a dispatch for Martin from Dartmouth. The governor was to assign the munitions to Lieutenant Colonel Allen Maclean to aid him in raising a battalion of Highlanders in the province. Martin's rank as lieutenant colonel was not restored; Maclean would be in command. Dartmouth advised Martin of the king's approval of Martin's plan to grant titles for the lands of those South Carolinians who once lived in the province, and, thus, attempt to resolve the boundary line dispute and gain support for the Crown.[1]

On July 18 Martin presided at a council meeting on board the *Cruizer*. The councillors present were James Hasell, Lewis De-Rosset, and John Sampson. They discussed the revolt in Mecklenburg and the coastal counties. The governor advised the council that he had received a report that the people of Bladen were following the example of Mecklenburg. The president of the council, James Hasell, argued that every lawful measure in the power of the governor should be used to suppress the unnatural rebellion. The council concluded that the deluded people of North Carolina would see their error and return to their allegiance to the Crown, and, therefore no violence should be used against them. Meanwhile, the radical leaders pursued their goal toward self-government. In response to the congressional delegates and the several committees, Samuel Johnston issued a call for a provincial convention to meet at Hillsborough on August 20. In his letter to the committee of Wilmington, Johnston reported that two Highland officers, McCloud and McDonnel, had arrived at Edenton on their way to visit "some of their countrymen in your river." Johnston suggested that these two officers were on an "errand of base nature."[2]

In July Martin encouraged the loyalist leaders in Anson County to resist the violent activities of the radicals there. He replied to a letter from Lieutenant Colonel James Cotton which referred to the dictatorial activities of Samuel Spencer to force the people to sign the association. Martin urged Cotton and the other loyalists to "unite against the seditious as they do against you in firm assurance that you will be soon and effectually supported." The governor was confident that His Majesty's army had reduced the spirit of rebellion in New England, another reference to Bunker Hill. He added: "I wait here to forward the purposes of the friends of Govt., or I would have been among you." This letter was intercepted by the radicals and read to the provincial congress at Hillsborough on August 29.[3]

The activities of the loyalists, such as James Cotton, and Samuel and Jacob Williams, in resisting Colonel Samuel Spencer, can be found in the depositions they made on the *Cruizer*. They were signers of a protest against the proceedings of the Continental Congress and harassment by the local committee. Colonel Spencer threatened to butcher the loyalists and seize their estates. Jacob Williams' depositions reflected the fear of being forced to embrace Catholicism; a rumor spread by the radicals that Lord North was a Catholic and the king was about to establish "Popery on all the Continent of America" because he had recognized Catholicism in the Quebec Act. After spending eight days on the *Cruizer*, Cotton and the two Williams departed only to be stopped by the committeemen. They were forced to sign the "association."

Some of the radical leaders used the pulpit as a platform for propaganda in North Carolina. If a minister did not support them in 1775, he was either severely reprimanded or dismissed, usually the latter, which in many cases left the minister impoverished.

The New Bern committee recommended that the Church of England minister and the governor's rector, James Reed, be suspended from pastoral duties and that his salary be stopped because he refused to hold services celebrating the fast day ordered by Congress. The Pitt committee recommended that the Reverend Nathaniel Blount withdraw from his twenty year agreement with his parish so that the people of Pitt County could unite and support the patriot cause. The Rowan committee forced the Baptist preacher the Reverend William Cook to recant "in the most explicit and humiliating Terms" for signing the protest against the cause of liberty which had circulated in the forks of the Yadkin River. The committee apparently was satisfied and Cook continued to serve as a minister to his flock.[4]

The patriots also used propaganda to discredit John Stuart, the Crown's Indian Agent for the Southern Department. They started rumors that Stuart would stir up the Indians and free and arm the Negroes. Stuart thought that the radicals had planted the rumors against him as a ploy to isolate him and limit his influence. He was forced to flee to St. Augustine to avoid capture by some of the South Carolina committeemen; they held his family hostage. Stuart was ill and he asked Dartmouth to help restore his family to him. Meanwhile, the propaganda organ for the Wilmington committee, the *Cape Fear Mercury*, reported on August 7 Stuart's alleged activities "to take up the hatchet against us," and his flight to Georgia. The *Mercury* informed its readers that a "strong party" had been sent after Stuart. Apparently, the editor and the committee did not know Stuart had escaped to Florida.[5]

Although the patriots were mistaken in accusing Governor Martin and John Stuart of inciting and arming the Negroes and the Indians, their fear that the Crown might arm the Indians was correct. The Carolinians and the Georgians had accused the wrong men, but it was useful propaganda to discredit the Crown's servants, Martin and Stuart. Unknown to Martin, Stuart and the radicals, the Crown decided in July 1775 to use Indian auxiliaries. This decision was made near the end of July because Dartmouth on August 2 sent dispatches to both Dunmore and General Gage about the use of Indians. Dartmouth told Dunmore: "The hope you held out to us in your letter of 1st of May that with a supply of arms and ammunition you should be able to collect from the Indians negroes" and other persons a force sufficient if not to subdue rebellion "at least to defend Government was very encouraging. . . . "[6]

Dartmouth advised Gage that His Majesty intended to have an army of 20,000 men, exclusive of Canadians and Indians, in North America by the spring of 1776. For the Indian units, Dartmouth told Gage: "The steps which you say the rebels have taken for calling in the assistance of the Indians, leave no room to hesitate upon the propriety of you pursuing the same measure." For this purpose Dartmouth enclosed a letter to the Indian Agent for the Northern Department, Colonel Sir William Johnson, containing His majesty's commands for engaging a body of Indians. Dartmouth promised to send a large assortment of trade goods for presents for the Indians, which Gage should safely convey to Johnson. Later similar promises were made to John Stuart. Unknown to Martin, the Crown and the radical leaders believed that the other side planned to use Indians. At the end of 1775, Stuart ordered the Creeks and the Cherokees to support the loyalists.[7]

Responding to the radicals' activities and the calling of a provincial congress at Hillsborough, Martin issued a fiery proclamation on August 8. He urged the people to reject the illegal and "traitorous acts of the wicked and flagitious" councils of men "who were misleading them through false assertions and insinuations of oppression in order to gratify for a moment their own lust for power and lawless ambition." Martin listed the "outrageous and false publications" of the *Mercury*, denounced John Ashe's letter signed "The People" and his leading the mob to burn Ft. Johnston, condemned the Mecklenburg Resolves as "treasonable," branded the report of the Congressional delegates to the committees as the source of sedition, and declared the imminent provincial congress illegal and subversive. Martin offered to pardon the people of the province if they returned immediately to their duty to king and government. Furthermore, he offered ample rewards for the surrender of "the few principal persons who seduced them to the reasonable outrages hereinbefore recited to be dealt with according to Law." One immediate effect of Martin's proclamation was that the Wilmington committee vetoed his request to Dr. Thomas Cobham for medicines which the doctor "readily agreed to on being called into committee." Another effect was that the provincial congress declared Martin's proclamation to be false and seditious libel and ordered it to be "burnt by the common Hangman."[8]

The North Carolina provincial congress met at Hillsborough from August 20 through September 10. Samuel Johnston was chosen president and Andrew Knox secretary. All three delegates to the Continental Congress appeared as provincial delegates from their local districts. The major problem that the provincial congress had to solve was the creation of a quasi-legal provincial government to take the place of the royal government. In a sense local governments had already been created by the various safety committees, and their delegates were present in Hillsborough to create on the provincial level what they had done on a local level. The provincial delegates proceeded to create a new government for North Carolina.[9]

In order to justify creating their own provincial government the patriots had to discredit fully the royal government and Governor Martin. On August 23 the delegates appointed a committee declaring that among other things Governor Martin had refused to exercise his office. The committee members, Hooper, Howe, Caswell, Hewes, and Maurice Moore, were instructed to write an address in a familiar, easy style, and calling upon the colonists to unite in defense of "American Liberty," and vindicating, from a necessity to which "Administration has reduced us, the taking up Arms," and assuming the "Controul of the Militia," and ascribing "the silence of the Legislative powers of Government to his Excellency the Governor refusing to exercise the Functions of the Office by leaving the Province and retiring on Board a Man of War, without any threats or violence to compel him to such measure." The accuracy of the last clause in this quotation could be questioned. For example, the presence of the New Bern committee at the head of a mob forcing themselves on Martin in the palace and demanding that the ritual cannon be remounted was not a gentle request, but pregnant with implied violence which Martin correctly interpreted as such. One historian has interpreted the New Bern mob at the palace as an abortive attempt to kidnap the governor. Another such example can be found in the Wilmington mob burning Ft. Johnston to prevent Martin from using it as his residence and forcing him to retire to a man of war, the *Cruizer.*

Late in August, the provincial congress appointed a committee to prepare a plan for maintaining law and order by making an arrangement in the civil police "to supply in some measure the defect of the executive powers of Government arising from the absence of His Excellency Governor Martin." The committee was further instructed to reorganize and establish the internal government of North Carolina and in early September it organized the legislature and determined when it should meet. The provincial council was to meet every three months; the legislature would meet annually beginning on November 10. Delegates were required to take an oath prescribed by this congress. As an assurance to the local patriots, the safety committees in the various towns and counties were to continue to help with the work of the provincial government. To unify and increase their support the delegates in the provincial congress early in their session resolved that the Regulators should be protected from every attempt to punish them for the late insurrection. The congress also appointed committees to convince religious pacifists and the Highlanders to unite with them in defense of their rights "which they derive from God and the Constitution." About the same time the delegates provided for a census of the inhabitants of the province for the collection of taxes on slaves, and, possibly to determine the number of delegates for each district. An exact list of the inhabitants within their respective counties and towns was to be compiled by the local committees. The chairman of the local committee was to certify the list to the president of the congress on or before the first day of November, 1775.[10]

The provincial congress reappointed Hooper, Hewes, and Caswell as delegates to the Continental Congress beginning September 5. Richard Caswell asked to be relieved since he had been made treasurer of the southern district of North Carolina, and placed in charge of the new currency approved by the provincial congress. Congress had approved the issuance of 125,000 dollars in bills of credit for the North Carolina currency. John Penn was appointed in the place of Caswell as a delegate to the Continental Congress. Then the provincial congress turned its attention to a plan of union presented to them by the Continental Congress. On Thursday, August 24, a draft of "Articles of Confederacy proposed for the Consideration of the several Colonies in North America" was brought before the provincial congress and read. This plan provided for a temporary union of the colonies or central government until the terms of reconciliation proposed in the petition of the Continental Congress were agreed to; the restraining and intolerable acts withdrawn; reparations to Boston and the burning of Charles Town; for the expenses of this "unjust war;" and all the British troops were withdrawn. Once these terms were accomplished the colonies were to "return to their former Connection and Friendship with Great Britain, but on failure thereof, this Confederacy to be perpetual." Copies of the plan were to be furnished the delegates for each county and the plan was to be studied.

A fortnight later, the provincial congress resolved itself into a committee of the whole house to take into consideration the plan of the confederation and after some time in discussion they came to a resolution. President Samuel Johnston resumed the chair and the chairman, the Reverend Henry Patillo, reported that the delegates were of the opinion that the plan of confederacy was "not at present Eligible." The committee thought the delegates to Congress should be instructed not to consent to any plan of confederation which may be offered in any ensuing Congress until it had been laid before and approved by the provincial congress. They were of the opinion that the present association ought to be further relied on for bringing about a reconciliation with the mother country and a further confederacy ought only to be adopted in case of the late necessity. Near the end of the session the provincial congress unanimously approved "An Address to the Inhabitants of the British Empire." This address was an appeal to public opinion to persuade the king (for whom they professed to have "an affection bordering upon devotion") and Parliament to restore the United

Colonies, to the State in which we and they were placed before the year 1763." It was more likely this address was intended for provincial persuasion and consumption.

While the radicals were willing to usurp the functions of the provincial royal government, they were unwilling to leave the British empire unless they did not get the terms they had requested from the king. It will not be until November 15, 1777, that the Continental Congress formally adopted the Articles of Confederation, and sent them to the states for ratification. Complete ratification did not occur until March 1, 1781.

Governor Martin was the convenient scapegoat of the provincial congress because he was near at hand while the king and Parliament were across the Atlantic Ocean. Besides laying his intercepted correspondence before the delegates and a written report about the hostile intentions of Martin, the provincial congress seized an opportunity to further humiliate him. James Biggleston, Martin's secretary, had written Samuel Johnston asking the favor of the provincial congress to give sanction and safe conduct to the removal of the most valuable effects of the governor on board the man of war, and his coach and horses to be sent to Farquhard Campbell for safekeeping. The congress resolved that safe conduct be granted Governor Martin's personal effects since the congress had a regard for property, but because Farquhard Campbell, a member of the congress, had expressed a desire that the coach and horses should not be sent to his house in Cumberland, they could not grant safe conduct to the coach and horses. The congress further took the opportunity to express their surprise at the governor's "having deserted the palace, he might have enjoyed all the conveniences of the same in a state of perfect security without insult or injury to his person or property." The patriots resolved that Farquhard Campbell had conducted himself as a friend to the American cause and that any remarks made by Governor Martin or his friends that they could rely on Campbell against the American cause had been without any encouragement from him.[11]

After the provincial congress had adjourned, Martin wrote Dartmouth on October 16 that he had learned to his great surprise and concern that the Highlanders on whom he had such firm reli-

148

ance had declared themselves for neutrality. He attributed this change in attitude of the Highlanders to the influence of Farquhard Campbell. After the burning of Ft. Johnston, Martin had been advised by some of the Highlanders to communicate with Campbell to learn of his ideas about the alarming state of the country. Campbell expressed to Martin his abhorrence of the violence that had been done at the fort and other instances. He gave the governor strong assurance of his own loyalty and that of his countrymen so that Martin did not suspect dissimulation and treachery on the part of Campbell. Responding to Campbell's words, Martin told him of the encouragements he was authorized to hold out to His Majesty's loyal subjects in the colony. Campbell seemingly approved and assured Martin he would consult with his countrymen. He would advise the governor of their determination. From the time of their conversation in July, Martin had heard nothing from Campbell until after the congress adjourned at Hillsborough. Martin discovered that Campbell, as a delegate from Cumberland County, had "unasked and unsolicited and without provocation of any sort" revealed the confidential July conversation to the other delegates. Martin said that Campbell had promised sacredly and inviolably to observe" the "confidential secrecy" of their conversation, but Campbell compounded the situation by the "aggravating crime of falsehood in making additions of his own invention and declaring that he had rejected all my propositions." Martin thought it was fortunate that Campbell could discover nothing new because "the public here were already fully acquainted" with the contents of Dartmouth's letter to which his conversation with Campbell referred. Copies of the Dartmouth letter had been circulated in the province by the committee at Charleston who had intercepted and detained the original. Martin was disappointed because he saw all the promising advantages with the Highlanders wrested from him "by the machinations of sedition for want of all necessary means to use and improve them."[12]

Dartmouth told Martin that the Crown approved his seeking refuge aboard the *Cruizer*, but he thought Martin's idea of taking the province by force of arms was not well founded. The Privy

Council, however, was willing to consider a future invasion providing General Gage thought it advisable. Therefore, 10,000 stands of arms and six light field pieces would be sent to Gage for use in the province should further intelligence prove Martin's plan possible. The colonial secretary thought the Highlanders should be used by Martin in the province, but should that fail he urged Martin to recruit the Highlanders into the British North American army.[13]

Apparently Martin received his information piecemeal about the decisions made by the provincial congress for in his dispatch to Dartmouth he discussed much of what the provincial congress had done. He stressed that the local congress had planned to raise an army of one thousand men, and that they had approved a plan to print paper currency. He noted that the Continental congressional delegates threatened the mercantilist system by planning to open the ports to foreign trade unless Britain acceded to their demands. He also enclosed copies of the province's two newspapers, the *Gazette* and the *Mercury*, with articles about the new colony of "freebooters," Transylvania, that had sent a delegate to the Congress in Philadelphia; and the story about William Hooper laying before the Hillsborough congress the plan for the Articles of Confederation for the United Colonies. Martin reminded Dartmouth that Hooper and the other two delegates to Philadelphia were the signers of the inflammatory letter addressed to the committees in the province that he believed the first cause of violence in the colony.

Before he received Dartmouth's dispatch of October 27 advising him of the Crown's plans for the southern expedition, he wrote to his brother Samuel. He said that he had a prospect of restoring law and order in the colony "by its own internal strength," but an unavoidable delay to furnish him "with the necessary means to exert that strength effectually, has given time for Sedition to work a great change" in the affairs of the colony. He believed if he had a small force to open communication with the large body of "well affected People" of the interior he could overcome the seditious activities of "the rebellious spirits among them." Martin concluded: " . . . there is a great Game depending between Britain and her Colonies; and my King now risks on his playing his part boldly."

The southern expedition of 1775-1776 had its origins in the suggestions of Governors Martin, Dunmore, and Campbell, of North Carolina, Virginia, and South Carolina respectively in the spring of 1775. The original idea behind this expedition was that the Crown would supply a small army together with the navy to support the loyalists in the back country of North Carolina. Once order was established, the Crown's armed forces could leave the loyalists in firm control of the province. After receiving similar suggestions from Lord Dunmore in Virginia, and Lord William Campbell in South Carolina, the Crown's ministers and the king began to consider seriously the proposal for a southern expedition. The one factor which remained constant throughout the development of the plans for a southern expedition was the belief in the essential loyalty of many parts of the southern colonies. Early in October 1775, Lord North and George III became interested in the expedition and ordered appropriate instructions sent to General Howe.[14]

When the Crown was disappointed in a bid for Russian troops for service in America, Lord North announced that a quick end to rebellion in America depended on immediate use of the available British forces. By early October, 1775, the loyalists had assumed prime importance in the Crown's hastily conceived American plans. While final instructions for the expedition were being prepared, George III explained that the southern expedition's purpose was to land first in North Carolina and to call forth those who had a sense of the duty they owed their mother country. It was to restore British government in that province and to leave behind a battalion of provincials formed from the back country settlers under the command of the governor. Moreover, the expedition was "to collect such men as may be willing to serve in the British Troops in America" and then proceed to Virginia or South Carolina as intelligence "may incline the commander to think most advisable." Provincial corps would be left for the protection of the civil magistrates, and when this business was completed the regiments were to proceed to New York.[15]

Dartmouth sent General Howe detailed instructions for the expedition in a dispatch dated October 22, 1775. The expedition was composed of five regiments under convoy of a naval force commanded by Sir Peter Parker, carrying ten thousand stand of spare arms for the loyalists. It was to sail from Cork, Ireland, for the Cape Fear River about December 1. These troops were to be met off Cape Fear by a small force directly from Boston, under a general officer appointed by Howe to command the operation, and by whatever loyal refugees Governor Martin had already under arms. Specific operations would be left to the general in command, on the basis of the latest local intelligence. Governors Martin and Dunmore had already carefully studied certain possible maneuvers, "and Governor Lord William Campbell of South Carolina and Southern Indian Superintendent John Stuart would join the expedition off Cape Fear."[16]

On October 27, Dartmouth advised Martin that the king had ordered regiments to the southern colonies to leave Cork about December 1 and proceed to the Cape Fear River. Martin's personal emissary to Dartmouth, Alexander Schaw, had listened with interest to the discussions held in Dartmouth's office respecting the employment of troops destined for the southern provinces. He had participated in the discussions of the kind of operations needed to subdue the rebels. Schaw argued that Martin thought he could keep up his authority, once it was re-established, without the assistance of regular troops, thus Schaw urged the necessity of conquering North Carolina first. Dartmouth still had doubts whether the expedition would be successful. In the same dispatch, Dartmouth informed Martin that he would be instructed by one of Howe's officers as to the plan and conduct of the expedition. Martin would have to raise a corps of provincials by his authority and he would have the rank of provincial colonel with the same pay as a colonel in the regular army, but without any rank or claim to half pay after the war. Martin, moreover, was to arrange secretly for a number of pilots to be put aboard the vessels that would cruise the coast until the fleet and transports arrived. He was also to secure carriages and draft horses for the use of troops in the province. Later, Dartmouth advised Martin that he should send his emissaries out to the back counties with authority and commissions to the principal persons of trust and confidence for recruiting men. Those recruited should have land grants and regular army pay. He cautioned that the transports with a "large Draught of water" might have difficulty landing troops in the Cape Fear because of the bar. If this proved correct, Dartmouth advised Martin that the expedition would proceed to Charleston in order to restore the government of South Carolina. Dartmouth's dispatch of November 8 to General Howe is similar to the one sent to Martin except that Dartmouth was still not sure the expedition would be successful, but should it fail Dartmouth believed it would not weaken the Crown's operations to the northward.[17]

From Philadelphia, Joseph Hewes advised Samuel Johnston in November that Congress did not expect reconciliation with Britain. Congress had decided to send four regiments to defend South Carolina and Georgia. Their enlistments were to end on December 31, 1776. On the 28th, Congress further accelerated defense plans for North Carolina. The two battalions in the colony were recognized as part of the Continental Army and they were to be paid by the United Colonies for one year. Congress had granted money to North Carolina to purchase drums, fifes, and colors for their battalions and Hewes advised that North Carolina could purchase gunpowder from the safety councils of Pennsylvania and South Carolina, and that the Carolina gunsmiths should be employed immediately in making muskets and bayonets according to the approved congressional standard. Hewes urged that two clergymen should be employed to go among the former Regulators and Highlanders and explain the nature of the dispute between Britain and the colonies.[18]

While the radicals were planning to win over the Highlanders, Martin reported to Dartmouth that 302 Highlanders had arrived in the mouth of the Cape Fear. He had given them permission to settle on the king's land. Another group of Highland immigrants asked the Virginia convention for aid so that they might go to the Cape Fear where they intended to settle. They were permitted to pass by land unmolested to North Carolina.[19]

The war sloop *Scorpion*, commanded by Captain John Tollemache, R.N., arrived in the Cape Fear on November 12 with dispatches for Governor Martin and Captain Francis Parry. The *Scorpion* had convoyed the transport *Palliser* to the Cape Fear so that she could take on board "the Cannon and other Ordnance Stores at Ft. Johnston." Gage's dispatches were old and no longer pertinent to the changing situation, although his dispatches did discourage Martin from expecting aid from him. Vice Admiral Samuel Graves advised Martin that Captain Tollemache would relieve Captain Francis Parry and he would patrol the coast of North Carolina after he had delivered dispatches to Charleston. The unfavorable November weather prevented the transport *Palliser* from returning to Boston. The presence of the king's ships in the river disturbed the Wilmington radical leaders, particularly when they learned that the transport was to pick up the artillery which they claimed belonged to the colony. They interpreted the securing of the artillery as another example of Martin's "open and avowed contempt" and violation of justice. The Wilmington committee planned to buy old ships, boats, and chains to sink in the channel to obstruct the passage of the king's ships. The Wilmington committee prepared for defense and called up the militia because they thought the man of war at Ft. Johnston would attempt to burn Brunswick, and afterwards Wilmington. The Wilmington leaders ordered that an inventory list be compiled of the buildings and property in the city. "Lead, saltpetre, and brimstone" were to be collected and given to Solomon Hewitt to manufacture ammunition. Hewitt was ordered to produce the two two-pound pieces he had in his possession and deliver them to the committee as soon as possible. The committee rejected Samuel Campbell's application to send provisions down to the *Cruizer*. The radicals declared that no provisions should be sent to any other ship belonging to the king.[20]

As the radicals began to draw the net tighter around the governor, he wrote his brother Samuel that "I still continue in an inglorious captivity on board a small vessel." The frustration of being cooped up on a small ship and waiting for supplies and troops that never seem to arrive sharpened Martin's sense of survival. He told his brother that Tryon was ill and was about to retire from the governorship of New York. One of Martin's friends, John Blackburn, an American merchant in London and a consultant on American affairs for Dartmouth, had spoken to the secretary abut giving the New York governorship to Martin. Blackburn had advised Martin that Dartmouth seemed to favor him as a replacement for Tryon. Martin asked his brother to talk to Blackburn and to contact William Knox, one of the undersecretaries of state in Dartmouth's office, who had been secretary for the province of New York. Martin justified his request to Samuel by arguing that the first principle he himself should follow was provision for and preservation of his family.[21]

Martin's sense of preservation and survival manifested itself in his attempts to recruit Highlanders to help him re-establish the authority of the royal government in the province. Captain Alexander McLeod, an ex-officer of the Marines, visited Martin and informed him that both he and his father-in-law, Allan Macdonald, had each raised a company of Highlanders in response to Martin's earlier encouragement. Both men were related to the Scottish heroine, Flora Macdonald; Allan the husband and Alexander the son-in-law. Allan had purchased a plantation named Killiegray eighteen miles north of present day Rockingham and two miles north of Capel's Mills on Mountain Creek. Allan Macdonald had met with Martin on July 3 to plan the raising of a battalion of Highlanders. McLeod told Martin that Gage's assistant, a Major Mc-Donald, wanted to recruit McLeod and Macdonald for a battalion to be commanded by Lieutenant Colonel Allan McLean. They accepted on the condition that should the Crown not approve Martin's proposal they would be free to accept Major McDonald's offer. Martin explained his quandary to Dartmouth. If McLeod and Macdonald were recruited by Gage their influence over the rest of the Highlanders would be lost and so would the Highlanders as supporters of the royal government in North Carolina. Moreover, the turncoat Farquhard Campbell's conduct was governed by his jealousy of the influence of McLeod and Macdonald over the Highlanders in the colony. The governor thought he might be able to reconcile the interests of all the parties whenever he had the power to act and could bring them together. He thought the Crown should accept only unconditional submission and not to trust the rebels. Dartmouth, Dunmore, Hillsborough, and Germain all agreed with Martin's view.[22]

As if to signal an important change in American policy, the Crown, on November 10, 1775, appointed Lord George Germain as a commissioner of trade and plantations and secretary of state for the colonies in place of Dartmouth. Germain was an unbending exponent of unconditional colonial submission to the Crown and Parliament. Germain was a scion of the noble family of Sackville. After receiving his M.A. at Trinity in Dublin, his career carried him from a captaincy to a major generalship and a self-publicized court martial. His public image was rehabilitated after he was empowered by an act of Parliament to assume the name of Germain, in accordance with the provisions of the will of Lady Betty Germain in 1770. He received further public approval when he fought a duel with Captain George Johnstone, late governor of Pensacola and then M.P. for Cockermouth. Their honor satisfied; the two men parted amicably. From this nadir Germain rose again to royal favor under George III as one of his chief ministers.[23]

The major responsibility for the Crown's southern expedition finally rested on two men, Lord Germain and Major General Henry Clinton, who, during the prosecution of the war, came to be closely identified with plans to use the loyalists. Clinton, the son of a former governor of New York, was appointed by Howe on January 6, 1776, to command the land forces of the southern expedition. These two men were to play important roles in many subsequent campaigns because Germain continued in his office until 1782, and Clinton, who later succeeded Howe, served as commander in chief in North America from May 1778 to May 1782. According to one historian, neither man distinguished himself in the planning or execution of the 1776 expedition to the southern colonies.[24]

The problem of defense against the imminent British invasion concerned the patriot council that met at the Johnston County Courthouse, December 18 through the 24th, 1775. The president of the council, Samuel Johnston, and ten members attended: Thomas Jones, Samuel Ashe, James Coor, Thomas Eaton, Abner Nash, John Kinchen, Whitmill Hill, Waightstill Avery, Samuel Spencer, and the former Regulator, Thomas Person. The councillors resolved that the treasurers should pay for the completion of fortifications at Edenton, Hanging Point on the Neuse River, and DuBoise's Mill on the Cape Fear. On paper the council created a navy when they appointed commissioners in three ports, Beaufort, Brunswick, and Roanoke, to purchase and supply an armed vessel for each of these ports to protect trade and commerce. On December 21, the delegate to Congress, Joseph Hewes, was advised of the action to guard the inlets of the province.[25]

Germain wrote Martin and referred to Dartmouth's dispatch of November 7 that had instructed Martin on the plan for the southern expedition. He informed Martin that the expedition was ready to proceed to America. The troops were to be accompanied by a naval force of nine of His Majesty's ships commanded by Sir Peter Parker. Germain advised Martin: "If this Dispatch should reach you before the arrival of the Armament, which is however uncertain," he was to exert every effort to execute the orders contained in Lord Dartmouth's letter. Martin was to "take every necessary preparatory step for collecting a Corps of Provincials to serve with the King's Troops and to join them upon their landing" at the Cape Fear. Martin received Germain's dispatch on March 18, 1776, after the battle of Moore's Creek bridge.[26]

Among the preparations for war there was one voice that spoke for peace; Judge Maurice Moore, a Whig who supported the radical leaders. He echoed Lord North's speech when he appealed to Martin to call an assembly to profess loyalty to the Crown and return to the conditions of 1763 before the King's Proclamation and the new tax programs were initiated. When he received Moore's letter, the governor had already issued a proclamation in which he raised the Royal Standard and summoned all loyal Carolinians to support him in subduing the rebels and traitors. He promised all rebels who would swear allegiance to the Crown would be forgiven, Committed to the crown and its plans, the dubious Martin asked Moore to produce evidence that the people of the province

157

wished to return to British authority "by dissolving all combinations of rebellion among them." Martin did not report to Germain the suggestion of Moore for reconciliation until May 17, 1777, when the governor was convalescing on his uncle's estate on Long Island. As his health improved Martin reviewed his Carolina papers and discovered the Moore letter of January 11, 1776. He explained to Germain he had not forwarded the letter earlier because he had "considered it of too trifling a nature to deserve notice." In Martin's dispatch are two valuable portrait sketches of Maurice Moore and Samuel Johnston. Both men had been educated in New England which Martin regarded as a hotbed of democracy. He thought Moore was fickle and desired to be popular, and thus a democrat who was capricious, whereas he thought Johnston had a good private character but his democratic ideas encouraged him to accept the office of moderator in the illegal assembly and the assembly's gift of the office of treasurer of the colony. Johnston, moreover, had been in uniform opposition to every measure of government during Martin's administration. Martin saw Moore as a "principal instrument of dethroning Justice in North Carolina, full two years before the total subversion of Government, by Rebellion," which in the colony, "may almost be said to have been forerun by anarchy."[27]

When the *Scorpion* arrived in the Cape Fear on November 11, 1775, Martin made it his headquarters in order to relieve the overcrowded conditions on the *Cruizer*. He was concerned when he discovered that the *Scorpion* was ordered to proceed to Charleston to help defend the city against an expected rebel attack. His concern was based on the belief that it was necessary to have a warship in the river for his base of operations. The *Cruizer* was scheduled to leave for Charleston for much needed repairs. Martin went with the *Scorpion* to Charleston to make sure that she would return to her station in the Cape Fear. With a transport under her convoy, the *Scorpion* arrived in Charleston harbor on November 30. Lord William Campbell, the royal governor of South Carolina was on board the *Cherokee* in Charleston harbor which he called "Rebellion Road." Although Lord Campbell realized that his position was similar to Martin's, he was distressed when he learned that the *Scorpion* was to return to the Cape Fear with Martin. Captain Edward Thornburg, R.N., at Charleston, honored Martin's request to return the ship to the Cape Fear. Contrary winds detained the ship so that Martin was absent from North Carolina a month, although the governor hastened to tell Dartmouth that "happily" nothing of consequence had occurred during his enforced absence. In the Cape Fear, Captain Tobias Furneaux of the *Syren* gave the returning governor a thirteen gun salute on the morning of January 4, 1776.[28]

While Martin was in Charleston, he and Campbell conferred about their problems with the rebels. Campbell told Martin that the loyalists in the interior of South Carolina had defeated a large body of rebels and they expected further advantages if the rebels in North Carolina did not intervene. After his return to the Cape Fear, Martin learned that 600 men under the leadership of Alexander Martin and Thomas Polk had marched from Mecklenburg and Rowan Counties and helped the South Carolina rebels disarm some loyalists. Despite the rebel victory, Martin thought that once the expedition arrived he could restore the lost authority of the royal government. He expected between two to three thousand former Regulators to support him. Colonel Alexander McLean was recruiting Highlanders and Martin assured Germain that he would support McLean's endeavors among the Scots emigrants. He also advised the secretary that the Cape Fear harbor would receive frigates drawing not more than six feet of water which the naval officers said would be sufficient to cover the landing of the troops. Since Martin did not expect opposition to the landing parties, he thought it was "immaterial whether Men of War come into this River or not." Martin was concerned because he had "a violent disorder" in his eyes and he had no "Amanuensis." He could not send the colonial secretary duplicates of his last two dispatches which he thought were probably waiting in Charleston for a packet boat. Archibald Neilson, who had been his secretary, left for England on the *George* with Janet Schaw and the Rutherford children on November 10, 1775.[29]

The presence of the *Scorpion* controlling the river traffic and serving as a base of operations for Governor Martin was a great cause of anxiety and concern among the radical leaders in the lower Cape Fear. The ship's presence spurred them to seek ways to usurp Martin's power over army officers and the control of the members of the royal council. On January 6, 1776, the Wilmington committee ordered the Highlander, Captain Alexander Maclean, not to wait on the governor but to write to him. He had to show the committee his letter before sending it to Martin. On January 10, Martin issued his proclamation condemning the rebels and exhorting His Majesty's faithful subjects to repair to the King's Standard. On the same day, Martin issued orders to General Donald McDonald, the Highlander, for raising the King's Standard in the back counties. On the 16th, the committee reprimanded Captain Maclean for visiting Martin because the captain had ignored their earlier orders to him.[30]

When Martin called a meeting of the Royal council on board the *Scorpion* on January 27, the Wilmington committee refused permission for the members to attend, announcing that it was not consistent with the safety of the country. Furthermore, the committee tried to usurp the royal navy's powers of clearance of ships by ordering on February 2 that no vessel could be cleared from its port unless it had an order from the committee. While they could control the council members responding to Martin's call for a meeting, the radicals would have a much more difficult time controlling a man-of-war. Opposition to Martin's plans came not only from the local radicals, but unknown to him, from the king's general in Boston. Major General William Howe in his dispatch to Dartmouth on January 16 argued that the priority of the troops of the southern expedition should be given to New York rather than the southern provinces. He thought the rebels in New York should be defeated before "designs of less importance are taken up." Howe was critical of the southern governors because he thought that the rebels would have been less able to defend themselves had they not been aroused by the conduct of their governors, none of whom possessed the power to suppress the rebellion and re-establish the royal government. The general resented the interference of civilian governors urging that regiments be sent southward: "It is remarkable that the destination of the regiments to the southward was promulgated here by private letters from England, that came in the same ship with your Lordship's Dispatch relative to them." Howe advised Dartmouth that Major General Sir Henry Clinton was ready to leave Boston for the Cape Fear in the *Mercury* with a sloop and two transports, "that had two companies of light infantry and some Highlanders." He hoped the Highlanders would be useful in "getting men in North Carolina, if Governor Martin is not deceived in his expectations, of which I do not presume to judge." Howe had not yet received Martin's letter referred to by Dartmouth in his dispatch of October 22.[31]

The New York committee advised their delegates in Congress that Clinton had arrived in New York on February 4 on his way southward. They also had happier news, the patriot General Charles Lee, ill with gout, had arrived at the same time with 700 men. Lee had ordered the patriot regiment under General William Alexander (sometimes called Lord Stirling) to join him. Lee reported to Washington that Clinton had arrived in New York with only two companies of light infantry from Boston and he expected to meet five regiments from England in North Carolina. The witty Lee thought that Clinton communicating "his full plan to the enemy is too droll to be credited." Lee, second in command to General Washington, had known Clinton when they were both officers of the king. With the intelligence reports from the northern committees, the safety committees of North Carolina, early in February, accelerated their defense preparations against Clinton and the southern expedition. The Tryon County committee ordered every third effective man to join the patriot forces and any man who refused to do this should be judged an enemy to his country. The New Bern committee raised the alarm that the former Regulators were in the field against the patriots. Colonel Richard Caswell would lead men to put down this insurrection. This proved to be a rumor. The Rowan committee took depositions from two patriots that they had heard read in William Field's camp at Dillos, the Manifesto of Brigadier General Donald McDonald of His Majesty's forces in North Carolina in which he urged the loyalists to support him and he promised them safety for their women and children.[32]

In Philadelphia, the delegate John Penn reported to Thomas Person that Brigadier General Richard Montgomery had been killed in the unsuccessful attack on Quebec on December 31. He also reported that Clinton consulted with Governor Tryon as to what measures he should pursue when he arrived in North Carolina. He commented that Governor Martin at last had his wish: the Crown had agreed to send seven regiments to him. Penn concluded that the Crown's ministers hoped to gain greater success in the southern provinces than to the northward. Unknown to Penn and about the same time he wrote Person, another loyalist manifesto was issued by Colonel Thomas Rutherford of the Cumberland militia on February 13. Rutherford summoned the loyalists to the King's Standard to meet at Cross Creek on or before the 16th of February.[33]

Lieutenant Governor Cadwallader Colden of New York apparently was privy to many of the plans the British had made for the subjugation of the rebels. In a letter to an unidentified correspondent, Colden described the secretary of state for the colonies, Lord Germain, as a despicable politician. He then discussed the plans of the British army in America. He said that 15,000 Hessians and 18,000 British soldiers were to be used against the Americans. He thought the British army was of a poor quality because it was made up of "boys and debilitated manufacturers." Lord Cornwallis was sailing from Cork, Ireland, to Virginia, with his regiments and he was to place them under the command of General Clinton. Clinton expected help from the Scots in Virginia and North Carolina under the command of General Donald McDonald. Colden added that Lord Howe would blockade the American coast and he hoped to get possession of New York and the Hudson River so that the South would be cut off from communicating with the northern colonies. Aware of the rumors that the British fleet might attempt to blockade the American coast, the New Bern committee was spurred to action to protect the town against attack by an armed vessel. The committee called up over one hundred men and officers of the militia when they received intelligence from the Wilmington committee that a British armed vessel had been fitted out by the man-of-war in the Cape Fear.[34]

There are several cryptic entries in the journal of the sloop *Cruizer* made by Captain Francis Parry for the month of February that suggest that Parry tried to contact the loyalist Highlander army that was thought to be on its way to Wilmington and a meeting with Martin. The entry on Wednesday the 14th of February reads "Came on board Govr. Martin at Noon Snows Point bore NW½W." Martin had learned that his emissary from Brunswick had been captured in the back country of the province, and that he had turned "rebel" as soon as he was caught. This meant that the rebels had Martin's list of loyalists on whom he could depend, and this made them worthless in a military sense. However, "a Mr. Reed" brought Martin intelligence that there were about 3,400 loyalists and they expected them to come down from Cross Creek and hold Wilmington. It is possible that Martin's meeting with Parry was to request that he cruise up the river and fire signals so that the loyalist army could be ferried down to Wilmington. Other cryptic entries in Parry's log suggests preparations and search for the loyalist army. In the next two days Parry took on fresh water and four quarters of beef. On Saturday, the 17th, Parry set sail at "7 A.M." and sailed up the river in the company of the schooner *Lady William* and anchored at 11 a.m. at the entrance of the North West River. At 4 p.m., he sailed "into the N.W. River and tow'd up about 3 miles" and anchored where the sloop went aground. On Sunday the 18th, he floated the sloop and sailed down the river where he anchored her at 8 a.m. off the entrance to the North West River. On Monday the 19th, Parry was moored for twenty four hours while he fired "5, 3 pounders for Private Sigls." On Tuesday the 20th, Parry fired several guns as private signals, and then sailed down the river at 4 p.m. Were these private signals that Parry fired meant to be communication signals for the HIghlander army? Evidence suggests that he was searching for the loyalist army. One historian has interpreted the signals fired by Parry as an attempt by Martin and the captain to effect a junction with the Highlanders and the Regulators.[35]

The patriot colonel, William Purviance, reported to the provincial council that he had skirmished with the troops and sailors from the *Cruizer* and the *Scorpion* when they raided plantations and pillaged what was left of Ft. Johnston. Foodstuffs, livestock, and furnishings were taken from John Ancrum's plantation but they did not steal the Negroes because they had run away. Ancrum was a major radical leader in the Wilmington area. The sailors were driven off by patriot rifle fire, and patriot riflemen forced the *Cruizer*, who was sailing up the river towards Wilmington, to turn back to the flats below Brunswick. Parry's entries in his log for Thursday the 22nd and Friday the 23rd stated that the *Cruizer* anchored abreast of Brunswick and on the 23rd she was joined by the *Scorpion*. Captain Tollemache's log for the *Scorpion* confirms the meeting with the *Cruizer* on the 23rd, but there is no mention of receiving patriot rifle fire or the raid on the plantations. Earlier Parry had entered in his log that grape shot had been fired at rebels when they appeared in the woods while his men were removing cannon from the fort. There were also entries that the *Cruizer* had anchored off the fort and later sailed towards Wilmington with two armed tenders. There is no mention of "pillaging" the fort or returning to the flats below Brunswick because of patriot rifle fire.[36]

Purviance advised the provincial council he had disarmed and confined the Tories in Wilmington and he had evacuated and fortified the town. Another precaution that the colonel took was to order a boom to be built at Mount Misery on the northwest branch of the Cape Fear River (Parry's North West River) to halt the march of the "Regulators and Highland Banditti" going to meet Governor Martin. Purviance received an express rider from Colonel James Moore's headquarters at Rockfish near Cross Creek on February 24 that reported the loyalists had crossed the river at Campbelton and camped on the eastern side. Moore thought they might attempt to come down, either by the Black River road, or through Duplin, and so he dispatched an express rider to Colonel Richard Caswell who had passed Black River on his way to the main body with about 1200 men. Caswell returned and marched downwards to secure the most important position. He gave orders to break the bridges on the approach of the enemy. The men in Duplin had already partially demolished the bridges. They were prepared to complete their work once it became necessary. Purviance then sent a strong detachment to the important pass of Her-on's Bridge on the northeast and another 120 men to Mount Mis-ery to stop the loyalists who had all the boats at Cross Creek. Both Purviance and Martin thought that the loyalists might try to trans-port their men, provisions, and ammunition by water. The loyalist army consisted mostly of "Highland Banditti," according to Pur-viance, and there were not more than 200 of the former Regula-tors. Purviance said this army had about 900 men because they were carefully counted by patriot scouts as they marched to Campbelton. Colonel Moore's army was about 1500 men. Purvi-ance believed that the immediate reason for the loyalists sudden march was that Colonel Alexander Martin was within a few miles of Cross Creek with almost 2000 men on the night of February 20.[37]

While the loyalist army was marching toward Wilmington to rendezvous with Governor Martin and Clinton's promised forces, Martin began another phase of the struggle for power in and around the town of Wilmington. From the *Cruizer* on February 27, Martin sent a message to the town of Wilmington requiring its citizens to furnish His Majesty's service with one thousand barrels of flour at the market price. He wanted the flour delivered on or before Saturday, March 2. Martin was supporting Captain Parry's demand for provisions for "His Majesties Ships" that had not been received. Parry in his letter to the Wilmington leaders advised them that he would be off Wilmington with the *Cruizer* and "other armed vessels under my Command to know the reason of their not being supplied." Parry expected the supplies by six p.m. on February 27; Martin had changed the demand date to no later than March 2. The Wilmington committee replied to both notes from Martin and Parry on February 27, and it directed the chair-man, John Ancrum, to sign the replies. To Martin, the committee members replied that they were astounded at the quantity of flour requisitioned because they could not understand why His Majesty would require so much flour in the Cape Fear region. The com-mittee argued that in peaceful times, it would have been difficult to get a large quantity of flour to Martin in so short a time. More-over, the committee added that this was the time when His Excellency had raised and commissioned an army that had for some time the possession of Cross Creek and the surrounding country-side "from whence only we can expect the Article you have thought proper to Demand.[38]

The committee members argued that Martin's request was a prelude to his intended destruction of the "devoted Town of Wilmington." The citizens of Wilmington, according to the committee, had to defend their property and if they did not accede altogether to Martin's wish, they had one consolation left. Wilmington's friends would within a few days have it in their power to make ample retribution against the Highlander army. The committee boldly declared that the Highlander army was now surrounded by three armies. Moreover, the town of Cross Creek would make some, though inadequate, compensation for the destruction of Wilmington. From the committee, Captain Parry received a list of the injuries caused by the naval flotilla in the river, the trade of the colony had been distressed by the ships, the seizing of military stores, the plunder of plantations, capture of livestock, and the pursuit of slaves. Moreover, the committee said that Parry had for the second time brought the *Cruizer* and several armed vessels to cover the landing of an army of "highland banditti" whom it claimed he would never see unless as fugitives imploring his protection. Parry was assured by the committee that thought he might threaten the town he could not expect any other answer than what it had given him.

Martin again wrote to the magistrates and people of Wilmington on February 28. He informed them that the requisition for supplies was not made as a prelude to the destruction of the town, but "as a test of the disposition of its inhabitants, whose sence I am unwilling to believe is known to the little arbitrary Junto (stiling itself a Committee) has presumed to answer for the People in this and other Instances." Martin told them that the revilings of the friends of government by the rebels gave him little reason to expect respect from the "Chairman of a Combination founded in Usurpation & Rebellion," a reference to John Ancrum. Immediately the Wilmington committee replied that it had not only been chosen by the people, but on this occasion the freeholders had been consulted on the propriety of the answer to Governor Martin. It pleased the committee to learn that His Majesty's service did not require a great amount of flour. The committee declared that the citizens of Wilmington did not deserve the epithets of rebels and traitors that the governor had called them.[39]

While Governor Martin and the Wilmington committee were negotiating, the loyalist army was marching toward Wilmington and a planned rendezvous with Martin and Clinton's promised forces. On the night of February 27, Colonel Richard Caswell arrived at Moore's Creek bridge. He found minute men and militia from the counties of Craven, Dobbs, Johnston, and Wake, and the towns of New Bern and Wilmington. They were under the command of Colonel Alexander Lillington. Colonel Purviance and others had been tracking General Donald Macdonald and the loyalist army for sixty miles from Cross Creek. Some of the patriots had heard rumors that there were three thousand men with Macdonald across the creek from them.[40]

In the early morning hours an alarm gun was fired which began the battle of Moore's Creek Bridge. Scarcely leaving the patriots a moment to prepare, Captains Alexander McLeod and John Campbell attacked the positions of Colonels Caswell and Lillington. General Donald Macdonald was ill in his tent. In the half-light McLeod and Campbell saw what they thought to be a small entrenchment next to the bridge that was empty on the patriots' side. They assumed that the patriots had abandoned their post. In the dark they made another fatal assumption. They charged across the bottomless and greased rail bridge only to flounder in the water. They advanced within thirty paces of the patriot breastwork and artillery where they were caught in a heavy enfilade and cut to pieces. McLeod and Campbell were among those slain. The patriots won this short and bloody battle.[41]

The effects of the battle of Moore's Creek Bridge were many. There were several major effects. It turned neighbors against neighbors in a civil war. It confirmed the patriots' confidence that they could win a battle with the provincial forces of the royal governor, although the battle was over before he knew about it. Governor Martin, nonetheless, had some reasons for optimism, 1500 loyalists had answered his call to the Royal Standard; more than he predicted. For the patriots, the battle encouraged them to continue in their struggle for their rights, yet the patriots' victory did not discourage Governor Martin. The battle renewed Martin's confidence in his cause and strengthened his determination to regain the lost authority of the royal government. Perhaps the most significant effect of the battle was that neither the patriots nor the loyalists could foresee that the battle would dissuade the Crown from invading North Carolina for several years, and that Martin would continue to play a role in the desperate gamble for the South.[42]

VIII. The Desperate Gamble in the South

The effect of the battle of Moore's Creek Bridge on Governor Josiah Martin was much greater than he initially realized. At first the loyalist defeat did not depress him, rather it renewed his confidence because the loyalist response had exceeded his predictions. That the Highlanders had rallied at all was more than Martin expected. Yet he was critical and rightly so that the southern expedition had been so tardy in arriving at the Cape Fear two weeks after the battle. In his first official dispatch to Lord George Germain on March 21, 1776, he gave a long report on his attempts to restore the royal government in North Carolina, and he carefully analyzed the reasons for the failure at Moore's Creek bridge.[1]

Martin did not receive Germain's first dispatch of November, 1775 until March 18, 1776. Germain's dispatch developed further the ideas and plans for the expedition to the southern colonies contained in Dartmouth's instructions of November 7. The unfortunate delay of the armament from Cork, Ireland, "contravened" Martin's plan to restore law and order in the province. The governor described for Germain the events leading to the battle of Moore's Creek Bridge, already discussed. He related how he had conferred with Captain Francis Parry of the *Cruizer* and how they made the decision to go up the river and carry the loyalist troops in small vessels down to Wilmington. As Parry made his preparations and consulted with the river pilots, intelligence was received that the loyalists had been checked seventeen miles above Wilmington at Moore's Creek bridge. Martin learned that "near 20 men killed and wounded" and the rest of the loyalists dispersed. He soon had this intelligence confirmed when four loyalist warriors, Maclean, Campbell, Stuart, and McNichol, sought refuge on the *Scorpion* off Brunswick. These men told the governor that they thought the reasons for the defeat were a lack of "prudent concert" and a deceit practiced by the rebels upon the country people. The deceit was a reference to a rumor circulated by the rebels that Martin was at Cross Creek with one thousand regular troops, and when he did not appear it had shaken the confidence of the country people, and disappointed the Highlanders. This deceit had destroyed all faith and confidence between the loyalists and their leaders and caused the reduction of the promised five thousand men to about 700 to 800 at Cross Creek.

If the deceit had not occurred, the governor thought the Highlanders and the country people could have restored peace and order without the immediate aid of His Majesty's troops. Martin, nonetheless, told Germain he was convinced that the delay of the southern expedition, which he had hoped would arrive at the beginning of February, was one of the major reasons for the defeat of the loyalists. Martin, however, still believed that victory could be achieved by use of British troops because "the little check the loyalists here have received I do not conceive . . . will have any extensive ill consequences." He added: "all is recoverable by a body of Troops penetrating into this country." Martin concluded that if the king's troops were to act in the province they must meet the loyalists in the country instead of at the sea shore. He asked Germain to urge the Crown to offer security for the loyalist families and for the wounded and disabled.

What Martin did not know is that Germain had changed the original objective of the southern expedition in December 1775, when he directed Sir Henry Clinton "not to make North Carolina the focus of operations, and, instead, authorized him to consider another location where the expedition might still be carried out." Germain's reasoning behind this important change was that he learned that an army could not safely land at Cape Fear because of the bar at the mouth of the river. Thus, a landing could not be supported by the navy. Later this information proved erroneous. When Germain received Martin's dispatch to Dartmouth of August 28, 1775, he learned that rebel control of the province extended almost one hundred miles inland. Germain had received Martin's dispatch on November 20 after he had succeeded Dartmouth as secretary of the colonies. One historian has commented that since the entire plan of the southern expedition rested upon Martin's supposed strength in North Carolina, Germain's decision seriously undermined the fundamental purpose of the expedition.[2]

The successful execution of the plan for the southern expedition depended upon an efficiency of organization and a degree of cooperation between British governmental departments, which did not exist. After incredible bureaucratic bungling, the expedition set sail four months after its organization began only to have stormy weather scatter its transports. The first of Clinton's flotilla from Boston, the *Glasgow* packet with soldiers, arrived in the Cape Fear on Tuesday, March 12. Sir Henry Clinton arrived two days later in the *Mercury*. Clinton conferred with Martin and discovered that a large body of North Carolina loyalists had been defeated at Moore's Creek bridge two weeks earlier. News of the loyalist defeat and the depressing information that the rest of the southern expedition from Cork had been seriously delayed, compelled Clinton to examine new proposals.

Martin defended his loyalists to Clinton. He argued that they would have done better if they had received the expected support of the southern expedition. He urged Clinton to use the troops when they arrived to establish a strong beach head around which the loyalists could rally. He argued that this should be done immediately upon their arrival "or the Climate" would "consume" them after the month of May. Clinton agreed with Martin about the dangerous hot weather, and refused to abandon hope that a partial victory might yet be achieved. Clinton's earlier talks with Governor Dunmore off Hampton Roads, and his communications with Governors Martin and Campbell on board the *Mercury* had convinced him that the southern loyalists were "still overflowing with zeal" and awaiting support of His Majesty's troops. Because the loyalists were located in the back country, Clinton concluded that they would be of little help until a British base had been established on the coast. Moreover, a few troops could be spared for this purpose, and the only realistic alternative left to him, he concluded, was the possibility of seizing some area which might "be held with a small force, and where the King's persecuted subjects and his officers might find an asylum until the proper season for a southern American campaign returned." His proposed solution of a British enclave conditioned planning in the following months and it was retained until the final failure of the expedition.[3]

Lord Cornwallis was on board the *Bristol*, Commodore Sir Peter Parker's flagship. Of the fourteen ships with Parker only six or seven were troop transports; Parker did not arrive at the Cape Fear until May 3. The main body did not land until May 12, and the camp was not organized until May 15. On May 16 Cornwallis reported to Germain that Clinton intended to move from the Cape Fear as soon as the transports were watered. He expected the army would join Howe in New York. Cornwallis advised Germain that he lamented the "fatal delays that prevented the armament from arriving in time" as he was convinced that it would have produced "the most happy effects in this and probably in the other southern colonies."[4]

Clinton informed Germain that he thought there was no immediate hope for success in North Carolina. He explained he had no water carriage, and there was a shortage of horses and wagons. Moreover, he would have to penetrate at least a hundred miles into country every inch of which would probably be defended. Georgia was not possible for climatic reasons. Charleston would be difficult to capture and it would contribute little to the re-establishment of law and order. Yet, after some discussion and thought Clinton committed his forces to the operation against Charleston. Clinton said later that he made his decision to attack Charleston because of letters from General Howe indicating that he did not need him yet and that Howe was interested in having some military operation take place in the south. Clinton, moreover, had received an intelligence report that the works on Sullivan's Island, "the key to Charles Town Harbour," were imperfect and unfinished. Because of these reasons, Clinton was induced to attempt the reduction of Charleston by a "coup de main" on a proposal from Admiral Sir Peter Parker. The expedition left the Cape Fear on May 31 accompanied by Governor Lord William Campbell and Governor Josiah Martin. Martin had to leave some of his loyal followers in a merchant ship in the Cape Fear protected by the

Cruizer and Captain Francis Parry.[5]

Martin not only left behind his faithful followers, but also the victorious but disgruntled members of the provincial congress that met at Halifax from April 4 to May 14, 1776. In a petition to the congress at Halifax, Joseph Woods and his partners asked for an order to dispose of the effects of Martin because they claimed his officers had seized goods on their sloop, the *Joseph*, when it was brought into the Cape Fear by a British privateer, the *General Gage*. This petition referred to Martin as "the late Governor of this province." Woods claimed they lost £1,500 current money of Pennsylvania. Besides their hatred for Martin, another reason the Halifax congressmen listened sympathetically to the Woods petition was because the property of two patriots, William Dry, former collector of the port of Brunswick, and General Robert Howe, was destroyed and confiscated shortly after the British army arrived in the Cape Fear.[6]

The Whig leaders in the provincial congress at Halifax moved towards the final step of divorcing themselves from the Crown on April 12. Under the guidance of Samuel Johnston, the provincial congress resolved that the colony's delegates to the Continental Congress should be empowered to concur with the other delegates in "declaring Independency and forming foreign alliances." The members of the provincial congress reserved the right to form their own constitution and laws for North Carolina. This is the reason why the North Carolina State flag bears the date of April 12, 1776.[7]

Johnston on April 13 told the Carolina delegates in Philadelphia that General Henry Clinton had arrived in the Cape Fear, and that he was preparing to land. It was thought that Clinton had no more than 400 troops, though this number was not verified. Robert Howe reported to General Charles Lee on April 10 from Halifax that Clinton had no more than 700 troops, but that he was expecting more troops hourly. Johnston told the delegates that they expected a formidable attack on the province and that the provincial congress had ordered the raising of four regiments. Howe informed Lee that General James Moore with his force of 1800 minute men and militia were watching Clinton, and that

Colonel Caswell with 600 men was within a few miles of Moore. Clinton was daily training his troops in "street fighting" on Battery Island under the guns of the men-of-war but too far away to be "annoyed" by the patriots.[8]

Meanwhile, Robert Howe again planned an attempt to capture Governor Martin. Howe's plans were based on wishful thinking. He reported to General Lee on April 10 that he had sent to the southward in search of Admiral Esek Hopkins, "who I heard was at Bulls Island in South Carolina, and have it much to lament that the report was not true, as I had given information" of the situation of "our good friend Governor Martin and the set of Infernals with him, and how easy and beneficial a conquest, the weakness of their ships," and the great quantity of military stores with which "they were freighted would make them." In a second letter the same day, Howe advised Lee of a rumor that the patriot fleet had captured Martin. If Lee received the news of the capture of Martin, the anxious Howe wanted Lee to advise him immediately. His expectations about the capture of Martin were frustrated because the governor was with Clinton at the Cape Fear.[9]

On June 28 Governor Martin witnessed the attack on Sullivan's Island from the snow *Peggy* "within the Bar off Charles Town." Clinton had proposed a sudden strike at Charleston that might be made with advantage, but, "owing to a train of unlucky circumstances" a month passed "before any attempt was made upon the enemy." Under the direction of General Charles Lee, the Americans beat off the attack and forced Parker to withdraw at nightfall with all his ships damaged and over 200 casualties. Clinton's troops failed to achieve their objective and had to withdraw.[10]

Martin believed that Parker's failure was in part caused by the pilots who deceived the British by not guiding their ships closer to the enemy's works on Sullivan's Island, where artillery could have pounded the rebels. Despite the British failure in the Carolinas, Martin praised Clinton's plan for conquest, probably because it was based on an earlier plan he himself had submitted to the Crown. Martin interpreted Clinton's plan as requiring British forces to attack the towns on the coast while the loyalists inland would attack the rebels' other flank. He thought that the "friends of the government" he had left on board a transport in the Cape Fear could correspond with British officials and encourage the loyalists in North Carolina. Should this basic plan fail, Martin thought that the conquest of the southern provinces would be hopeless. For the first time Martin was doubting that royal government could be restored in the South. His desire to see his family in New York, and the series of frustrations may have affected his health. He was ill and he asked permission from Germain to accompany the fleet to New York City where he could rejoin his family on Long Island. He was much concerned about their safety and feared rebel reprisal against them.[11]

The summer of 1776 saw the end of the royal government in the colonies except for New York City which the British army occupied on September 15 after the victory on Long Island. In the thirteen colonies all British authority except for the army and navy came to an end. The abandonment of North Carolina and their failure at Charleston ended active operations by the British in the southern theatre for more than two years. Thus, the defeats at Moore's Creek bridge and Charleston encouraged patriots to believe they could win, and, as for Martin, he saw his dream of the recovery of the lost province turned into a nightmare of frustration and depression.

Why was the southern expedition a failure? One historian, who has analyzed the expedition, argued that in its lack of coordination, its changes of character and objectives, its delays, and its misunderstanding of the position of the loyalists, the expedition typified many of the British military operations of the War for American Independence. It revealed how ill-suited for the conduct of war was the eighteenth-century system of government in Great Britain. There was a lack of co-ordination between departments and in the supervision of preparations. "Co-ordination was essential if expeditions were to be prepared and dispatched with speed; its absence meant delay and inadequacy." Each department of government was separate and self-contained and its minister in charge responsible directly only to the king. These conditions "rendered the carrying into effect of a vigorous policy more difficult—such a system could not grapple either with the problems of

strategy or with those of organization, supply and transport."
Moreover, the successful execution of plans depended upon an efficiency of organization, and a degree of co-operation between departments, which did not exist.[12]

Martin's hopes for 1775 had been destroyed by bureaucratic
bungling and bad weather. The tactful Germain chose to blame
the failure on bad weather. According to one historian it was a
"performance which was to be repeated too often by the British
during the War for American Independence." Still another historian believed the expedition "had not been defeated—it had been
abandoned—and the original assumptions which gave it birth
were not refuted." He noted that despite "failure and frustration,
incompetence and irresolution, schemes to use American loyalists
in the south to restore royal authority persisted, eventually dominating British strategic planning after 1778."

While waiting for the British fleet to go to New York City, Martin tried to help Thomas Macknight, a loyalist merchant and former assemblyman, regain part of his lost fortune. Macknight,
fearing assassination by the patriots, had fled to Martin in the
Cape Fear and then accompanied him when the fleet went to
Charleston. Macknight, who represented the counties of Currituck and Pasquotank in the second provincial convention, had lost
a fortune valued at £30,000. Martin sent Macknight to Germain
with a private letter asking Germain to help him recover the value
of his lost property. Martin also asked his brother Samuel to aid
Macknight in London in his application for aid at the Public Office. Although Macknight lost his property, he was one of the more
fortunate loyalists to escape the Carolina patriots. Lord Francis
Rawdon at Charleston wrote to the Earl of Huntingdon on July 3
and reported that all the leading loyalists of North Carolina had
been captured in their attempts to join Governor Martin. The governor told his brother Samuel that since he could be of no further
use "in my own Govt., and that General Clinton concurred in
opinion with me" that he would accompany the fleet to New York
to "rescue my Wife, and family out of the danger" from the rebels
he thought they were exposed to on Long Island. Clinton had
asked Martin to see Sir Peter Parker and advise him of the condi-

tions in North Carolina. Martin added that if he had to send his family to England, would his brother look after them?[13]

When Martin wrote his brother Samuel from Charleston harbor, he did not know that the Continental Congress had declared the United Colonies free and independent. News of the Declaration of Independence was received by the council of safety in session in Halifax on July 22. They resolved immediately that each of the committees of the colony should receive a copy of the Declaration and proclaim it publicly to all the good people of the colony. The patriot government was beginning to consolidate its control over the new state, although a mutiny among the patriot troops had to be quelled early in July. The new district of Washington, comprising the settlements of Watauga and Holston, on July 22 successfully petitioned the council for annexation by North Carolina.[14]

While the British had abandoned North Carolina, Martin still had plans for regaining his government. He had hired the merchant vessel *Jenny* to house the loyalists who had fled to him at Cape Fear. The *Jenny* left with the king's ships and Martin told Germain that he expected it would soon be arriving with the fleet from Charleston. He advised Germain that he had organized the loyalists and the Crown's servants into provincial troops who were ready to serve the king in such corps as the commander in chief should be pleased to assign them. After burning their tenders, the king's ships left the Cape Fear and the elated Samuel Ashe reported to the council that "the terror of Cape Fear," the *Cruizer*, was likewise burnt. Although Wilmington was now an open port, Ashe feared it would not remain so unless the council would "hurry down" some ammunition.[15]

Martin arrived in New York harbor with Clinton and the fleet on August 1. From the transport *Sovereign* in the narrows of New York harbor, Martin told Samuel that he was only twenty miles from his family on Long Island, but could not see them because of rebel activity on the island. Washington had shifted his army from Boston to the New York area in the latter part of March. General Sir William Howe had landed 10,000 men unopposed on Staten Island on July 2, and his brother, Admiral Lord Richard Howe had arrived with a strong fleet and 150 transports on July 12. Governor Martin had learned that the operations of the army had been suspended until the arrival of all the Hessian troops, "one ship of them only yet come in." Martin hoped soon to rescue his family and he awaited the outcome of "the issue of a contest in which I am sure I have had my share of suffering, and I believe you will think so when I tell you that I have now spent nearly fourteen months on board various ships, under every circumstance of distress & inconvenience." Besides his worries about his family, Martin had a report from a gentleman from Antigua "that our good and aged father had fallen ill on a false report of my Captivity, and ill usage by the Rebels: and Heaven knows where my woes are to end."[16]

After the Battle of Long Island, Governor Martin was reunited there with his tormented family on September 1. Their tormentors were rebel soldiers who were quartered in their house. Martin related to his brother Samuel how "an army of ragamuffins terrorized my family" but now they were safe. He spoke of friends being taken hostage to New England and even their family doctor had been taken as a hostage to Philadelphia, but was released three weeks later. The joy of Martin's homecoming was enhanced by the birth of his daughter Augusta on September 5. With peace and harmony restored to the family circle, Martin turned his attention to his duties as governor. He reported to Germain the success of British arms in securing good winter quarters in New York City and on Long Island. The island was fairly secure except for the raids of the rebels from New England on the northern coast when they seized loyalists and drove off their cattle. In a reflective mood Martin assessed for his brother the previous two years when fortune at first seemed to smile on him, but he had not given up because he expected to return to his government in North Carolina. He regretted the decision of Lord Howe to recall the ships from the southern provinces because this meant he could not return to North Carolina and await "on board ship, the orders of Government." Martin was worried about the expense of his family, and the loss of his property when he left North Carolina. He expected the Crown to continue his salary. Lord Granville had died and the governor had sent a bill for his services to Granville's merchant broker in London. Martin thought that if he could not be a civil governor, he hoped to get his "superior military rank" restored to him.[17]

The success of the rebels in unseating the civil governors was the cause for Martin's financial troubles. Depressed, Martin told his brother Samuel: "Nothing can be more contemptible than the situation of the outcast Civil Governors, which have rendevoused here to the number of five." New York City was a haven for loyalist refugees including governors long before William Tryon was superseded as governor of New York when Sir William Howe occupied the city on September 15, 1776. Probably the five Martin referred to was himself, Lord William Campbell, Lord Dunmore, John Wentworth, and James Wright. The summer of 1776 saw the end of royal governors in the thirteen colonies save for Wright of Georgia who regained his office temporarily when Sir Henry Clinton campaigned in the South in 1780. In New England, General Thomas Gage of Massachusetts and the Americans John Wentworth of New Hampshire and Joseph Wanton of Rhode Island had left their posts by October, 1775. Like Martin, Campbell of South Carolina, Dunmore of Virginia, and Wright of Georgia had to flee their capitals and take refuge on a nearby British warship. Both Robert Eden of Maryland and John Penn of Pennsylvania left their proprietary posts peaceably. Lord William Campbell, wounded at the siege of Charleston, returned to England with his American wife. William Franklin, the estranged son of Benjamin, was arrested by General William Alexander ("Lord Stirling") of the New Jersey militia and sent to house arrest in East Windsor, Connecticut, where he remained for two years until he was exchanged for the patriot governor John McKinley of Delaware. Franklin went to New York City in 1778.[18]

Before they arrived in New York City, the two Howe brothers, General Sir William and Admiral Lord Richard, expected to use the refugee governors there to support them with the peace negotiations. The two Howe brothers were appointed by the king on May 3 as peace commissioners with powers to pardon and protect those Americans who swore allegiance to the king, but without authority to negotiate with any colony until all the extralegal congresses and conventions had been dissolved. A fortnight after the Declaration of Independence, a forthright Congressional committee, on July 19, resolved that a copy of the "Circular Letters, and the declaration inclosed from Lord Howe to Mr. William Franklin, Mr. Penn, Mr. Eden, Lord Dunmore, Mr. Martin, and Sir James Wright, which were sent to Amboy by a flagg, and forwarded to Congress by General Washington" be published in the newspapers so that the people of the United States could be informed "of what nature are the Commissioners, and what the terms, with expectation of which the insidious court of Britain" had endeavored to amuse and disarm them. The committee resolution concluded that the few people who still believed in the justice of the "late King" may be convinced "that the valour alone of their Country, is to save its Liberties."[19]

After the Battle of Long Island, the Howes sent their prisoner, General John Sullivan, to Congress to deliver a proposal that an informal peace conference be held. A committee was appointed to meet with Lord Howe; its members were Benjamin Franklin, John Adams, and Edward Rutledge. The meeting took place on Staten Island on September 11, but it proved to be fruitless because Howe's demand for a revocation of the Declaration of Independence as a necessary preliminary to negotiations for peace left no ground for further discussions. Most of the plans for the peace conference were made before Martin arrived in New York harbor on August 1. He was preoccupied with caring for his family after his reunion with them on September 1. If he learned of Lord Howe's circular letters to the governors about the peace conference, it was after the fact. There are no references to the conference or the letters in Martin's extant correspondence.

While Martin was caring for his family and looking after his refugee North Carolina loyalists in New York City, the war went on. Lord Cornwallis was pursuing General Washington and General Nathanael Greene across New Jersey. In North Carolina the rebels were moving to establish a permanent government. Martin told Germain that the rebels "were so infatuated with the idea of being an independent State, as declared by Congress" that they printed £500,000 paper currency with a liberal hand. They had spent nearly all of it. He commented on a resolution of the committee of safety that was calculated to complete the distress of the loyalists and add to the wealth of the rebels: "My effects in that country it seems were previously plundered, and under the sanction of this Act I suppose will be confiscated with the estates of all the obnoxious. To what an extreme of madness is this People arrived!" His property was sold by order of the congress at New Bern on February 6, 1777. He identified the rebel leaders, Cornelius Harnett, Willie Jones, and Thomas Jones as "all very guilty characters." Many North Carolina loyalists had arrived in New York with Martin and the fleet. Some of them would join the king's army; others, he thought, should be able to make a living without being a charge on the board of treasury. Martin had recommended to General Sir William Howe the services of Major Alexander McLeod and Captain William Campbell with five subalterns and a few volunteers.[20]

The governor admitted to his brother that he had broken his promise to him of spending public money by drawing on the board of treasury £450 sterling "to satisfy the cravings of some miserable provincial officers & Soldiers just arrived from Carolina in the utmost Distress & need." Howe was not available at this time for approval of the payment. With Howe out of the city, Martin felt it was necessary to draw on the board of treasury to help the needy loyalists. While Washington crossed New Jersey with Cornwallis in pursuit, the patriots in North Carolina issued a Declaration of Rights and announced a new constitution on December 17-18. During this time while Martin was dreaming and planning about returning to his government in North Carolina, the patriots passed on December 18 an "Ordinance for appointing a Governor, Council of State, and Secretary, until the next General Assembly." It seemed most unlikely that his Majesty's governor would ever return to the palace at New Bern.

There was little military activity after Washington's victories at Trenton and Princeton for the British and American armies went into winter quarters. Martin became seriously ill during the winter of 1776-77 and was preoccupied with the health of his family.

He wrote to his brother Samuel in April that ill health for three months had kept him from going to New York City to settle his governmental accounts. His father had died in Antigua, and his father-in-law, Uncle Josiah, had "fallen into a second state of childhood." Martin had volunteered for the army but was kept out by ill health, and he added that this was a source of embarrassment. The governor was grateful to his brother for securing the king's leave to go to England, but he had indicated to Germain that he would stay on at Long Island to watch the issue of the spring campaign which everyone believed would soon begin. He did not plan to go to England "until better times return." As Martin's health improved, he was able to visit New York City where he resumed friendship with the military officers and the other refugee American governors living there. He discovered that all the governors had received the same optional king's leave, return to England or stay in America. Martin was not sure whether he wanted to stay in America, but he would rely on his brother's judgment on that subject.[21]

Samuel had been apprehensive that Martin would be tempted again "to try the strength of the Loyalists in North Carolina." The governor told him that he had changed his opinion of the loyalists; he had learned more about them since Moore's Creek bridge. He related again the story of the eager solicitations of the loyalists, the treachery of Farquhard Campbell, and the small number of loyalists who rose in defense of the government. Martin wrote "from better information" received since, "I have not reason to think so favorably as I then did of the behavior of those People," he added "(I mean the Scotch Officers who have escaped from confinement, & joined the Army) forfeited my good opinion by their avidity for money, and the high price they put upon their short & ineffectual service in No. Carolina that they really seem to compute above all reward."

The governor attempted to salvage as much of his financial loss as he could by requesting his brother's help in obtaining indemnification for the loss of his personal property. Martin estimated that the property confiscated by the rebels amounted to £3,000. Mrs. Martin was able to save the silver plate and a small amount of clothing, but "her departure was too sudden to admit of her packing anything else, and indeed nothing very bulky would have escaped the vigilance of the Committee Line." She had a couple of small trunks held up by the "Congress Inquisitors," but a servant helped recover them for her. In his appeal to Samuel for advice, Martin indicated that he had not given up the idea of being restored to his government in New Bern. He believed that the recovery of his station in Carolina as the king's governor and the proprietor's agent would ease his financial burdens.

Martin's personal financial worries were alleviated for a while when his brother Samuel told him he was to receive £1000 sterling from their father's estate. Their father had died on December 21, 1776. Josiah's children were to each receive £250 and some bank stock. Colonel Samuel's plantation at Antigua had not been evaluated nor had his taxes or funeral expenses been deducted, but presumably there would be more money from the estate in the future.

Looking forward to the day when he would be restored to his province, Martin submitted to Germain a plan for constitutional governmental reforms for the province. This plan was similar to the one he had sent earlier to Dartmouth. He urged creation of a system that would offer justice for all. Martin commented that the patriot leaders saw that they had only to oppose obstinately any regulation of government to have it revoked. He believed that the "Government's" compliance had reduced it to a "very Phantom in the Colonies" because the continual usurpation of the assemblies had drawn all the real power into their hands. He thought this to be particularly true in North Carolina where the power of the purse exercised by the assembly had reduced the governor's power. Nonetheless, Martin's hopes, in June, were raised by the news about the plans for two British campaigns against the Americans.[23]

The first British plan sought to isolate New England by invading upper New York state through the lake district and down the Hudson River to New York City. Germain approved this plan and General John Burgoyne was given command of the main army which was to move from Canada to New York City. Germain also approved a second plan by General Howe on March 3 for a campaign to capture Philadelphia by sea. Apparently Germain's reason for approving two plans at the same time was his belief that Howe could capture Philadelphia in time to go to the aid of Burgoyne. Howe occupied Philadelphia on September 26 but failed to support Burgoyne and the Northern Campaign which ended in defeat when his 5700 men surrendered their arms to General Horatio Gates at Saratoga on October 17, 1777.

The stunning victory at Saratoga had important effects upon the British, the Americans, and the French. France recognized the independence of the United States of America on February 6, 1778, and Congress ratified the two treaties of alliance and commerce with the king of France on May 4. In June there was a clash between French and British naval forces and the two empires were at war. This new development aided the Americans because the British would have to send most of their forces against their European enemies. The American agony at Valley Forge ended on June 19 when Washington decided to harass Clinton's army as it marched across New Jersey towards New York City. Clinton had replaced Howe as commander at Philadelphia on May 8. When he received reports that a French fleet was heading for New York he decided to evacuate Philadelphia. Washington ordered General Charles Lee to attack the British army near Monmouth Court House. The Americans nearly lost the battle. Washington's timely arrival checked the flight of Lee's men and Clinton's attacks were beaten back. The British stole away during the night of June 28-29, and marched toward Sandy Hook where they boarded transports and sailed to New York.

Martin was discouraged by these developments when he wrote Samuel on July 7: " . . . unless the King's Govt. be restored here, you will see with me the impossibility of my remaining here in any condition of life, and I am utterly at a loss what course to pursue." Samuel had always discouraged Martin about settling in England because economic opportunities were more limited there than in the colonies. Martin concluded that the prospect was gloomy on every side.[24]

Despite the gloomy prospects, ill health and separation from his government, Martin remained in New York caring for his family. Unfortunately, tragedy struck at Martin again. His wife, Elizabeth, died in October, 1778, a month before her father (Uncle Josiah). His grief was blunted by his devotion to his motherless children and his work for the North Carolina loyalists in New York City. Meanwhile, William Eden, manager of the British Secret Service in Europe, had made a trip to America to survey the possibilities of using loyalists as militia against the rebels and to bribe patriot leaders. Returning to England, Eden persuaded the king to appoint a council to assist Sir Henry Clinton in New York. Eden proposed that the council should include, two royal chief justices, William Smith of New York and Frederick Smyth of New Jersey, and John Tabor Kempe, attorney general of New York. To these the king added Cornwallis, James Robertson the newly appointed royal governor of New York, and the two royal governors, Franklin of New Jersey and Martin of North Carolina. Apparently Clinton did not use the services of this council to any extent. For over seventeen months Martin pursued his various duties until December 1779 when Clinton raised his hopes for better employment. Clinton asked him to be the temporary civil governor of South Carolina, after the fleet conquered Charleston. In the new campaign in the South, Martin was to hold dual governorships of both North Carolina and South Carolina.[25]

Early in December the governor was elated over the news that the French and "their rascally allies" were defeated in Georgia. In September General Benjamin Lincoln and his troops had joined with the French to besiege the city of Savannah held by General Augustine Prevost and his British troops. After the Franco-American assault on the city on October 9 in which the Allies suffered over 800 casualties to Prevost's 155, Comte D'Estaing withdrew his fleet and the initiative passed to the British. The lifting of the siege of Savannah had delivered Martin "from a gloom that had for sometime hung over us, in our long torpid state of inaction." Martin was anxious for action which he hoped would once more make him an active governor. The British expedition to the South had been delayed because Comte D'Estaing's fleet had sailed to the Chesapeake Bay to collect supplies and provisions. Martin did not have long to wait. He left New York with Clinton and 8,000 troops on December 26, 1779. Charleston was again their target.[26]

The expectation of returning to his role as an active royal governor encouraged Martin to make plans for his family and for the time when he would return to New Bern. He notified Samuel that he was sending his son, Josiah Henry, to England for his education. The seven year old lad was to be accompanied by Martin's servant, James Burnside. His brother Henry was to supervise the lad's education, but should Henry not be able to take "My Dearest little boy," he would put him in the care of his aunt, Mrs. Henrietta Fitzgerald. He left the other children in the care of their older sister, Mary Elizabeth, and their uncle, Dr. Samuel Martin, at Rockhall.

Martin arrived off Charleston with Clinton and his troops on February 1, 1780. By April 11, Clinton's 14,000 soldiers had completed the investment of the city. On May 6, Ft. Moultrie fell, and General Benjamin Lincoln capitulated on the 12th. At the cost of 255 casualties, Clinton captured the 5,400 man garrison and four American ships; this was Britain's greatest victory of the American war and the most expensive American defeat. In the euphoria of the victory at Charleston, Governor Martin's hopes were dashed by Clinton. Sir Henry advised Martin that his promise to him that he would be the civil governor of South Carolina "would have to fall to the ground." Sir Henry's commission had been superseded by a joint commission with Admiral Marriot Arbuthnot, and apparently the admiral had another candidate for the governorship of South Carolina. The conflict between Clinton and Arbuthnot later developed into a feud; another illustration of the diverse personalities within the British war command and how disorganized the overall war command was. Martin was disappointed, he said, because many people expected him to be the civil governor, but he admitted that he would rather be back at his old position as governor of North Carolina.[27]

Clinton issued a proclamation on June 3 urging all Americans to take an oath to His Majesty's government, and cautioning that all persons who afterwards failed to take an oath of allegiance would be considered in rebellion and treated accordingly. Clinton's critics argued that persons on parole who had quietly accepted their positions as neutrals were now forced to choose between professed loyalty and open rebellion. He did not deny that the proclamation had unfortunate consequences, but argued that "I gave the loyalists an opportunity of detecting and chasing from among them such dangerous neighbors" as the rebels. For one historian, the June 3 proclamation "was the point upon which the continuance of the Revolution in South Carolina turned."[28]

Clinton had other plans for Governor Martin. The general left for New York on June 8 satisfied that South Carolina had been recovered for the Crown. He left Cornwallis with 8,000 men to maintain and to extend British control. Cornwallis was to lead an expedition into North Carolina and Governor Martin was to accompany him where he could use his influence to rally the loyalists. Cornwallis was to establish a small post at Cape Fear when he began his invasion "to give countenance" to the North Carolina loyalists. Martin began recruiting North Carolina loyalists for the British army despite his keen disappointment over the loss of the civil governorship of South Carolina. He advised Germain from headquarters at Camden, South Carolina that he thought the majority of the North Carolinians would return to their allegiance. He was basing this statement on his correspondence and intelligence reports from North Carolina. Two loyalists from that province had promised to put 400 men under arms as soon as their district should be protected by the royal forces and he was confident they would do it.[29]

The British hold on Georgia and South Carolina was not seriously challenged although guerrilla bands led by Francis Marion, Andrew Pickens, and Thomas Sumter prevented the British from consolidating their strength, until General Horatio Gates was commissioned by Congress to lead a southern army against the British. Gates took over his command at Coxe's Mill, North Carolina on July 25, 1780. He began a slow march against the British post and supply base at Camden, South Carolina. Cornwallis, with about 2,400 men, made a surprise contact with Gates' forces early on August 16 north of the town and defeated them. American losses were almost 900 killed, and 1000 captured. Gates fell back to Hillsborough, about 160 miles north of Camden.

Martin was delighted that 1400 loyalists from North Carolina had joined the army at Camden after the battle, including almost 800 men under Colonel Samuel Bryan of Rowan County. Bryan and his men "rose at the forks of the Yadkin and after a long & difficult march joined Major Archibald McArthur at the Cheraws." Martin argued that 800 men were "great proof" of the loyalty of the North Carolinians. What Martin did not know is that Bryan and his men were to be drafted into the rebel militia and they fled to safety in South Carolina. The Bryan experience illustrates how the rebels had been rapidly organizing militia units to combat the British throughout the Carolinas.[30]

Cornwallis reported to Germain on his victory at Camden, the skirmishes with General Sumter, and his attempts to strengthen the British control of South Carolina. Cornwallis told Germain "I likewise had settled good channels of correspondence with our friends in North Carolina, and had given them positive directions to attend to their harvest, and to remain quiet until I could march to their relief." In this business Cornwallis advised Germain, "I was greatly assisted by Governor Martin from whose abilities and zeal for the service I have, on many occasions, derived great advantages, and which I must beg that your Lordship will please to represent in the strongest terms to his Majesty." Governor Martin, Cornwallis told Germain, "became again a military man, and behaved with the spirit of a young volunteer."[31]

Colonel Banastre Tarleton's victory over Thomas Sumter at Fishing Creek, South Carolina, on August 19 opened the way for a British invasion of North Carolina. Six weeks after the battle of Camden, Cornwallis reached Charlotte, North Carolina, and on September 27 he issued a proclamation requiring the inhabitants to deliver up their arms and to accept a military parole in exchange for receiving the protection of the army. Their lack of response indicated a fear of rebel reprisals, and so Governor Martin tried his luck with a proclamation on October 3. He announced the triumph of the king's arms, the suppression of the rebellion, the restoration of the royal government, and called upon all faithful subjects to rally to the defense of the royal standard. Martin's proclamation may have been a test to prove for potential loyalist reaction or at least to propagandize among the patriots in what has been called "the Hornet's Nest" of the Revolution in Mecklenburg County. Charlotte was a stronghold of the Revolution and it had no supplies for Cornwallis' army. While waiting for supplies from Camden before continuing to Hillsborough, Cornwallis received an intelligence report of a rebel attack on Augusta, Georgia, which if successful, would have destroyed British control throughout the backcountry. On Cornwallis' left was Major Patrick Ferguson in Gilbert Town, North Carolina, with a few provincials and several hundred loyalist militia. Ferguson had already scattered some parties from the mountains marching to join the rebels, and he was on his way to cut off the retreat of the rebels if they escaped Colonel John Harris Cruger and his militia on their way from Fort Ninety-Six to relieve Augusta. Recognizing an opportunity to destroy Ferguson and his hated loyalists, the mountain men quickly assembled under Colonels Isaac Shelby and John Sevier from the Watauga settlements and started tracking their enemy. The mountain men trapped Major Ferguson and his unit on October 7 on a spur of King's Mountain. They killed Ferguson, one of his two mistresses, 200 of his men and captured the rest. This battle was to have large consequences.[32]

The shock of Ferguson's defeat on King's Mountain and the concern for the backcountry of South Carolina caused Cornwallis to abandon his march to Hillsborough. On October 14 he withdrew to Winnsboro, South Carolina, between Camden and Ninety-Six, where he assessed his situation. His army was greatly weakened by fever. The rebel militia had set the South Carolina backcountry aflame and were energetically challenging his every move. Moreover, his first experience with North Carolina loyalists had been a complete failure; the loyalists repeatedly failed to cooperate with him and Governor Martin. The conduct of the loyalists did not support the belief that a majority of North Carolinians were tired of their oppressors and were waiting hopefully for the appearance of the British army. Cornwallis commented to Clinton:

. . . we have cause to be convinced, that many of the inhabitants wish well to his Majesty's arms; but they have not given evidence enough

189

either of their number or their activity *to justify the stake of this province, for the uncertain advantages that might attend immediate junction with them."*

In winter camp, Cornwallis began to plan a return to North Carolina while Governor Martin went to New York City for a few weeks to care for his family and secure medical treatment.[33]

When Martin arrived in New York City late in October, 1780, he learned about General Benedict Arnold's defection to the British and the capture, trial, and execution of Clinton's adjutant, Major John Andre, as a spy. The Andre affair may have been in the minds of the members of the new Board of Associated Loyalists when Martin met with them on October 28. The other board members were William Franklin "together with Messrs. Ruggles, Wanton, Cox, Ludlow, Lutwische, Rome, and Leonard." The board was created by Clinton at the express command of the king to raid the seacoasts and harass the patriot trade in the states of Connecticut and New Jersey. Benjamin Franklin's estranged son, the former governor, William Franklin, of New Jersey, was president of the board. Both Franklin and Clinton held low opinions of each other. The board was to act as an intelligence gathering agency and to organize groups of 50 warriors each to attack the patriots but it seems clear that Franklin and some of the other loyalists on the board had guerrila warfare in mind. Atrocities were committed on both sides of the Revolution and the board soon went to extremes in committing atrocities which culminated in the Joshua Huddy affair of 1782. The Associated Loyalists got Clinton's permission to take Captain Joshua Huddy of the New Jersey militia out of the provost in New York on the pretext that he was to be exchanged for one of the loyalists held by the Americans in New Jersey. Instead they hanged him in revenge for the death of the loyalist, Philip White. The Huddy case discredited the Board of Associated Loyalists in the eyes of Clinton and it involved Washington, Sir Guy Carleton and many others. However, Josiah Martin was not actively involved on the board because he returned to Cornwallis in the South in December, 1780, and when the Huddy affair broke he was in London. It is doubtful that Martin would have approved of any atrocity because of his earlier experience in denying the patriots' charges of using slaves or Indians against them. Moreover, there are no references to the board or the Huddy affair in the extant Martin correspondence.[34]

When the war in the Carolinas resumed in December, 1780, Governor Martin returned to serve as a volunteer under Cornwallis. Cornwallis began his long delayed march on January 7, 1781, three months after his withdrawal to Winnsboro. Conditions in the South had changed drastically and Cornwallis realized that the fall of Charleston and the battle of Camden had produced a widespread sentiment for peace. The Americans had gained a new and able commander in the South, Major General Nathanael Greene. The British established a camp near Wilmington on January 29. Major James Henry Craig reported to Cornwallis that the entrenched rebels near the town were scattered, and the "notorious rebel," Cornelius Harnett had been captured and imprisoned. An address of the inhabitants of Wilmington was forwarded to Governor Martin on April 21.[35]

Working from their bases in the southern ports, the British again tried to extend their conquests by invading the Carolina piedmont. They hoped to achieve this through the use of the British army and aid from the loyalists in the interior. Some members of Martin's former Highland regiment under Cornwallis tried to raise a regiment of Highlanders, telling the governor he could be their colonel. The recruiting for this proposed regiment was unsatisfactory for only about 100 men came to the colors, and these in two companies, under Captain Forbes at Charleston in 1781, and Captain McArthur at Fort Arbuthnot in 1782. The two companies were compelled to remain on guard duty; Martin remained with Cornwallis.

General Nathanael Greene moved from Charlotte to Cheraw, South Carolina, but he was too weak to attack Cornwallis' main camp at Winnsborough. He detached General Daniel Morgan with about 800 men for a sweep to the west and Henry Lee for guerrila activity between Cornwallis and Charleston. Cornwallis' march to North Carolina was now threatened from each flank by a determined enemy and so he detached Colonel Tarleton and ordered him to drive Morgan back against the main British force. Tarleton caught up with Morgan before he could safely cross the Broad River. Morgan chose a position near Cowpens on January 17, 1781, and by skillful handling of his forces won a smashing victory. The Cowpens victory lifted the spirit of the rebels and caused Cornwallis to attempt a desperate maneuver to save dwindling British power and prestige. He regrouped his forces and began the pursuit of Morgan's retreating force, but the alert Morgan quickly joined Greene's main army before he could be intercepted. Cornwallis again changed plans and tried to cut off Greene from Virginia but Greene fled northward across the Dan River and lured Cornwallis far beyond the source of his rapidly diminishing supplies. Lacking boats and supplies, Cornwallis had to abandon his pursuit at the Dan River. Carefully, he assessed the situation and decided to continue with his original plan despite failure to destroy Greene's army. Cornwallis ordered the army to march in easy stages to Hillsborough, the patriot capital of North Carolina, where he could propagandize among the citizens and secure supplies. He issued a proclamation on February 20 that he had driven the enemy from North Carolina. He invited all faithful and loyal subjects "to repair, without loss of time, with their arms and ten days provisions, to the Royal Standard." Cornwallis assured them that he would suppress the rebellion in the province and reestablish "good order and constitutional government."[36]

Josiah Martin tried to persuade some of the citizens of Hillsborough to volunteer for the loyalist militia. There was no response. Cornwallis' proclamation had little more effect. Three days later on February 23 a force of two hundred loyalists under Colonel John Pyle was completely crushed by an enemy detachment. Thus, the futility of Cornwallis' guarantees was exposed. That same day Greene's main army recrossed the Dan River into North Carolina. At once it began to harass Cornwallis and to intimidate the loyalists. Pyle's defeat and Greene's appearance brought to an end Cornwallis' plan to recruit North Carolina loyalists.[37]

Hillsborough and the countryside were drained of supplies and Cornwallis had to look for other sources. He decided on Cross

Creek where supplies could be brought up the Cape Fear River from Wilmington, but he had to delay this move because Greene's army was growing in numbers and he began to track Cornwallis and threaten potential loyalists. Cornwallis concluded that he would have to attack Greene because he was convinced that it would be impossible to succeed in "that great object of our arduous campaign, the calling forth the numerous loyalists of North Carolina, whilst a doubt remained on their minds of the superiority of our Arms."

The two armies met near Guilford Court House on March 15. Cornwallis won the field but at a cost of almost 100 killed and over 400 wounded; a loss he could ill afford. He issued a proclamation to the Highlanders of Cumberland, Bladen, and Anson Counties urging them to join the service now that Greene was defeated and had fled into Virginia. In his reports to Germain, Cornwallis stressed the difficulties of a defensive war in South Carolina and the lack of support of North Carolina loyalists. He described how the geography of North Carolina made reduction of the province difficult. Cornwallis recommended that if the prosecution of the war in the South was desired he urged that a serious attempt upon Virginia was necessary. He pointed out that strong reinforcements were sent to Greene by Virginia despite Arnold's presence in the Chesapeake area; an indication to Cornwallis that Virginia was not frightened by small expeditions.[38]

Because of the scarcity of provisions, Cornwallis decided to march to Cross Creek. On arrival he discovered that only small boats could navigate the Cape Fear River and since they would have to pass through hostile territory there was little chance supplies could get through. He decided to abandon the Carolinas to Greene and march to Wilmington. With this decision, the Carolina campaign ended. Cornwallis had altered the basic concept of the war in the South. This decision brought on a pamphlet war between him and Sir Henry Clinton known as the Clinton-Cornwallis Controversy. Cornwallis' proclamation of March 18, 1781, was to be the last serious British effort to rally the American loyalists in the South. With this decision by Cornwallis died the plans of the Crown's ministers for the southern expedition and the dreams of Josiah Martin to recover his lost authority in North Carolina. Neither Cornwallis nor the ailing Governor Martin fully realized the significance of the general's decision until much later.[39]

In his dispatches to Germain, Cornwallis praised his troops and the zeal of Josiah Martin as contributions to the campaign. Whether the looters after the Guilford Court House battle knew about Martin's zeal as a volunteer, they did find his hat floating in a nearby creek. The loss of his hat may have been caused by the gusty March winds or Martin's zeal in the fighting; only Martin could tell us and he has departed. Cornwallis praised Martin to Germain: "I have constantly received the most zealous assistance from Gov. Martin during my command in the southern districts. Hoping that his presence would tend to incite the loyal subjects of this province to take an active part with us," and he has "cheerfully submitted to the fatigue and dangers of our campaigns; but his delicate constitution has suffered by his public spirit, for, by the advice of the physician, he is now obliged to return to England for the recovery of his health." He referred Germain to Martin for more details on the campaign and the Guilford Court House battle.[40]

With Cornwallis' permission to leave the army at Wilmington, Martin returned to his motherless family in New York in April. He spent the spring with his family at Rockhall on Long Island. Seeking better medical treatment, the governor and his family save for his eldest daughter Mary Elizabeth, sailed for London. Mary Elizabeth chose to remain with her relatives at Rockhall. Martin expected to give his personal report of the southern expedition in the Carolinas to the Crown's ministers.[41]

Most of the Crown's governors in the thirteen colonies were forced to abandon their offices and were not active in the Revolution save for Lord William Campbell, William Franklin, William Tryon, Sir James Wright and Josiah Martin. After the first invasion of the south, Campbell soon returned to England; Franklin, exchanged for an American officer, worked as chairman of the Associated Loyalists in New York City but after the Luddy Affair he too went to England; Wright returned for a brief time as governor of Georgia but soon he had to leave. William Tryon remained in New

York for awhile but he was assigned to the army and participated in the raids on New England and New Jersey. Only Martin remained as governor and he was active in the two invasions of the southern colonies. Compelled by medical reasons in 1781 to return to England, Martin missed the fateful meeting at Yorktown. In London, he still persisted in his attempts to participate in the "great game depending between Britain and her colonies."

IX. A Postlude for Governor Josiah Martin

Although Martin had been forced to withdraw from the "great game depending between Britain and her colonies," he continued his life-long role of devotion to his country and his people. Before he landed in Britain on June 3, while he was on board the transport *Delight* at Spithead, England, Martin occupied himself writing a letter to his friend Francis, Earl of Huntingdon. He described General Greene's defeat at Hobkirk's Hill, South Carolina, on April 19, and that Lord Rawdon had attacked and routed Greene's army again on April 26. Martin advised Huntingdon that Rawdon's health, like his own, was seriously impaired.[1]

Depressed because of his ill health and frustrated because of his loss of his government, and the turn of military events in America, Josiah Martin resigned his governorship. Germain advised William Knox, the undersecretary of the American Department, on June 9 that Martin had resigned as governor. Germain analyzed the reasons for Martin's resignation: "Governor Martin must naturally despond when he is disappointed in his expectations of immediate assistance from the inhabitants of N. Carolina. These poor people have suffered sufficiently from the cruelty of the rebels," and those who have been induced to declare in "our favor have not been protected, so that I cannot suppose many will expose themselves to be murdered till they see the King's troops able to drive Mr. Greene out of their province," and proceed to punishment and not to proclamations of pardon in consequence of victory. "If Martin sees the case desperate, he is right to inform the King's ministers, but I hope he will not proclaim it to the public. If his health is the cause of his resigning, it may lead him to see things in an unfavourable light."[2]

While Germain's analysis is perceptive in some ways, it is probable that he could not clearly see the frustration and disappointment experienced by Governor Martin and his loss of political power, prestige, and property. Germain had prestige and power and men so favored are often blind to the problems of others, although Germain rose from disgrace to his position as one of the king's friends. In January, 1782, Germain lost his position in a reorganization of the government that led to the fall of Lord North's ministry after news of the Yorktown defeat. Thus, both Germain and Martin lost power and prestige in the desperate British gamble in the southern colonies.

Much of the governor's time was spent in trying to secure financial aid for the loyalists who had suffered and sacrificed for the defense of the Crown in North Carolina. Martin enlisted the aid of his brother Samuel and his powerful friends in and out of Parliament, the former secretary of war, Welbore Ellis, Sir Guy Carleton, Lord Dartmouth, General Sir Henry Clinton, and the Lords of the Treasury. In London, he presented his cases to the American Loyalist Claims Commission. With memorials and evidence given personally in the presence of the board, Martin argued for his North Carolina loyalists and himself. Although the patriots had won a great victory at Yorktown on October 19, 1781, Martin persisted in the belief that the rebels could be conquered by British arms. He submitted to Germain's successor, Welbore Ellis, on March 7, 1782, a plan for forming a regiment from North Carolina Highlanders who were refugees in England. Nonetheless, Martin spent most of his declining energy and his time trying to secure financial aid for his loyalists who had suffered and sacrificed for the defense of the Crown in North Carolina.[3]

By October 1782, 315 American loyalists were receiving aid from Parliament in the amount of £40,280 yearly. There were 135 postwar claims of loyalists from North Carolina. This group included Josiah Martin who had been granted £500 a year from July 6, 1777; Henry McCulloch, father and son, had each received £200 a year since April 5, 1777; Chief Justice Martin Howard, £250 annually since midsummer 1777; and Neil Snodgrass, £100 a year since January 5, 1778. Concern for the enormous amount of money paid by Parliament to the loyalists caused Lord Shelburn in the summer of 1782 to ask John Wilmot, M.P., to examine the claims of the loyalists for fraud. Wilmot chose Daniel Parker Coke, M.P., to assist him in the examination.[4]

Of the 315 claims, the allowances of fifty six persons who failed to appear before the Wilmot committee were suspended. Twenty five persons were found to be ineligible for relief on the grounds for which relief was to be granted, an active loyal defense of the crown. Ninety persons had their allowance reduced because they appeared to be receiving too much in comparison with the others. Ten persons had a modest increase in their allowance. In the meantime, fresh claims were accumulating and in the spring of 1783, 438 new claims were examined so that by June over £17,000 was added to the amount granted to the loyalists. The articles of peace of the provisional treaty between Britain and the United States were ratified by Congress on March 13, 1783. On April 26, 7,000 loyalists sailed from New York, the last of nearly 100,000 who had departed for Britain, Canada or the British Caribbean islands.

While the Wilmot committee was in session, the North Carolina loyalists living in London met in March at the London Coffee House. James Parker acted as chairman. The purpose of this meeting was to advise Henry McCulloch, Sr., their representative in London, about claims of the loyalists from North Carolina. A committee of Thomas McKnight, Lewis Henry De Rosset, Alexander Morrison, James Monroe, and Arthur Banning, decided that the property losses amounted to £256,000. Four months later they held another meeting at the same coffee house with Lewis De Rosset in the chair. The purpose of this meeting was to help the commissioners distinguish between those who were "legitimate objects of bounty and those who were pretenders." Their decision in most cases was favorable. The new ministry in Westminster approved the temporary provision which had been made for the loyalists, and also introduced a bill for appointing a new commission. In 1784 sixty two men and women from North Carolina were receiving regular annual pensions including Josiah Martin. When those loyalists died, payments were made to their widows and heirs down to the year 1832.[5]

Martin estimated that his salary, with the perquisites of the governor's office, was worth from 1700 to 1800 pounds sterling a year. His furniture, he valued at 2400 to 2500 pounds; his books at 500 to 600 pounds. His horses, two carriages, and the lands which he as governor had granted to himself and his children, 10,000 acres, were worth altogether 3500 pounds. The British Treasury had been paying Martin a salary of 1000 pounds a year since July, 1775. Martin was granted 500 pounds a year by the Treasury as a temporary allowance in 1777. Until October, 1783, Martin had his salary, but after that date the 500 pounds allowance seems to have been his only payment from the British Crown, except for the compensation for losses, which was a little over 2913 pounds. In 1785 Martin reported that he had received only 840 pounds of that amount.[6]

In London Governor Martin established his motherless family in a townhouse in the fashionable area between Hanover and Grosvenor Squares where many wealthy sugar planters and the upper echelon of the Crown's civil servants lived. In 1782, he lived on South Milton Street, just off Oxford Street, later he resided at 56 James Street, and in Grosvenor Square. The governor had a country estate near Richmond, in Surrey. He was within easy traveling distance to his son, Josiah Henry, at preparatory school, and to his sister and brothers. Josiah's older brother Samuel lived in retirement on his estate at Great Canford near Wimborne; his brother Henry, soon to be knighted, was a naval commissioner at Portsmouth; the youngest brother William Byam was soon to resign his Residency to the Mogul Court at Delhi and return to his estate at Whiteknights in Berkshire. The governor's sister, Henrietta, the wife of Colonel John Austin Fitzgerald, lived near him in London.[7]

Josiah Martin had finally achieved his youthful Antiguan dream of being a resident of the imperial city of London, a hard earned reward which he enjoyed the rest of his short life. Governor Martin died intestate ten days short of his forty-ninth birthday on April 13, 1786. He was buried in the cemetery of his parish church, St. George's in Hanover Square. Elizabeth, the governor's wife died on Long Island in 1778; the governor never remarried.[8]

The governor had eight children: Mary Elizabeth born on

Long Island; two daughters who died shortly after their birth on Long Island; Sarah born on Antigua, Alice and Samuel born on Long Island; Josiah Henry in North Carolina, and Augusta after her mother fled from the rebels in North Carolina. Little Samuel died in North Carolina, and Augusta in England before 1788. The others were all living in 1795. Josiah Henry was appointed registrar of the court of appeals in Benares, India, where he died unmarried in 1799. Apparently the governor's eldest daughter, Mary Elizabeth, several years older than the other children, remained on Long island and did not go with the family to London in 1781. She lived with her uncle and his family at Rockhall plantation, Long Island. Letters of Administration, dated June 20, 1786, and February 17, 1789, regarding the governor's estate, are among the records of the Prerogative Court of Canterbury in the Administration Act Books for those years. Sarah, Alice, and Josiah Henry Martin were the beneficiaries in both grants because Mary Elizabeth had renounced all claim to a share in her father's estate. In the grant of 1789 she was mentioned as residing at Black Rock in North America, a misreference to Rockhall. Mary Elizabeth's maternal grandfather, Josiah, had given £200 to her in his will in 1779. The governor's father, Colonel Samuel Martin of Greencastle, Antigua, and his brother Samuel Martin, Jr. made generous bequests in their wills for the governor's children, and many other relatives and friends.[9]

One historian has stated that Mary Elizabeth remained in Long Island, but the archives at St. George's Hanover Square lists a Mary Martin as a daughter of Governor Martin. She was buried on March 21, 1820 in the burial ground on Bayswater Road; she was 57 years old at the time of her death. It is possible that Mary Elizabeth Martin went to London, shortly after her father's death, to care for her sisters and brother. Sarah and Alice both lived to a venerable old age. Sarah died at the age of 85 on March 6, 1851 and Alice at the age of 83 on May 29, 1852. Both were buried with their sister Mary Elizabeth in the burial ground on Bayswater Road.[10]

With the death of the governor's last child in 1852, there seems to be no direct descendants of Governor Martin. There were, however, descendants of the governor's two brothers, Henry Martin, the first Baronet of Lockynge, and William Byam Martin. The sons of William Byam served the Crown as warriors and diplomats. The eldest, Samuel Coote Martin, had a commission in the Grenadiers and died in action near St. Jean de Luz in December 1813. The second, William Byam II, rose rapidly in the diplomatic and civil service in his father's footsteps. He became Governor of Amboyna, Resident of Hyderabad, Resident at the Mogul Court at Delhi, and the third member of the Supreme Council of India. Several of Sir Henry's sons and their descendants served the empire faithfully and one of his sons and his descendant rose to eminence in the Navy as an admiral. Sir Henry's daughter, Sarah Catherine Martin (1768-1826) was the author of *The Comic Adventures of Old Mother Hubbard and Her Dog*, "Published June 1, 1805, by J. Harris, Successor to E. Newbery, Corner of S. Paul's Church Yard." The success of this publication was instantaneous and it was pirated by many chapbook publishers. The British Museum catalog lists twenty-six titles of "Old Mother Hubbard" under Sarah Catherine Martin's name. There is evidence that the public believed it to be a political squib and this may have contributed to its immediate popular success. Miss Martin gained some notoriety when Prince William Henry (afterwards William IV) fell in love with her while he was a naval cadet at Portsmouth. Sir Henry, the naval commissioner, sent his daughter to the country to escape the prince's ardent courtship for they knew he could never marry her. The last known male descendant of Sir Henry, an admiral, died early in this century. The descendants of William Byam and Sir Henry Martin are traced through the female line. Many of them have contributed their services to the British armed forces and the civil service. Still others have held the office of High Sheriff in their counties or excelled in scholarly pursuits, and some have practiced law as their ancestors did.[11]

Governor Josiah Martin: An Assessment

The life of Governor Josiah Martin illustrates many themes in the eighteenth century British empire, government, politics, economics, and social life, that were familiar to the gentry class that staffed the Crown's bureaus and provided officers for the armed forces. The story of the Martin family relates what the empire meant to them and why they gave their allegiance to the empire. The Martins had a long tradition of service to the Crown since the Conquest in 1066. It was also a part of a network of gentry families who were joined together by financial and marriage alliances. The Martin family members shared a set of interests, political and commercial connections, mutual support of each other, critical skills and insights, and a sense of their own ability and importance which the empire encouraged and rewarded. This Anglo-Irish family, with its economic bases in Britain and the Caribbean Islands, sought advancement and wealth within the new empire whether it was in Britain, India or on the American mainland.

Josiah Martin lived at a time when the British empire was going through a transitional phase of its development. The new empire provided many opportunities for the gentry families. When the governor's astute brother, Samuel accomplished the "miracle" of the appointment to the governorship of North Carolina the Martin family was delighted and proud. Josiah Martin differed in some ways from the average placeman in that he was interested in reform of imperial institutions and administration. Like Henry Ellis and Thomas Pownall, he sought to modify imperial institutions and practices, and like them he came to grips with medieval concepts that prevented solutions to problems that were caused by the emerging democratic concepts of government as practiced by the American colonists. Martin was impatient with laxity and corruption, yet he shared with other placemen many of their attitudes towards the empire.

Only a few isolated placemen were groping to find ideas that we would recognize today as democratic principles of government and the efficient management of men and materials. Habits of mind of the men around the Crown prevented them from seeing that a new more flexible organization was necessary to govern the new empire. These ministers made the policies that the governors had to apply to the changing ideas of the colonies, what has been called "government by instruction." The fundamental weakness of the system of government by the king's instructions (his commissions to the governors) was its rigidity which forced the governors to follow a predetermined course expressed in the inflexible form of instructions. The king's planners refused to give their governors in America that discretion and latitude of action which were essential to success in political and military operations. The board of trade, the secretary of state, and the privy council did not, and probably could not, appreciate the actual conditions under which the governors labored. The king's ministers were ignorant about America because most of them had never been there. Apparently they could not anticipate the changes in the local situation which might have taken place before their long deliberated orders should reach the governor. Because of the planners' attitudes, the governors were often placed in a dilemma. They must violate their instructions in order to accomplish some immediately necessary end, thus incurring the displeasure of the planners or else they must blindly adhere to their orders in spite of changed conditions submitting if necessary to defeat on some vital issues when a little more freedom of action might possibly have enabled them to save the situation. Consequently, the Crown would suffer a loss of prestige and the colonists would tend to grow more estranged from the home government. Moreover, the governors would have to endure the severe criticism of the planners for their apparent failure to support the medieval concept of the royal prerogative.[12]

Criticized from both sides, administrators developed habits of mind they hoped would produce compromise in every situation they faced, but they did not always please their critics. Conscious of this phenomenon, administrators often were hampered in effecting pragmatic solutions to problems instead they became caretakers and satisfied no one save for those who wished to avoid disruption. Thus, there developed a frame of mind that could be called the administrative mind which sought a safe but oftentimes innocuous position. They satisfied no one because the administrators of the past and the present have feared to "rock the boat" and they have become easy prey for dissidents, revolutionaries, and those ambitious men who wish to advance themselves at the expense of others. Pressured by these groups the American colonial governors retreated to a middle of the road stance or in a few cases counterattacked the radicals and used all the force that was available to them. Such governors as Lord Dunmore of Virginia, Tryon of New York, and Martin of North Carolina tried to block and did oppose the radicals who were intent upon forcing the Crown's ministers to accept American rights and wishes in provincial government. As the American constitutional crisis developed into a full fledged revolution, all the governors were defeated in their attempts to maintain the medieval concept of the royal prerogative.

Josiah Martin came to his governorship after the first two Anglo-American crises, the Stamp Act of 1765 and the Townshend Duties of 1766, and before the third crisis, the Boston Tea Party of 1773. Martin soon discovered that when the planners insisted on a rigid adherence to their policies this often inhibited him from making pragmatic decisions needed for the serious problems facing him. He learned also that distance and time were important factors that delayed his receiving instructions from the secretary of state and sometimes the delays prevented practical solutions to his problems. Consequently, Martin was caught between the planners in Westminster and the colonists' needs and wishes in times of crisis. When he applied the planners' policies the colonists reacted. Martin, like the other governors, became a caretaker and he was conscious of defending his position against both the planners and the colonists. This position often irked him for he was conscientious about enforcing the planners' policies and yet concerned about the colonists' needs. This was particularly true when the controversy erupted over the attachment law and courts which eventually led to his loss of office.

Josiah Martin was reared in an atmosphere dominated by management ideas of men, materials, profit, prestige and property. As a lad, the governor was trained by his father to manage a successful sugar plantation on Antigua. His father, Colonel Samuel Martin, belonged to that fraternity of contemporary gentlemen farmers who applied science to agriculture to increase their wealth and some of them used their profits to invest in the emerging industrial revolution. They were groping toward the concept of modern efficiency in management which they did not fully realize and that was unknown to most leaders in the British government. British inefficiency in the executive departments of the royal government can be seen in the cliche "muddling through" used to describe bureaucratic efforts and in the wasteful planning and execution of the Southern Expedition for the invasion of the southern colonies. The executive departments of the armed forces competed with each other rather than cooperate with each other in this expedition, and this seemed to be the general practice in many of the Crown's bureaus.[13]

British inefficiency in the executive departments of the royal government can be seen in the careers of the three colonial secretaries that Martin served under: the venality of Hillsborough, the inefficiency of Dartmouth, and the competitive ambition of Germain. It would appear that George III selected his ministers for their personalities and not their abilities. They were called the "King's Friends." It was believed that Hillsborough and his friends had deliberately kept the attachment law out of North Carolina because they did not want to have their property attached by Carolinians. One scholar has declared that Dartmouth was "entirely without any administrative capacity." On the other hand Germain was partly to blame for the failure of the southern expedition because he meddled in and opposed the other participating executive departments. On the gubernatorial level Martin had to compete with the Carolina leaders' high regard for former Governor William Tryon and his alleged influence with the royal ministers in London. William L. Saunders saw Tryon as a "con" man when influencing North Carolinians:

Tryon's supposed influence at home seems to have been his principal if not his entire stock in trade. That he unduly magnified that influence is now apparent, for not one of his currency bills became a law.[14]

"At home" means London.

Martin's interest in the management of plantations and in increasing the export of cash crops for the province can be seen in his communications with Lord Hillsborough and later with Lord Dartmouth in 1772. He suggested a method of improving the major export, salt pork, when he asked Hillsborough for permission to use salt from Portugal and Spain so that his planters could compete with the northern provinces. He thought, too, that the salt could be used for the fishery on the Roanoke River. The suggestion to use salt from outside the empire may have given cause for Hillsborough to defend the mercantilistic system and ignore Martin's request for the extant records do not include his reply. Nonetheless, Martin's concern for a threatened famine in the province caused him to issue a proclamation on August 25, 1772, placing an embargo on wheat, rye, Indian corn, and flour. He had the support of his council but not of Dartmouth. The secretary cautioned him not to place an embargo on these items to England because they were of "great concern to this Kingdom," and they had been the object of attention in the current session of Parliament. Earlier, Martin was pleased to note to Hillsborough and later to Dartmouth the increase in the production of cash crops of rice and indigo in the lower Cape Fear River region "after the example of South Carolina and in emulation of its prosperity principally derived from those valuable productions."[15]

Closely related to his interest in increasing the export of cash crops was Martin's interest in improving the port of New Bern. He tried to persuade Hillsborough to help him secure money to improve the navigation channels there. He described the "little Town or rather village of New Bern growing very fast into significance in spite of the great natural difficulties of the navigation leading to it" and its importance would become greater as the "spirit of improvement begins to dawn among the neighboring planters. . . . " The poor navigation of the "river Neuse and the Bar of Ocracock, will much retard its growth" unless measures were taken to improve the harbor, and then it would soon become "a City not unworthy of notice in the great and flourishing Empire." His analysis of the drawbacks that have kept New Bern from developing into a major seaport are prophetic, although he could not have anticipated the development of the deep draft modern ocean-going ships.

It was second nature to Martin as an administrator to manage men, materials, and society in an efficient and effective manner but he was hamstrung by the king's planners in their "government by instruction" and by the radicals who planned to have at least home rule. Martin possessed the qualities of comprehension, tact, persuasion, and firmness which were needed to be a successful administrator but again these qualities were taxed by the provocative actions and program of the radicals. Many people can be pleasant and cooperative when things are going smoothly but when one is challenged by critics again and again it taxes one's patience and causes frustration. If one assails his critics they charge him with lacking tact and comprehension and present him in the worst light as the radicals did to Martin and some historians have adopted this view. Conscious of the need for consensus, Martin nevertheless did not hesitate to upset the status quo if he thought it was necessary, especially as the revolutionary crisis grew in North Carolina.

Unfortunately for Governor Martin he came to the governorship of North Carolina at a time when the colony was burdened with some very serious problems left by Governor William Tryon and his predecessors and a tradition of the royal prerogative blocking the wishes and needs of the assembly. Unlike Tryon, Martin did not try to persuade the assembly that he had influence in Westminster so that the North Carolinians could have a paper currency and the attachment of debtors' property. Nevertheless, Martin was able to work out with the assembly the problem of the debenture notes, and thus helped provide them with a substitute paper currency.

After investigation and study of the Regulator troubles, Martin saw that they had been exploited. He talked to former Regulators when he visited Hillsborough. Unlike Tryon, Martin listened to the Regulators instead of only listening to their critics, the county officers. The governor tried to persuade the former Regulators to support his government by promising to remedy some of the malpractices of the county officers who had ruthlessly trampled over their rights. At the same time, he managed to get the men in Tryon's army paid for putting down the Regulator revolt. Martin, like Tryon, issued a proclamation that directed the county officials to publicly post the fees that they would charge for their services. Many of the county officials ignored Martin's proclamation while some of the county leaders were alienated by Martin's reconciliation with the Regulators.

Martin was interested in securing the attachment of debtors' property which the privy council frowned on. In his willingness to work out a compromise on the attachment law (he sympathized with the colonists), Martin came into conflict with the privy council and the colonial radical leaders in the assembly. The radical leaders seized the issue of the attachment law and used it against the Crown and Martin to oppose and usurp the royal prerogative. By refusing to pass a new judiciary law without the attachment law, the radicals could argue that it was the Crown and Martin who were responsible for no courts in the province.

Proroguing the assembly was a power used by all royal governors, and Martin's proroguing the assembly when it did not agree with the policies of the Crown added to his difficulties. Martin's use of this power was one of the criticisms levelled at him when the radicals usurped the royal prerogative and called their own convention in defiance of the Crown and Martin. Other weapons available to Martin were the veto, proclamations, appointive offices, persuasion, and the prestige of the Crown. Unlike Tryon, he could not call up the militia to oppose a geographic minority such as the Regulators because the radicals who opposed him were spread throughout the colony. Many of the radical leaders were already members of the office-holding oligarchy and they could use their positions to influence and mold public opinion against Martin. They isolated him from the neutral colonists and those merchants and Highlanders who would support him.

Martin saw the radicals as a minority and, at first, a group that he could control. The governor's underestimation of the radical leaders was a serious mistake for he let them grow in power and they persuaded many of the colonists to join them. Faced by a defiant assembly, a fearful council, and a vociferous minority who called on him at the palace, Martin wisely sent his family to New York. A few hours later, the governor accompanied by Archibald Neilson rode in his coach through open country to Cross Creek and then down the river to Ft. Johnston where he established his new capital.

If Martin had commissioned a Highland police unit earlier, he could have arrested Caswell, Johnston, Harnett, Harvey, Howe, and the other radical leaders and sent them out of the colony when the first resistance began to grow. He could have quelled the radicals temporarily, but that was not the way he wanted to govern nor would the Crown's planners have permitted it. Again on the deck of the *Cruizer* in the dark of the night, Martin watched the flames leap up toward the sky and outline the dark figures of the radicals as they applied the torch to Ft. Johnston. Ignoring the suggestion of the ship's captain, he refused to order the *Cruizer* to shell the patriots as long as they did not attempt to remove the king's artillery lying on the shore. Part of his hesitation may have been based on prudence and the knowledge that he did not have troops to use against the arsonists and he knew the fort was decrepit and of no value to him. Yet, he argued that he would not use the guns of the *Cruizer* against the radicals because he did not wish to begin hostilities against the people.

Isolated on the *Cruizer*, Martin began to change his mind. He assessed the situation and decided to make the best of it. He denounced the rebel leaders in private and public correspondence and summoned the good people of North Carolina to support him in his several proclamations. He called the council and corresponded with the Highlander leaders to rally their support but the radical leaders successfully isolated him and hampered his efforts. Martin correctly saw that Cornelius Harnett and Robert Howe were his mortal enemies and he persuaded Cornwallis to proscribe these men in his proclamation at Wilmington. Disappointed with Clinton's decision not to invade North Carolina, Martin agreed to go to Charleston with him where he hoped to rally support to regain North Carolina for the Crown. It was for a similar reason that Martin later accompanied Cornwallis to Charlotte, Hillsborough, and Guilford Court House. Moreover, it was Martin's plan of conquest that first encouraged the Crown to try to regain the southern colonies. As a loyal governor, Martin then moved against the radicals as could be expected from any governor who attempted to maintain law and order in a period of rebellion.

Despite the frustrations of being forbidden by the Crown's

ministers to make concessions to the assembly and the defiance of the radical leaders, Martin was sincere in his desire to reform the judicial system of North Carolina. Before and after he left the colony, he continued to plan for the judicial reforms. He was convinced that once law and order was reestablished in North Carolina that the majority of the colonists would work with him as governor. He also continued to work to help the North Carolina loyalists gain some compensation for their losses of property in the province.

Some of the royal governors saw political office as a property right rather than as a public trust. Martin was not venal as Lords Hertford and Hillsborough were alleged to be. Early in his career, Martin, like other governors, saw the governorship as a stepping stone to a better and higher office within the empire, but as he gained more experience in the problems of the colonists he began to regard the governorship as a public trust. Perhaps this was a manifestation of his ethical training as a youngster and the traditional *noblesse oblige* of his family. Despite his desire to improve himself financially and to add lustre to his prestige, Martin did concern himself about the welfare of the colonists, particularly in the restoration of the Regulators, the Debenture Notes, and the necessity for an adequate judicial system in North Carolina.

If Martin had been governor in a relatively peaceful period, he could have been one of the better royal governors of North Carolina because he did have talent and a humanitarian concern for the colonists but the times and circumstances did not permit him to exercise it to the fullest for the benefit of the Crown, North Carolina, and himself. Thus, Josiah Martin was defeated by the Crown's planners, the radical leaders, and by his own ill-health aggravated by the problems he faced. By maintaining his role as a determined royal governor, Josiah Martin unwittingly contributed to the American Revolution in North Carolina when the radicals used him as a scapegoat and a symbol of tyranny as exercised by the Crown and Parliament. George III was too far away for the radicals to reach but Josiah Martin was near at hand.

Martin made sacrifices for his office of governor of North Carolina, some North Carolinians, and his family. In addition to financial losses, his health was broken, he had lost three children in the province, and the health of Mrs. Martin had deteriorated so much that she went to an early grave in New York. Broken in health but not in spirit, Martin gathered his motherless children and went to the imperial city of his youthful dreams, London. He resigned his office in which he had invested all of his energies and dreams; an act that must have been traumatic for him. He spent the remainder of his dwindling energy working for the compensation of the North Carolina loyalists until he too went to an early grave.

History does not often regard the defeated in compassionate terms, for example, some historians today consider Josiah Martin as a symbol of British tyranny. Nevertheless, Governor Martin changed North Carolina in several ways. His resistance to the radical leaders spurred them on to accomplish the revolution and create a state. Perhaps the most important change is that the present governor does not have the veto power. The patriots would not give the veto power to their governors and they reduced the office to a ceremonial one. A more positive contribution by Martin was his humanitarian concern for the Regulators and his attempt to reconcile them to the royal government. His actions forced the radicals to court the Regulators for their support. The radical leaders incorporated most of the desired Regulator reforms into the new state government after the Revolution. Martin's indirect contribution here has proven to be a positive and constructive one. The governor's family name was memorialized in Martin County when it was formed in 1774 from Halifax and Tyrrel Counties. Probably the county's name would have been changed "like those of Dobbs and Tryon but for the popularity of Alexander Martin, who was governor, 1782-1785 and 1789-1792." The irony of the public confusion here does not need to be elaborated on. Flora MacDonald, another famous loyalist, has become a folk hero in North Carolina but she was not as much of a threat to the radical leaders as Josiah Martin. Josiah Martin was fortunate to have friends as well as enemies because his critics have kept his memory alive for over two centuries. Perhaps other Americans should be that fortunate?[16]

Endnotes

Chapter I

1. This and the following paragraphs are based on the genealogical records and correspondence of Colonel Samuel Martin and his sons in the British Museum, London, Manuscript Collections, Additional Manuscripts, and will be cited as Martin Papers, with the proper numerical designations. Martin Papers, Add. MSS, CXXIX, 41474, f. 56. The motto "Pro Patria" is taken from the Martin Papers; it differs from V. L. Oliver, who has identified the Martin motto as "Auxilium ab Alto," Vere Langford Oliver, *The History of the Island of Antigua* (London: Mitchell and Hughes, 3 volumes, 1894-1899), II, 240-251, III, 320, hereinafter cited as Oliver, *History of Antigua*. Additional genealogical material was given the author by the pre-Columbian scholar and author, Nigel Davies, whose uncle, Colonel Warburton Davies, compiled a typescript of genealogical materials on the Martin family in 1936, hereinafter cited as Davies, "The Martins." Chapter I is based on Vernon O. Stumpf, "Josiah Martin and His Search for Success: The Road to North Carolina," *North Carolina Historical Review*, LIII (January, 1976), 55-79.

2. For this and the succeeding paragraph refer to the following: Janet Schaw, *Journal of a Lady of Quality; Being the Narrative of a Journey from Scotland to the West Indies, North Carolina, and Portugal, in the Years 1774 to 1776*, edited by Evangeline Walker Andrews with the collaboration of Charles McLean Andrews (New Haven: Yale University Press, 1922, 104, hereinafter cited as Schaw, *Journal of a Lady of Quality*; Martin Papers, Add. MSS, CXXIX, 41474, f. 56; Herbert and Carole Schneider (eds.), *Samuel Johnson, President of King's College, His Career and Writings* (New York: Columbia University Press, 4 volumes, 1929), IV, 35, 221, hereinafter cited as Schneider, *Samuel Johnson*; Warburton Davies, "The Martins." Oliver, *History of Antigua*, II; 240.

3. This and the succeeding paragraph refer to the following: Martin Papers, Add. MSS, CXXIX, 41474, f. 56; Davies, "The Martins."

4. Martin Papers, Add. MSS, CXXIX, 41474, f. 56, 41475A, f. 57; A. R. Newsome stated that Colonel Martin had twenty-three children, but it is possible that Newsome used as his source the journal of Janet Schaw rather than the Martin Papers. A. R. Newsome, "Josiah Martin," in Allen Johnson, Dumas Malone,

and others (eds.), *Dictionary of American Biography* (New York: Charles Scribner's Sons, 20 volumes, 1928; index and updating supplements), XII, 343, hereinafter cited as *DAB*. Schaw, *Journal of a Lady of Quality*, 105, 262-264; Sir Lewis Namier and John Brooke, *The History of Parliament, the House of Commons, 1754-1790* (London: Published for the History of Parliament Trust by Her Majesty's Stationery Office, 3 volumes, 1964), III: 114-117, hereinafter cited as Namier and Brooke, *History of Parliament*; F. A. Inderwick and others (eds.), *A Calendar of the Inner Temple Records* (London: Published by Order of the Masters of the Bench, 5 volumes, 1896-1936), IV, 231, 321; Franklin B. Wickwire, *British Subministers and Colonial America, 1763-1783* (Princeton: Princeton University Press, 1966), 63-64, 77-78; Davies, "The Martins."

5. Namier and Brooke, *History of Parliament*, III, 114-117. There may be a clue to the identity of the mother of Samuel's son in his will: "£30 a year to Mrs. Smith of the Isle of Wight," Oliver, *History of Antigua*, II, 244. A photograph of the Hogarth portrait of Samuel Martin, Jr., is in Ronald Paulson, *Hogarth: His Life, Art, and Times* (New Haven and London: Published for the Paul Mellon Centre for Studies in British Art [London], Ltd., by the Yale University Press, 2 volumes, 1971), 246, 312, 366, 367, 420, hereinafter cited as Paulson, *Hogarth*. Hogarth bequeathed the Martin portrait to Samuel in 1764, Paulson, *Hogarth*, 508. In his will Samuel Martin bequeathed "my vol. of Hogarth prints given me by the author" to his brother Henry and his portrait by Hogarth to his brother William Byam Martin, Oliver, *History of Antigua*, II, 244. The portrait has ben listed as missing for a number of years, but the author discovered it in a private collection in the British Isles in 1977.

6. For a fuller discussion of the concepts of the empire and political advancement and ambition, see Richard Koebner, *Empire* (Cambridge: At the University Press, 1961); Jack P. Greene, "An Uneasy Connection: An Analysis of the Preconditions of the American Revolution," in *Essays on the American Revolution*, ed. Stephen G. Kurtz and James H. Hutson (Chapel Hill: University of North Carolina Press for the Institute of Early American History and Culture, Williamsburg, Virginia, 1973), 32-80; John Shy, "Thomas Pownall, Henry Ellis, and the Spectrum of Possibilities, 1763-1775," in *Anglo-American Political Relations, 1675-1775*, ed. Alison Gilbert Olson and Richard Maurice Brown (New Brunswick, Rutgers University Press, 1970), 155-186, hereinafter cited as Shy, "Pownall and Ellis"; Robert M. Calhoon, "The Floridas, the Western Frontier, and Vermont: Thoughts on the Hinterland Loyalists," in *Eighteenth Century Florida Life on the Frontier*, ed., Samuel Proctor (Gainesville: University of Florida, 1976), 1-15, hereinafter cited as Calhoon, "The Floridas"; Malcolm Frieberg, "How to Become a Colonial Governor: Thomas Hutchinson of Massachusetts," *The Review of Politics*, 21 (October, 1959), 646-656, hereinafter cited as Frieberg, "Thomas Hutchinson."

7. Richard B. Sheridan, "Samuel Martin, Innovating Sugar Planter of Antigua, 1750-1776," *Agricultural History*, 34 (July, 1960), 128-130, 137-138; Rich-

ard B. Sheridan, "The West Indian Antecedents of Josiah Martin, Last Royal Governor of North Carolina," *North Carolina Historical Review*, LIV (July, 1977), 259n; and Richard B. Sheridan, *Sugar and Slavery: An Economic History of the British West Indies, 1623-1775* (Baltimore: Johns Hopkins Press, 1973); 200-203, 360-361, 378-380, hereinafter cited as Sheridan, *Sugar and Slavery* Colonel Martin to Samuel Martin, Jr., May 22, 1748, and Colonel Martin to Josiah Martin, December 15, 1763, Martin Papers Add. MSS, VIII, 41346, f. 1, and 41353, ff. 69-70.

8. Josiah Martin to Samuel Martin, Jr., December 21, 1752, Martin Papers, Add. MSS, XVI, 41361, f. 1.

9. Colonel Martin to Samuel Martin, Jr., November 30, 1752, April 8, August 4, September 29, 1753, January 28, 1754, Martin Papers, Add. MSS, VIII, 41346, ff. 43, 51, 71, 88, 91. Josiah Martin to Samuel Martin, Jr., December 15, 1752, Josiah Martin to Henry John Forfer, August 6, 1754, Josiah Martin to Samuel Martin, Jr., December 14, 1754, Martin Papers, Add. MSS, XVI, 41361, ff. 7-8. Charles Rollin, *The Method of Teaching Belles Lettres . . . Translated from the French* (London: Printed for W. Strahan, J. and F. Rivington, et. al [Seventh Edition], 4 volumes, 1770.

10. For this and the succeeding paragraph see Colonel Martin to Samuel Martin, Jr., February 6, December 20, 1754; March 28, May 20, 1755, Martin Papers, Add. MSS., VIII, 41346, ff. 93, 126, 132, 135.

11. For this and the succeeding paragraph see Colonel Martin to Samuel Martin, Jr., December 20, 1754; March 25, May 20, 1755, Martin Papers, Add. MSS, VIII, 41346, ff. 126, 132, 135; E. Alfred Jones, *American Members of the Inns of Court* (London: The St. Catherine Press, 1924), 155-157.

12. Josiah Martin to Samuel Martin, Jr., 1757, Martin Papers, Add. MSS, XVI, 41361, f. 11.; Colonel Martin to Samuel Martin, Jr., January 23, December 28, 1759, January 18, 1760, Martin Papers, Add. MSS, VIII, 41347, ff. 7, 19, 27.

13. Colonel Martin to Samuel Martin, Jr., January 18, 1760; Josiah Martin to Samuel Martin, Jr., October 11, 1760, Martin Papers, Add. MSS, VIII, 41347, f. 27; XVI, 41361, ff. 13-14.

14. Colonel Martin to Samuel Martin, Jr., February 20, June 1, 1760; Samuel Martin, Jr., to Colonel Martin, August 28, 1760, Martin Papers, Add. MSS, VIII, 41347, ff. 35-36, 43, 56.

15. Uncle Josiah's Long Island estate had two names, Rock Hall and the Hermitage. In formal records it is called Rock Hall; in the Martin private correspondence it is sometimes called the Hermitage. Josiah Martin to Samuel Martin, Jr., January 6, 1760, Martin Papers, Add. MSS, XVI, 41361, f. 85. This letter is misdated; it should be dated 1761 because Martin mentions the recent death of King George II, who died in October, 1760. Colonel Martin to Samuel Martin, Jr., July 1, 1761, February 12, 1762, Martin Papers, Add. MSS, VIII, 41347, ff. 91, 122.

16. Josiah Martin's will dated March 30, 1773, "Abstracts of Wills on File in

the Surrogate's office, City of New York, January 7, 1773-February 7, 1783," *Collections of the New-York Historical Society for the Year 1900* (New York: Printed for the Society, 1901), IX, 55-56. Josiah Martin to Colonel Samuel Martin, June 23, 1761, Martin Papers, Add. MSS, XVI, 41361, ff. 19-23.

17. Josiah Martin to Colonel Samuel Martin, August 23, 1761, Martin Papers, Add. MSS, XCI, 41361, ff. 19-23; Colonel Samuel Martin to Samuel Martin, Jr., July 1, 1761, February 12, 1762, Martin Papers, Add. MSS, VIII, 41347, ff. 91, 122; Josiah Martin to Colonel Samuel Martin, November 20, 1761, Martin Papers, Add. MSS, XVI, 41361, ff. 24-25. William S. Price, Jr., "'Men of Good Estates': Wealth among North Carolina's Royal Councillors," *North Carolina Historical Review*, XLIX, (January, 1972), 77; Hereinafter cited Price, "Men of Good Estates."

18. Josiah Martin to Colonel Samuel Martin, April 23, May 26, 1762, Martin Papers, Add. MSS, XVI, 41361, ff. 26-29; James Sullivan and others (eds.), *The Papers of Sir William Johnson* (Albany: University of the State of New York, 14 volumes, 1921-1965), III; 950, hereinafter cited as Sullivan, *Johnson Papers.*

19. Colonel Samuel Martin to Josiah Martin, July 14, August 1, 1764, Martin Papers, Add. MSS, XVI, 41353, ff. 78, 80.

20. Colonel Samuel Martin to Josiah Martin, July 14, August 1, 1764, Martin Papers, Add. MSS, XVI, 41353, ff. 78, 80. John Singleton Copley told his half-brother, Henry Pelham, in 1771 that he had seen a miniature of Governor Martin "by Miers which cost 30 Guineas and I think it worth the money. The Governor says he sat at least 50 times for it." *Letters and Papers of John Singleton Copley and Henry Pelham, 1739-1776* (Boston: Massachusetts Historical Society, 1914), 128. Josiah Martin to Samuel Martin, Jr., August 2, September 17, 1764, Martin Papers, Add. MSS, XVI, 41361, ff. 30-31.

21. Josiah Martin to Samuel Martin, Jr., July 8, 1767, Martin Papers, Add. MSS, XVI, 41361, ff. 107-108.

22. Josiah Martin to Samuel Martin, Jr., August 7, 1767, Martin Papers, Add. MSS, XVI, 41361, ff. 110-113.

23. Philip Davidson, *Propaganda and the American Revolution, 1763-1783* (Chapel Hill: University of North Carolina Press, 1941), 170-171; hereinafter cited as Davidson, *Propaganda*, Arthur M. Schlesinger, *Prelude to Independence: The Newspaper War on Britain, 1764-1776* (New York: Random House, 1957), 72, 77, 81, 83, 100, 111 hereinafter cited Schlesinger *Prelude*; Josiah Martin to Samuel Martin, Jr., August 7, 1767, Martin Papers, Add. MSS, XVI, 41361, ff. 110-113.

24. Josiah Martin to Samuel Martin, Jr., August 7, 1767, Martin Papers, Add. MSS, XVI, ff. 110-113; Namier and Brooke, *History of Parliament*, III, 126.

25. James W. Hayes, "The Social and Professional Background of the Officers of the British Army, 1714-1763" (unpublished master's thesis, University of London, 1956), 125. For a definition of off-reckonings, see *A Treatise on Military Finance* (London: Printed for T. Egerton, at the Military Library, near Whitehall

Chapter I

[Revised Edition], 1796), 13, 17, hereinafter cited as *Military Finance*. This edition listed no author, but apparently it was based on John Williamson, *A Treatise on Military Finance*, published in London in 1782. In the revised edition the unnamed author wrote that his revision did not affect the off-reckonings and other deductions from the soldier's pay that had been practiced for a number of years. Josiah Martin to Samuel Martin, Jr., January 21, May 19, 1766, Martin Papers, Add. MSS, XVI, 41361, ff. 52-55, 58-59.

26. Josiah Martin to Samuel Martin, Jr., September 1, 1766, Martin Papers, Add. MSS, XVI, 41361, ff. 62-64; *Military Finance*, 6, 40; John Shy, *Toward Lexington: The Role of the British Army in the Coming of the American Revolution* (Princeton, N.J.: Princeton University Press, 1965), 234-235, 346, 348, hereinafter cited as Shy, *Toward Lexington*.

27. Josiah Martin to Samuel Martin, Jr., July 11, 1766, Martin Papers, Add. MSS, XVI, 41361, ff. 60-61.

28. W. L. Grant and James Munro (eds.), *Acts of the Privy Council of England, Colonial Series, The Unbound Papers* (London: Published for His Majesty's Stationery Office, 6 volumes, 1908-1912), VI, 433; Oliver, *History of Antigua*, II, 248. Colonel Martin to Samuel Martin, Jr., July 1, 1765, May 16, August 10, 1766, Martin Papers, Add. MSS, VIII, 41347, ff. 204, 224, 234. Josiah Martin to Samuel Martin, Jr., September 1, 1766, Martin Papers, Add. MSS, XVI, 41361, ff. 62-64.

29. Colonel Samuel Martin to Samuel Martin, Jr., September 4, 19, October 6, 1766, April 25, 1767, Martin Papers, Add. MSS, VIII, 41347, ff. 263, 267, 270, 280; Sheridan, *Sugar and Slavery*, 452-459; Josiah Martin to Samuel Martin, Jr., October 2, 30, 1766, Martin Papers, Add. MSS, XVI, 41361, ff. 69-71, 73-74.

30. Josiah Martin to Samuel Martin, Jr., November 25, 1766; Josiah Martin to Miss Irish, December 5, 1766; to Samuel Martin, Jr., December 3, 1766; to James Hammond, December 5, 1766; to Jas. Robson, December 5, 1776, Martin Papers, Add. MSS, XVI, 41361, ff. 75-82, 85.

31. Josiah Martin to Samuel Martin, Jr., December 3, 1766, March 3 and April 15, 1767, Martin Papers, Add. MSS, XVI, 41361, ff. 79-80, 97-100.

32. Josiah Martin to Samuel Martin, Jr., March 3, May 20, June 8, October 6, 1767; Samuel Martin, Jr. to Josiah Martin, January 30, 1768, Martin Papers, Add. MSS, XVI, 41361, ff. 97-98, 104-105, 121-127.

33. Colonel Samuel Martin to Samuel Martin, Jr., March 10, April 14, 25, September, 1767, Martin Papers, Add. MSS, VIII, 41347, ff. 263, 270, 278.

34. Colonel Samuel Martin to Samuel Martin, Jr., July 20, November 5, December 5, 1767, Martin Papers, Add. MSS, VIII, 41347, ff. 275, 292, 299.

35. Colonel Samuel Martin to Samuel Martin, Jr., November 21, 30, 1767, January 15, 30, October 18, 1768, Martin Papers, Add. MSS, VIII, 41347, ff. 294, 296, 41348, ff. 2, 4, 28-29.

36. Josiah Martin to Samuel Martin, Jr., May 4, 14, October 21, 29, 1768, April 17, May 23, 1769, Martin Papers, Add. MSS, XVI, 41361, ff. 134, 136-138, 146-148, 156, 158-159.

37. Josiah Martin to Samuel Martin, Jr., May 23, 1769, Martin Papers, Add. MSS, XVI, 41361, ff. 158-159; Colonel Samuel Martin to Samuel Martin, Jr., April 26, May 22, 31, 1769, Martin Papers, Add. MSS, VIII, 41348, ff. 45, 50, 54.

38. Governor William Woodly to Lt. Col. Josiah Martin, June 14, 1769; Lt. Col. Josiah Martin to Governor Woodly, June 27, 1769; Josiah Martin to Samuel Martin, Jr., July 27, 1769; Samuel Martin, Jr., to Josiah Martin, August 2, 1769; Martin Papers, Add. MSS, XVI, 41361, ff. 166, 164-165, 167-169. The purchase price of a lieutenant colonelcy was £3,400, Shy, *Toward Lexington*, 347.

39. Samuel Martin, Jr., to Josiah Martin, August 2, 4, 1769; Josiah Martin to Samuel Martin, Jr., October 14, 1769; Josiah Martin to James Meyrick, October 14, 1769; Martin Papers, Add. MSS, XVI, 41361, ff. 167-170, 178-182. For a discussion of the end of absentee officeholding in the colonies, see Helen Taft Manning, *British Colonial Government after the American Revolution, 1782-1820* (New Haven: Yale University Press, 1933), 30-31.

40. Josiah Martin to Samuel Martin, Jr., October 6, 1769, May 24, 1770, Martin Papers, Add. MSS, XVI, 41361, ff. 176-177, 187-190; *Journal of the Commissioners for Trade and Plantations* (London: Published by His Majesty's Stationery Office, 14 volumes, [April, 1704, to May, 1782], 1920-1938), VIII, 188, 190-200, hereinafter cited as *Journal of the Commissioners for Trade and Plantations*.

41. Josiah Martin to Samuel Martin, Jr., August 17, 1770, Martin Papers, Add. MSS, XVI, 41361, ff. 191-194.

42. Josiah Martin to Samuel Martin, Jr., August 17, September 7, 1770, Martin Papers, Add. MSS, XVI, 41361, ff. 191-96.

43. Josiah Martin to Samuel Martin, Jr., September 22, October 5, 1770; Colonel Samuel Martin to Samuel Martin, Jr., June 24, August 5, 13, September 17, 1770, Martin Papers, Add. MSS, XVI, 41361, ff. 197-202; VIII, 41348, ff. 82, 84, 88.

44. *Journal of the Commissioners for Trade and Plantations*, VIII, 115, 116, 218.

45. Josiah Martin to Samuel Martin, Jr., October 5, 1770, March 3, 1771, Martin Papers, Add. MSS, XVI, 41361, ff. 201-204. The English newspaper reporting the appointment has not been identified, but there is a reference to "Henry Martin, Esq. to be Gov. of North Carolina" in *Gentleman's Magazine and Historical Chronicle*, XL, (December, 1770), 501.

46. Josiah Martin to Samuel Martin, Jr., March 3, April 2, May 7, June 4, 1771, Martin Papers, Add. MSS, XVI, 41361, ff. 203-204, 205-208, 213-214; James Rivington, the New York editor, commented that Josiah Martin had been delayed in going to North Carolina because of the operation for a fistula. James Rivington to Sir William Johnson, May 6, 1771, in Sullivan, *Johnson Papers*, VIII, 98.

47. Josiah Martin to Samuel Martin, Jr., March 3, 1771, Martin Papers, Add. MSS, XVI, 41361, ff. 203-204. If the two governors exchanged portraits, they are not mentioned further in the extant records. There is no portrait of Governor

Martin in the current art collection of the Tryon family, Lady Tryon to the author, 14 July 1977.

48. For this and the following paragraph refer to: Colonel Samuel Martin to Samuel Martin, Jr., March 1, 3, April 25, 1771; April 10, 1774, Martin Papers, Add. MSS, VIII, 41348, ff. 139, 141, 145, 179.

49. Josiah Martin to Samuel Martin, Jr., March 3, 1771, Martin Papers, Add. MSS, XVI, 41361, ff. 203-204.

50. Josiah Martin to Samuel Martin, Jr., April 2, May 7, 1771, Martin Papers, Add. MSS, XVI, 41361, ff. 205-208.

51. Josiah Martin to Samuel Martin, Jr., May 16, 1771, Martin Papers, Add. MSS, XVI, ff. 41361 209-210. For a more detailed account of the Regulators, see William S. Powell, James K. Huhta, and Thomas J. Farnham (eds.), *The Regulators in North Carolina: A Documentary History, 1759-1776* (Raleigh: State Department of Archives and History, 1971), hereinafter cited as Powell and others, *Regulators*. Many references to the Regulators may be found in Powell, *The Correspondence of William Tryon*. See also Alonzo Thomas Dill, *Governor Tryon and His Palace* (Chapel Hill: University of North Carolina Press, 1955), 132-139, 141-147, 152-153, 166-167, hereinafter cited as Dill, *Governor Tryon*; George R. Adams, "The Carolina Regulators: A Note on Changing Interpretations," *North Carolina Historical Review*, XLIX (October, 1972), 345-352, hereinafter cited as Adams, "The Carolina Regulators."

52. Josiah Martin to Samuel Martin, May 16, June 4, 27, 1771, Martin Papers, Add. MSS, XVI, 41361, ff. 209-210, 213-214, 217-218.

53. Hillsborough to Martin, May 4, 1771, Powell and others, *Regulators*, 451.

54. Tryon to Hillsborough and Tryon to Board of Trade, June 29, 1771, William L. Saunders (ed.), *The Colonial Records of North Carolina* (Raleigh: State of North Carolina, 10 volumes, 1886-1890), VIII, 627, hereinafter cited as *Colonial Records*.

55. Josiah Martin to Samuel Martin, Jr., July 9, August 21, 1771, Martin Papers, Add. MSS, XVI, 41361, ff. 219-220, 223-224; Martin to Hillsborough, August 15, 1771, Powell and others, *Regulators*, 504.

56. Josiah Martin to Samuel Martin, Jr., July 20, 1771, Martin Papers, Add. MSS, XVI, 41361, ff. 221-222.

Chapter II

1. Martin to Hillsborough, August 15, 1771; Earl of Rochford to Tryon, August 2, 1771, Powell and others, *Regulators*, 498, 503-504; *Colonial Records* 8: 653.

2. Council Journal, August 12, 1771; Martin to Hillsborough, August 15, 1771, Saunders, *Colonial Records*, IX, 15-16, 16-17. The eight missing councillors were Lieutenant Governor George Mercer, William Dry, Alexander McCulloch, Robert Palmer, Lewis Henry deRosset, John Rutherford, John Sampson, and Samuel Strudwick. Powell, *The Correspondence of William Tryon*, II, 181-182, 4n-54.

Endnotes

3. Samuel A'Court Ashe, *History of North Carolina* (Greensboro: Charles L. Van Noppen, Publisher, 2 volumes, 1925), I, 396-397, hereinafter cited as Ashe, *History of North Carolina*; James Iredell to Henry E. McCulloh, March 5, 1771, Charles E. Johnson Collection, Archives, Division of Archives and History, Raleigh; Samuel Johnston to Thomas Barker, June 10, 1771, Calendar of Manuscripts in the Hayes Collection of John C. Wood, Southern Historical Collection, University of North Carolina Library, Chapel Hill.

4. Marshall DeLancey Haywood, *Governor William Tryon and His Administration in the Province of North Carolina, 1765-1771* . . . (Raleigh: E. M. Uzzell, 1903, reprinted 1958), 63-64, hereinafter cited as Haywood, *Tryon*, Dill, *Governor Tryon*, 112-127; Adams, "The Carolina Regulators," 345-352; Saunders, *Colonial Records*, VIII, xiii, IX, xv ff.

5. James P. Whittenburg, "Planters, Merchants, and Lawyers: Social Change and the Origins of the North Carolina Regulation," *William and Mary Quarterly*, XXXIV (Third Series, April, 1977), 221-231, hereinafter cited as Whittenburg, "Planters, Merchants, and Lawyers." Mancur Olson, Jr., has challenged the belief that rapid economic development is a deterrent to civil disorders. He asserts " . . . until further research is done, the presumption must be that growth, far from being the source of domestic tranquility it is sometimes supposed to be, is rather a disruptive and destabilizing force that leads to political instability." Mancur Olson, Jr., "Rapid Growth as a Destabilizing Force," *Journal of Economic History*. XXIII (December 1963), 552.

6. Powell and others, *Regulators*, xv-xvi; Lefler and Powell, *Colonial North Carolina*, 217-239; Petition of Inhabitants of Orange County to George III [May, 1768], *Colonial Records*, VII, 770-782; Petition of Inhabitants of Orange County to Tryon and the Council [May 21, 1768]; Regulators to Tryon and the Council, [May 21-May 30?, 1768], Powell, *The Correspondence of William Tryon*, II, 110, 113-115; Powell and others, *Regulators*, 579; Proclamation of Tryon, [July 21, 1768], Powell, *The Correspondence of William Tryon*, II, 164; A. Roger Ekirch, *"Poor Carolina": Politics and Society in Colonial North Carolina, 1729-1776* (Chapel Hill: University of North Carolina Press, 1981), 204-205, hereinafter cited as Ekirch, *"Poor Carolina*; Proclamations of Josiah Martin [August 22, 1771], *Colonial Records*, IX, 24-25; John S. Bassett, "The Regulators of North Carolina (1765-1771)," *Annual Report of the American Historical* Association for the Year 1894, Washington: Government Printing Office, 1895, 150-155.

7. Jack P. Greene's review of Powell and others, *Regulators*, in the *North Carolina Historical Review*, XLIX (April, 1972), 206-207; Whittenberg, Planters, Merchants, and Lawyers," 215-238; Peter H. Wood's review of Ekirch, *"Poor Carolina*," in the *North Carolina Historical Review*, LIX (April, 1982), 193: Powell and others, *Regulators*, xxvi; Elisha P. Douglass, *Rebels and Democrats: The Struggle for Equal Political Rights and Majority Rule During the Revolution* (Chapel Hill: University of North Carolina Press, 1955), 72-74, hereinafter cited as Douglas, Rebels and Democrats; Marvin L. Michael Kay, "The North Carolina

Chapter II

Regulation, 1766-1776: A Class Conflict," in Alfred F. Young (ed.), *The American Revolution: Explorations in the History of American Radicalism* (DeKalb: Northern Illinois University Press, 1976), 73-123, hereinafter cited as Kay, "The North Carolina Regulation"; Ekirch, "Poor Carolina," 166-168.

8. Ekirch, "Poor Carolina," 164-165; Tryon to Hillsborough, June 16, 1768, Powell, *The Correspondence of William Tryon*, II, 135; Powell and others, *Regulators*, 584-585; Assembly to Tryon, [January 25, 1771]; Tryon to Assembly, [January 26, 1771]; Proclamation of Tryon, [February 7, 1771]; "Journal of the Expedition against the Insurgents, April 20-June 21, 1771," entry for May 12; Tryon to Regulators, May 16, 1771; "Newspaper Accounts of the Battle of Alamance" (from the Williamsburg *Virginia Gazette*, June 13, 1771), [Newbern, May 24, 1771], 718, 739-740; Kay, "The North Carolina Regulation," 102-103.

9. Charles Grier Sellers, Jr., "Making a Revolution: The North Carolina Whigs, 1765-1775," in J. Carlyle Sitterson (ed.), *Studies in Southern History*, (Chapel Hill: University of North Carolina Press, 1957), 26, hereinafter cited as Sellers, "Making a Revolution;" Tryon to Hillsborough, March 12, 1771, Powell, *the Correspondence of William Tryon*, II, 628-629.

10. Lefler and Powell, *Colonial North Carolina*, 238, 289; Powell and others, *Regulators*, xxvi.

11. Kay, "The North Carolina Regulation," 104; Ekirch, "Poor Carolina," 205-206; Martin to Hillsborough, October 18, 1771; Hillsborough to Martin, December 4, 1771, *Colonial Records*, IX, iii, xx, 64-65; Powell, *The Correspondence of William Tryon*, II, 842-843, 844.

12. Hillsborough to Martin, December 4, 1771, *Colonial Records*, IX, 64-65.

13. Ekirch, "Poor Carolina," 205; Adelaide L. Fries, Douglas LeTell Rights, Minnie J. Smith, and Kenneth G. Hamilton (eds.), *Records of the Moravians in North Carolina* (Raleigh: North Carolina Historical Commission, 11 volumes, 1922-1969), II, 684-685, 737, hereinafter cited as Fries and others, *Records of the Moravians*; John L. Cheney, Jr. (ed), *North Carolina Government, 1585-1979: A Narrative and Statistical History* . . . (Raleigh: North Carolina Department of the Secretary of State, second, updated edition, 198), 59, hereinafter cited as Cheney, *North Carolina Government*.

14. Fries and others, *Records of the Moravians*, II, 654, 753-754.

15. Duane Meyer, *The Highland Scots of North Carolina* (Raleigh: Carolina Charter Tercentenary Commission, 1963), 32-33; Kay, "The Carolina Regulators," 103-104; Ekirch, *"Poor Carolina"* 201-202; see examples of newspaper accounts in Powell, *The Correspondence of William Tryon*, II, 833-841.

16. *Colonial Records*, IX, xii; Martin to Hillsborough, August 15, 1771, Hillsborough to Martin, December 4, 1771, Powell, *The Correspondence of William Tryon*, II, 828, 844; Council Journal, November 19-December 23, 1771; Assembly Journal, November 19-December 23, 1771, *Colonial Records*, IX, 101-136, 136-222.

17. Martin to Hillsborough, August 15, 1771, Powell, *The Correspondence of*

Endnotes

William Tryon, II, 829; Council Journal, December 7, 17, 20; Assembly Journal, December 6, 16, 19, 20, 21, 23, *Colonial Records*, IX, 114, 122, 127, 166-167, 169, 189, 196, 201, 208, 222.

18. Martin to Hillsborough, January 30, 1772; Council Journal, January 25, 29, 1772, *Colonial Records*, IX, 230-235, 228-229, 229-230; Alan D. Watson, "The Appointment of Sheriffs in Colonial North Carolina: A Reexamination," *North Carolina Historical Review*, LIII (Autumn, 1976), 385, 391.

19. Martin to Hillsborough, January 30, 1772; Hillsborough to Martin, December 4, 1771; Martin to Hillsborough, December 26, 1771; Council Journal, December 20-23, 1771, Assembly Journal, December 18-23, 1771. *Colonial Records*, IX, 231-232, 64-65, 75-78, 124, 127, 193, 194, 197, 203, 206-207, 208, 213, 222; Robert M. Weir, "North Carolina's Reaction to the Currency Act of 1764," *North Carolina Historical Review*, XL (April, 1963), 194-196, hereinafter cited as Weir, "Reaction to Currency Act," See also Hillsborough to Martin, April 1, 1772; Martin to Hillsborough, April 12, 1772, *Colonial Records*, IX, 275-276, 278.

20. Assembly Journal, December 21, 1771; Hillsborough to Martin, December 4, 1771, April 1, 1772; Martin to Hillsborough, April 12, 1772, *Colonial Records*, IX, 213, 65, 275-276, 278.

21. Assembly Journal, December 23, 1771; Martin to Hillsborough, December 26, 1771; Council Journal, December 23, 1771, *Colonial Records*, IX, 222, 217, 75-77, 136. See also Weir, "Reaction to Currency Act," 194-196.

22. "Royal order for running the South Carolina boundary Line," May 29, 1771, *Colonial Records*, VIII, 611-612; Assembly Journal, December 17, 21, 1771; Martin to Hillsborough, November 10, 1771, *Colonial Records*, IX, 191-192, 211-212, 48-49.

23. Assembly Journal, December 21, 23, 1771; Martin to Hillsborough, December 26, 1771; Hillsborough to Martin, April 1, 1772, *Colonial Records*, IX, 211-212, 220, 77-78, 276.

24. Council Journal, April 1, 1772; Martin to Hillsborough, April 12, 1772, *Colonial Records*, IX, 274, 279-280; Josiah Martin to Samuel Martin, Jr., February 5, 1772, Martin Papers, Add. MSS, XVI, 41361, ff. 231-232.

Martin to Hillsborough, June 5, July 8, 1772; Assembly Journal, March 3, 1773, *Colonial Records*, IX, 299-300, 312, 562.

26. Assembly Journal, March 3, 6, 1773, *Colonial Records*, IX, 563, 578.

27. Jack P. Greene, *The Quest for Power: The Lower House of Assembly in the Southern Royal Colonies, 1689-1776* (Chapel Hill: University of North Carolina Press for the Institute of Early American History and Culture, Williamsburg, Virginia, 1963), 205-206, 210-211, 217-219, hereinafter cited as Greene, *Quest for Power*; Council Journal, March 6, 9, 1773; Assembly Journal, March 6, 1773; Martin to Dartmouth, March 12, 1773, *Colonial Records*, IX, 447, 594-596, 587, 598-601.

28. Leonard Woods Labaree, *Royal Government in America: A Study of the*

British Colonial System before 1783 (New Haven: Yale University Press, 1930; reprint, Frederick Ungar Publishing Co., 1958), 396-401, hereinafter cited as Labaree, *Royal Government in America*. *Colonial Records*, VI, 245-251, 256; Martin to Hillsboro, March 7, 1772, *Colonial Records*, IX, 264-268.

29. Martin to Samuel Johnston, February 6, 1772, Martin to Dartmouth, December 24, 1773, *Colonial Records*, IX, 236-237, 300, 569, 589, 618-619, 1176.

30. Martin to Samuel Johnston, February 8, 1772, Martin to Dartmouth December 24, 1775, *Colonial Records*, IX, 236-237, 798-799; Cheney, *North Carolina Government*, 56, 57, 153; Martin to Samuel Martin, Jr., June 17, 1772, Martin Papers, Add. MSS, XVI, 41361, ff. 240-243.

31. Greene, *Quest for Power*, 341-342; Martin to Dartmouth, May 5, 1774, *Colonial Records*, IX, 992-993, Labaree, *Royal Government in America*, 399-400; Basic *Documents of English History*, ed. Stephen B. Baxter, (Boston: Houghton Mifflin Co., 1968), 114-115.

32. Greene, *Quest for Power*, 211, 219.

Chapter III

1. Walter Clark (ed.), *The State Records of North Carolina* (Winston and Goldsboro: State of North Carolina, 16 volumes, numbered XI-XXVI, 1895-1906), XXIII, 259, hereinafter cited as Clark, *State Records*.

2. Charles D. Drake, *A Treatise of the Law of Suits by Attachment in the United States* (Boston: Little Brown & Company, 1858), 699.

3. W. P. Courtney, "Richard Jackson," in Leslie Stephen and Sidney Lee (eds.), *The Dictionary of National Biography* (New York: Macmillan and Co.; London: Smith, Elder, & Co., 63 volumes, 1885-1900; updating supplements, Oxford University Press), XXIX, 104-105, hereinafter cited as *DNB*; Board of Trade to Tryon, December 12, 1770, *Colonial Records*, VIII, 265; H. Braughn Taylor, "The Foreign Attachment Law and the Coming of the Revolution in North Carolina," *North Carolina Historical Review*, LII (January, 1975), 21, hereinafter cited as Taylor, "Foreign Attachment."

4. Instructions to Martin, February 4, 1772; Hillsborough to Martin, July 1, 1772, *Colonial Records*, IX, 235-236, 308; Taylor, "Foreign Attachment," 21-22.

5. Martin to Hillsborough, July 11, 1772, *Colonial Records*, IX, 315-317, Martin to Hillsborough, October 25, 1772, *Colonial Records*, IX, 347-348.

6. Josiah Martin to Samuel Martin, Jr., December 3, 1772; February 21, 1773, Martin Papers, XVI, 41361, ff. 246-248.

7. G. F. Russell Barker, "William Legge," *DNB*, XXXII, 417-418; Dartmouth to Martin, November 4, 1772, *Colonial Records*, IX, 352.

8. Martin to Dartmouth, November 28, 1772, October 18, 1773, *Colonial Records*, IX, 357-359, 694.

9. Martin to Dartmouth, February 26, 1773; Council Journal, January 25, 27, February 3, 12, 15, 19, 1773; Assembly Journal, February 24, 25, March 1, 2, 6,

Colonial Records, IX, 377-378, 380-381, 387, 395, 399, 405, 534-535, 539-540, 551, 556-560, 579-580, 587; Josiah Martin to Samuel Martin, Jr., March 14, 1773, Martin Papers, XVI, 41361, ff. 250-251. See also Taylor, "Foreign Attachment," 22.

10. Josiah Martin to Samuel Martin, Jr., February 21, 1773, Martin Papers, XVI, 41361, f. 248.

11. Assembly Journal, March 6, 1773, *Colonial Records*, IX, 578-579; Taylor, "Foreign Attachment," 22-23.

12. Martin to Dartmouth, April 6, 1773, *Colonial Records*, IX, 625-626; Taylor, "Foreign Attachment," 23.

13. For this and the succeeding paragraph see Martin to Dartmouth, April 6, May 30, 1773, February 26, March 12, 31, October 8, 18, 1773; Dartmouth to Martin, August 4, 1773, *Colonial Records*, IX, 373-374, 598-601, 619-621, 625-632, 655-56, 690, 693, 680-682.

14. Extracts from Memoirs of Josiah Quincy, Jr., March 27-April 5, 1773, *Colonial Records*, IX, 610-613; Davidson, *Propaganda and the American Revolution*, 7, 57; James Truslow Adams, "Josiah Quincy," *DAB*, XV, 307-308.

15. Report of Richard Jackson, July 15, 1773; Dartmouth to Martin, August 4, 1773, *Colonial Records*, IX, 670, 681-682; Taylor, "Foreign Attachment," 24.

16. Dartmouth to Martin, August 4, 1773, *Colonial Records*, IX, 681-682; Taylor, "Foreign Attachment," 24-25.

17. Council Journal, March 16, 1773, *Colonial Records*, IX, 607; Martin Howard to James Iredell, March 8, 1773, Don Higginbotham (ed.), *The Papers of James Iredell* (Raleigh: Division of Archives and History, Department of Cultural Resources, 2 volumes, 1976), I, 133-134, 134n, hereinafter cited as Higginbotham, *Iredell Papers*.

18. "A Planter" [James Iredell], "Essay on the Court Law Controversy," Higginbotham, *Iredell Papers*, 163-165; Editorial Note, 165n-166n; Taylor, "Foreign Attachment," 25.

19. Martin to Dartmouth, October 6, 18, November 5, 1773, *Colonial Records*, IX, 685-687, 693-695. For a discussion of government by instruction, see Labaree, *Royal Government in America*, 420-448.

20. *Colonial Records*, IX, 701-704; Taylor, "Foreign Attachment," 25-26.

21. For this and the succeeding paragraph see Martin to Dartmouth, December 16, 1773, Council Journal, December 4, 1773, *Colonial Records*, IX:698-699, 706-709.

22. Ashe, *North Carolina*, I:404-495.

23. Council Journal, December 8, 21, 22, 1773; Assembly Journal, December 7, 9, 21, 1773, *Colonial Records*, IX, 710, 729-733, 790-791, 738, 742-743, 786-788; Taylor, "Foreign Attachment," 26.

24. For this and the succeeding paragraph refer to Martin to Dartmouth, December 16, 1773; Assembly Journal, December 6, 8, 1773, *Colonial Records*, IX, 698-699, 737, 740-741; Lefler and Powell, *Colonial North Carolina*, 257-259.

Chapter III

25. Assembly Journal, December 21, 1773, *Colonial Records*, IX, 786-787.

26. Martin to Dartmouth, December 24, 1773, *Colonial Records*, IX, 798-801; Committee of House to Tryon [on or after December 21, 1773], Powell, *The Correspondence of William Tryon*, II, 857-858.

27. Josiah Martin to Samuel Martin, Jr., January 27, 1774, Martin Papers, XVI, 41361, ff. 274-276; Council Journal, December 22, 1773, *Colonial Records*, IX, 791.

28. Josiah Martin to Samuel Martin, Jr., January 27, 1774, Martin Papers, XVI, 41361, ff. 274-276.

29. Martin to Dartmouth, January 13, 1774, *Colonial Records*, IX, 816-819.

30. Martin to Board of Trade, December 24, 1773, *Colonial Records*, IX, 795-797; Taylor, "Foreign Attachment," 27-28.

31. Martin to Dartmouth, January 28, 1774, *Colonial Records*, IX, 820; Taylor, "Foreign Attachment," 28.

32. Martin to Dartmouth, January 28, 1774, *Colonial Records*, IX, 821; Taylor, "Foreign Attachment," 28.

33. Journal, March 2, 5, 1774; Assembly Journal, March 5, 1774, *Colonial Records*, IX, 832-833, 835, 879; Taylor, "Foreign Attachment," 28-29.

34. Assembly Journal, March 9, 1774, *Colonial Records*, IX, 890-893; Taylor, "Foreign Attachment," 29.

35. Council Journal, March 11, 1774; Assembly Journal, March 11, 1774, *Colonial Records*, IX, 844, 901-902; Taylor, "Foreign Attachment," 29.

36. Council Journal, March 14, 16, 1774; Assembly Journal, March 15, 19, 1774, *Colonial Records*, IX, 849, 854, 915-916, 927-929; Taylor, "Foreign Attachment," 29-30.

37. Assembly Journal, March 24, 1774, *Colonial Records*, IX, 939.

38. Assembly Journal, March 21, 24, 1774, *Colonial Records*, IX, 929-931, 945-946; Taylor, "Foreign Attachment," 30.

39. Assembly Journal, March 24, 1774; Martin to Dartmouth, April 2, 1774, *Colonial Records*, IX, 940-941, 962; Cheney, *North Carolina Government*, 41, 46, 47, 48, 49, 51, 52; Taylor, "Foreign Attachment," 30.

40. Council Journal, March 28, 1774, *Colonial Records*, IX, 954-955.

41. This and the succeeding paragraph refer to Martin to Dartmouth, April 2, 1774, *Colonial Records*, IX, 962-964; Taylor, "Foreign Attachment," 30-31.

42. Martin to Dartmouth, April 6, 1774; Council Journal, March 19, 1774, *Colonial Records*, IX, 971-972, 830-831; Taylor, "Foreign Attachment," 31.

43. Martin to Dartmouth, April 6, 1774; Councillors (DeRosset, Rutherford, Sampson, Cornell, Dry) to Martin, March 25, 1774, *Colonial Records*, IX, 972, 975-980; Taylor, "Foreign Attachment," 31.

44. Martin to Dartmouth, April 6, 1774, *Colonial Records*, IX, 971-973; Taylor, "Foreign Attachment," 31.

45. Josiah Martin to Samuel Martin, Jr., June 17, 1772, Martin Papers, XVI, 41361, ff. 240-243; Martin to Dartmouth, April 6, 1774, May 27, 1773, *Colonial*

Records, IX, 973-975, 646-647.

46. Taylor, "Foreign Attachment," 31-32.

47. Dartmouth to Martin, May 4, 1774, *Colonial Records*, IX, 988; Taylor, "Foreign Attachment," 32.

48. Martin to Dartmouth, September 1, 1774, March 23, 1775, *Colonial Records*, IX, 1059, 1174-1175; Taylor, "Foreign Attachment," 32.

49. This and the succeeding paragraph refer to Alexander Elmsly to Samuel Johnston, May 17, 1774, *Colonial Records*, IX, 997-999; Taylor, "Foreign Attachment," 32-33.

50. Samuel Johnston to Alexander Elmsly, September 23, 1774, *Colonial Records*, IX, 1071; Taylor, "Foreign Attachment," 33.

51. Alexander Elmsly to Samuel Johnston, December 22, 1774, *Colonial Records*, IX, 1092, Taylor, "Foreign Attachment," 33.

52. Dartmouth to Martin, March 3, 1775, *Colonial Records*, IX, 1141; Taylor, "Foreign Attachment," 33.

53. Memorial of the North Carolina Assembly to the Earl of Dartmouth and the Board of Trade, n.d, [March, 1775?] *Colonial Records*, IX, 1147-1148; Taylor, "Foreign Attachment," 33.

54. Report of Richard Jackson to the Board of Trade, May 17, 1775, *Colonial Records*, IX, 1252-1253; Taylor, "Foreign Attachment," 34.

55. Board of Trade Journal, May 18, 1775, *Colonial Records*, X, 377-378; Taylor, "Foreign Attachment," 34.

56. Sellers, "Making a Revolution," 27, 30; Greene, *The Quest for Power*, 424.

Chapter IV

1. *Rebels and Demos*. 1-8; Alfred F. Young, *The American Revolution, Explorations in the History of American Radicalism*, (De Kalb, Northern Illinois University Press, 1976), ix-x111.

2. Robert L. Ganyard, "Radicals and Conservatives in Revolutionary North Carolina: A Point at Issue, the October Election, 1776," *William and Mary Quarterly*, 3rd Ser., (1967), 24:570-578, 582-587.

3. *The Revolutionary War in the South: Power, Conflict, and Leadership, Essays in honor of John Richard Alden*, edited by W. Robert Higgins, (Durham: Duke University Press, 1979), 80-84.

4. Pauline Maier, "Early Revolutionary Leaders in the South and the Problem of Southern Distinctiveness," *The Southern Experience in the American Revolution*, ed. by Jeffrey J. Crow and Larry E. Tise, (Chapel Hill, University of N.C. Press, 1978), 3-21, hereinafter cited Crow and Tise, *American Revolution*.

5. Catherine Drinker Bowen, *The Most Dangerous Man in America*, (Boston, Little Brown and Co., 1974), 230-243; Bernard Bailyn, *The Ordeal of Thomas Hutchinson*, (Cambridge, Massachusetts, The Belknap Press of Harvard University Press, 1974), 6, 76, 91, 223 ff, 285-287, 336, 350, 369; Alexander Elmsly to

Samuel Johnston, March 24, 1774, *Colonial Record* 9:828-30.

6. Hooper to Iredell, April 26, 1774, *Colonial Records*, 9:983-86: Higginbotham, *James Iredell*, I:230-233.

7. Samuel Johnston to William Hooper, April 5, 1774, *Colonial Records*, 9:968-69, 876.

8. Dartmouth to Martin, July 6, 1774, and Martin to Dartmouth, July 13, 1774, Colonial Records, 9:1007, 1009-10.

9. Fries and others, *Records of the Moravians*, II, 685f-685, 755, 808, 875$_n$. George Washington Paschal, *History of North Carolina Baptists* (Raleigh, General Board, N.C. Baptist State Convention, 2 volumes, 1930), I, 352$_n$, 422-425; *Colonial Records*, 7, 432, 8, 505.9, 6; Reverend James Reed to the Secretary of the Church of England Missions, July 19, 1774, *Colonial Records*, 9, 1014-1015.

10. *Colonial Records*, 9:1016-18, 1024-26.

11. *Colonial Records*, 9:1030, 1032, 1034, 1037-38.

12. Council Journal, July 29, 1774; Andrew Miller to Thomas Burke, July 29, 1774, *Colonial Records*, 9:1018-20, 1023.

13. *Colonial Records*, 9:1027-1041.

14. *Colonial Records*, 9:1041-49.

15. Andrew Miller to Thomas Burke, September 4, 1774, *Colonial Records*, 9:1063-64.

16. *Colonial Records*, 9:1043.

17. This and the succeeding three paragraphs are based on *Colonial Records*, 9:1041-49.

18. This and the succeeding three paragraphs are based on *Colonial Records*, 9:1050-61.

19. Andrew Miller to Thomas Burke, September 4, 1774, *Colonial Records*, 9:1063-64.

20. *Colonial Records*, 9:1072-75.

21. For this and the next paragraph, *Colonial Records*, 9:1079-81.

22. Andrew Miller to Thomas Burke, December 12, 1774, *Colonial Records*, 9:1102.

23. Samuel Johnston to Alexander Elmsly, September 23, 1774, *Colonial Records*, 9:1070-72.

24. This and the succeeding paragraph are based on Martin to Dartmouth, November 4, 1774; *Colonial Records*, 9:1083-87; Unsigned, "William Legge," *DNB*, XI, 858-860.

25. Martin to an unknown correspondent, November 5, 1774, *Colonial Records*, 9:1087-88.

26. Council Journal, October 8, 1774, and Martin to Dartmouth January 26, 1775, *Colonial Records*, 9:1078-79, 1114.

27. This and the succeeding paragraph are based on Archibald Neilson to Andrew Miller, January 28 and Martin to Dartmouth, January 26, 1775, *Colonial Records*, 9:1116-17, 1114-16; *Records of the Moravians*, II:863-68, 870-71.

28. This and the succeeding paragraph are based on Martin to Dartmouth, March 10, 1775, *Colonial Records*, 9:1155-59.

29. *Colonial Records*, 9:746-47, 1108-13, 1118-19, 1126-28, 1133-36.

Chapter V

1. Council Journal, April 2, 1775, *Colonial Records*, 9:117-78.

2. The Journal of the Proceedings of the Second Provincial Convention of North Carolina, Held at New Bern on the Third Day of April, A.D., 1775, *Colonial Records*, 9:1178-85.

3. *Colonial Records*, 9:1178-85, 1187-1205.

4. This and the next two paragraphs are based on Legislative Journals, *Colonial Records*, 9:1190-96.

5. This and the next paragraph are based on *Colonial Records*, 9:1201-04.

6. This and the next paragraph are based on *Colonial Records*, 9:1205.

7. *Colonial Records*, 9:1211.

8. This and the next three paragraphs are based on Martin to Dartmouth, April 7, 1775, *Colonial Records*, 9:1212-15.

9. Andrew Miller to Thomas Burke, April 6, 1775, *Colonial Records*, 9:1205-06.

10. This and the next paragraph are based on Alexander Elmsly to Samuel Johnston, April 7, 1775, *Colonial Records*, 9:1207-10. In a debate in the House of Lords on November 27, 1781, Hillsborough expressed hope that the "independence of America would never be admitted in that house." The Dobbs referred to is Governor Arthur Dobbs, 1754-65, who preceded William Tryon, and "Nash" is Abner Nash, attorney from Craven County.

11. William Cobbett and Thomas C. Hansard, eds., *The Parliamentary History of England . . . to 1803*, (London, His Majesty's Stationers Office 36 vols., 1806-1820), 22:661-62.

13. Gage to Martin, April 12, 1775 and Martin to Gage, April 20, 1775, *Colonial Records*, 9:1220, 1223-28.

14. Dartmouth to Martin, May 3, 1775, *Colonial Records*, 9:1240-42; and Dartmouth to Gage, May 3, 1775, Clarence E. Carter, ed., *The Correspondence of General Thomas Gage . . . 1763-1775* (New Have, Yale University Press two vols., 1931-33), II:196-97.

15. Messages from Safety Committees in the northern colonies to North Carolina Safety Committees, April 23 to May 9, 1775, and Henry Montfort to Thomas Burke, May 9, 1775, *Colonial Records*, 9:1229-39, 1245.

16. Martin to Dartmouth, May 18, 1775, *Colonial Records*, 9:1242-46.

17. This and the next three paragraphs are based on Martin to Dartmouth, May 23, 1775, *Colonial Records*, 10:41-42.

18. Schlesinger, *Prelude* 244.

19. This and the next paragraph are based on Martin to Dartmouth, Ft. John-

ston, June 30, 1775, *Colonial Records*, 10:41-50.

20. Schaw, *Journal of a Lady of Quality*, 186-87.

21. Martin to Dartmouth, New Bern, May 23 and Ft. Johnston, June 30, 1775; Sale of Governor Martin's Property, February 6, 1777, *Colonial Records*, 10:41-50, 22:880-889.

22. Martin to Dartmouth, June 30, 1775, *Colonial Records*, 10:50; Schaw, *Journal of a Lady of Quality*, 187; *South Carolina Gazette*, Tuesday, June 20, 1775.

23. *Records of the Moravians*, II:846; *South Carolina Gazette*, Tuesday, June 20, 1775.

24. Robert Salter to Colonel Richard Caswell, June 3, 1775, Calendar of Hayes Papers, Bundle 15, Southern Historical Mms. Colls., Chapel Hill; the Cogdell letter and the Extract are in *Colonial Records*, 10:14, 11-12.

Chapter VI

1. Martin to Dartmouth, June 30, 1775, *Colonial Records*, 10, 41-50.

2. This and the next paragraph are based on William B. Clarke, (ed.), *The Naval Documents of the American Revolution*, (Washington, U.S. Government Printing Office, 5 volumes, 1964-1970) I, 599, 618-619, hereinafter cited *Naval Docs.*; Martin to Dartmouth, June 30, 1775, *Colonial Records*, 10, 41-50.

3. *Naval* Docs., I, 675.

4. *Colonial Records*, 10, 43, 46; "Class, Mobility, and Conflict in North Carolina on the Eve of the Revolution," by Marvin L. Michael Kay and Lorin Lee Cary, Crow and Tise, *American Revolution*, 112-114.

5. For this and the next paragraph, *Colonial Records*, 10, 16-19.

6. This and the next paragraph are based on *Colonial Records*, 10, 16-19, 24, 26-29.

7. For this and the succeeding paragraph refer to *Colonial Records*, 10, 38-40.

8. This and the four succeeding paragraphs refer to *Colonial Records*, 10, 41-50; Alan D. Watson, "William Dry: Passive Patriot," Lower Cape Fear Historical Society, Inc., *Bulletin*, (October, 1973), XVII, No. 1, 1-5.

9. *Colonial Records*, 10, 51-60.

10. This and the two succeeding paragraphs are based on *Colonial Records*, 10, 20-23.

11. *Colonial Records*, 10, 61-64.

12. *Colonial Records*, 10, 85-86.

13. For this and two succeeding paragraphs refer to Colonel John Simpson to Colonel Richard Cogdell, July 15, 1775, *Colonial Records*, 10, 94-95; Jeffrey J. Crow, "Slave Rebelliousness and Social Conflict in North Carolina, 1775 to 1802," *William and Mary* Quarterly, 3rd Ser., (January, 1980), XXXVII, 79-80; Michael Mullin, "British Caribbean and North American Slaves in an Era of War and Revolution, 1775-1807," Crow and Tise, American Revolution, 235-237.

14. *Colonial Records,* 10:72-73; and *Report on American Manuscripts in the Royal Institutions of Great Britain* (London, His Majesty's Stationers Office 4 vols., 1904-09), I:4-5, hereinafter cited *Report on American Manuscripts.*

15. Martin to Dartmouth, July 6, 1775, *Colonial Records,* 10:66-68; Schaw, *Journal of a Lady of Quality,* 196.

16. This and the succeeding paragraphs see Martin to Samuel Martin, Jr., July 5, 1775, Martin Papers, XVI, 41361, ff. 286-88.

17. Martin to Dartmouth, July 6, 1775, *Colonial Records,* 10:69-71; and Schaw, *Journal of a Lady of Quality,* 196.

18. This and the succeeding paragraphs see Dartmouth to Martin, July 5, 1775, *Colonial Records,* 10:66-68.

19. Neilson to Iredell, Edenton, July 8, 1775, Duke University Mms. Colls.

20. For this and the succeeding paragraph refer to Hewes to Iredell, July 8, 1775, Duke University Mms. Colls.; *Colonial Records,* 10:103-06; White to Livingston, July 8, 1775 and Livingston to Thomson, July 8, and Hooper and Hewes to Livingston, July 8, *Colonial Records,* 10:74-75, 84.

21. Hewes to Johnston, July 8, 1775, *Colonial Records,* 10:85-86.

22. For this and succeeding paragraph refer to Martin to Dartmouth, June 30, 1775, *Colonial Records,* 10:48-50, 91-93.

23. Martin to Graves, July 8 and Collet to Gage, July 8, 1775, *Naval Docs.,* I:843-45.

24. This and the succeeding paragraphs are based on Martin to Dartmouth, July 16, 1775, *Colonial Records,* 10, 96-98; Schaw, *Journal of a Lady of Quality,* 187.

25. Martin to Dartmouth, Cruizer Sloop of War, July 17, 1775, and William Todd's deposition c. August 5, 1775, *Colonial Records,* 10, 100-102, 131-132.

26. For this and the succeeding paragraph refer to Edward Cheeseman's deposition, September 1; Samuel Cooper's deposition, undated, John Martin's deposition, September 4, and William Todd's deposition c. August 5, 1775, *Colonial Records,* 10, 132-133, 130-132, 133.

27. This and the next two paragraphs are based on Martin to Dartmouth, July 20, 1775, *Colonial Records,* 10, 102-104, 108-109.

28. *Colonial Records,* 10, 112-115, 139-140.

29. Davidson, *Propaganda,* 21, 232, 243; Schlesinger, *Prelude,* 186-187, 222-223, 244; Martin to Dartmouth, June 30, 1775, *Colonial Records,* 10, 41-50.

Chapter VII

1. Dartmouth to Martin, July 12, 1775, *Colonial Records,* 10:89-91.

2. Council Journal, July 18, 1775, and Samuel Johnston to Committee at Wilmington, July 21, 1775, *Colonial Records,* 10:106-07, 117-17.

3. This and the succeeding paragraph are based on Martin to Cotton, July 21, 1775; Journal of Provincial Congress, August 29, 1775, *Colonial Records,* 10:119,

125-29, 183; *Cape Fear Mercury*, August 25, 1775.

4. *Colonial Records*, 10:115-16, 134, 152; *History of N.C. Baptists*, II:122.

5. Stuart to Dartmouth, July 21, 1775, *Colonial Records*, 10:117-19. For more detailed information on Stuart's life, see John R. Alden, *John Stuart and the Southern Colonial Frontier, A Study of Indian Relations, War, Trade, and Land Problems in the Southern Wilderness, 1754-1775* (Ann Arbor, The University of Michigan Press 1944) and for Stuart's later attempts to organize the Indians against the patriots see James H. O'Donnell, III, *Southern Indians in the American Revolution* (Knoxville, University of Tennessee Press, 1973), 18, 19, 29, 33, 35, 49, 62, 64, 70, 81.

6. Stuart to Dartmouth, July 21, 1775, *Colonial Records*, 10:138a.

7. Dartmouth to Gage, August 2, 1775, *Colonial Records*, 10:141-51.

8. Martin's Proclamation, August 8, 1775, *Colonial Records*, 10:141-51, 160, 180.

9. This and the next paragraph are based on Journal of Provincial Congress, August 20, 1775, *Colonial Records*, 10:184-220; Schaw, *Journal of a Lady of Quality*, 187.

10. This and the succeeding paragraphs are based on *Colonial Records*, 10:184-220.

11. This and the succeeding paragraphs are based on *Colonial Records*, 10:184-220.

12. Martin to Dartmouth, October 16, 1775, *Colonial Records*, 10:285.

13. For this and the two succeeding paragraphs see Dartmouth to Martin, September 15, 1775 and Martin to Dartmouth, October 7, 16, 1775, *Colonial Records*, 10:247-48, 262-63, 265-74; Martin to Samuel Martin, Jr., September 9, 1775, Martin Papers, XVI, 41361, ff. 289-90.

14. Paul H. Smith, *Loyalists and Redcoats, A Study in British Revolutionary Policy*, (Chapel Hill, University of North Carolina Press, 1964), 18-31, hereinafter cited Smith, *Loyalists and Redcoats*. Eric Robson, "The Expedition to the Southern Colonies, 1775-1776," *English Historical Review*, 66 (1951), 545-60, hereinafter cited Robson, Expedition. North to George III, October 15, 1775; George III to North, October 16, 1775, Sir John Fortescue, ed., *The Correspondence of King George the Third from 1760 to December, 1783* (6 vols., London, His Majesty's Stationers Office 1927-28), IV, Nos. 1724, 1727.

15. A draft in the hand of George III, dated October 16-17, 1775 and quoted in Smith, *Loyalists and Redcoats*, 22; Precis Prepared for the King of the Events Leading Up to the Expedition Against the Southern Colonies, Dartmouth, Whitehall, October 22, 1775, *Naval Docs.*, II:769-74.

16. Smith, *Loyalists and Redcoats*, 23.

17. Dartmouth to Martin, October 27, November 7, Dartmouth to Howe, November 8, 1775, *Colonial Records*, 10:299-300, 306-08, 313-14; Alexander Schaw to Dartmouth, October 31, November 8, 1775, *The Manuscripts of the Earl of Dartmouth*, Great Britain Historical Manuscripts Commission (Fourteenth Re-

port, Appendix, Pt. X [London, H. M. Stationery Office, 1895], 397, hereinafter cited *Dartmouth Mss.*

18. Hewes to Johnston, November 9, 1775, Extracts from the Proceedings of the Continental Congress, November 28, 1775, Colonial Records, 10:314-16, 338; Hewes to Johnston, December 8, 1775, Calendar of Mms. in Hayes Coll., Bundle 1, Southern Historical Colls., Chapel Hill.

19. Martin to Dartmouth, November 12, 1775 and proceedings of Virginia Convention, Williamsburg, December 14, 1775, *Colonial Records*, 10:324, 346.

20. Graves to Tollemache and Graves to Martin, August 22, 1775, Naval Docs., I:1200-01, 1204-05; Martin to Dartmouth, November 12, 1775, Proceedings of the Safety Committee at Wilmington, November 20, 1775, *Colonial Records*, 10:327, 335-36.

21. Martin to Samuel Martin, Jr., November 15, 1775, Martin Papers, XVI, 41361, ff. 291-92.

22. For this and the succeeding paragraph are based on John P. MacLean, *Flora Macdonald in America* (Lumberton, N.C., A. W. McLean 1909). See chapters VI-IX for her adventures in North Carolina before and during the Revolution; Martin to Dartmouth, November 12, 1775, *Colonial Records*, 10:325-26.

23. "Lord George Germain" in *DNB*, 7:1110-14.

24. Smith, *Loyalists and Redcoats*, 23-24.

25. Journals of the Provincial Council, *Colonial Records*, 10:349-62; Samuel Johnston to Joseph Hewes, December 21, 1775, Calendar of Mms. in Hayes Colls., Bundle 18, Southern Historical Colls., Chapel Hill.

26. Germain to Martin, December 23, 1775 and Martin to Germain, March 21, 1776, *Colonial Records*, 10:364, 486-94.

27. Moore to Martin, January 9, 1776, Martin to Moore, January 11, 1776, Martin's Proclamation, January 10, 1776, and Martin to Germain, May 17, 1777, *Colonial Records*, 10:395-400.

28. Martin to Dartmouth, November 12, 1775, *Colonial Records*, 10:327; Campbell to Dartmouth, January 1, 1776, *Naval Docs.*, III:568, 622.

29. Campbell to Martin, and Martin to Campbell, December 1, 1775, *Naval Docs.*, II:1225-26; Martin to Dartmouth, January 12, 1776, *Colonial Records*, 10:406-09; Schaw, *Journal of a Lady of Quality*, 216.

30. Proceedings of the Committee of Safety, Wilmington, January 6, 1776; and Orders from Governor Martin and General McDonald for raising the King's Standard in North Carolina, January 10, 1776, *Colonial Records*, 10:389, 441-42.

31. Howe to Dartmouth, Boston, January 16, 1776, Proceedings of the Committee of Safety, Wilmington, January 16, 27, 1776, *Colonial Records*, 10:412-13, 424, 427.

32. New York Safety Committee to the New York delegates in Congress, February 4, 1776; Lee to Washington, New York, February 5, 1776, Proceedings of Tryon Safety Committee, February 6, 1776, Proceedings of New Bern Safety Committee, February 10, 1776, Manifesto of Brigadier General Donald Mc-

Donald, February 8, 1776, and Rowan County Proceedings, February 10, 1776, *Colonial Records*, 10:428-31, 443-45.

33. Penn to Person, February 12, 1776, Manifesto from Thomas Rutherford, Colonel of the Cumberland Militia, Cross Creek, February 13, 1776, *Colonial Records*, 10:448-50, 452.

34. Colden to an unknown correspondent, February 14, 1776, and Proceedings of New Bern Safety Committee, February 15, 1776, *Colonial Records*, 10:453-54, 456-57.

35. William B. Clarke sees the signals as an attempt to find the Highlanders, Journal of the Sloop Cruizer, Captain Francis Parry, *Naval Docs.*, IV:71-73; Martin to Germain, March 21, 1776, *Colonial Records*, 10:486-93.

36. Purviance to the Provincial Council, February 23, 1776, *Colonial Records*, 10:465-68; *Naval Docs.*, II:1054, IV:73, 105.

37. Purviance to the Provincial Council, February 23, 1776, *Colonial Records*, 10:465-68.

38. For this and the succeeding paragraph see Parry to the Magistrates and Inhabitants of Wilmington, February 27, 1776, *Naval Docs.*, IV:102-03.

39. Martin to the Magistrates and Inhabitants of Wilmington, February 28, 1775, *Naval Docs.*, IV:112-13; Safety Committee of Wilmington, February 28, 1776, *Colonial Records*, 10:486.

40. Caswell to Harnett, February 29, 1776 and James Moore to Harnett, March 2, 1776, *Colonial Records*, 10:482-84.

41. Christopher Ward, *The War of the Revolution*, ed., John R. Alden, (2 vols., New York, Macmillan 1952), II:662-64 hereinafter cited Ward, *Revolution*; Robert O. DeMond, *The Loyalists in North Carolina during the Revolution*, (Durham, N.C., Duke University Press, 1940), 88-97 hereinafter cited DeMond, Loyalists, and Hugh F. Rankin, "The Moore's Creek Bridge Campaign, 1776," *North Carolina Historical Review*, 30 (1953), 30-56.

42. Martin to Germain, March 21, 1776, *Colonial Records*, 10:486-93; and Smith, *Loyalists and Redcoats*, 30.

Chapter VIII

1. This and the succeeding two paragraphs are based on Martin to Germain, March 31, 1776, *Colonial Records*, 10:486-93.

2. Smith, *Loyalists and Redcoats*, 24.

3. This and the succeeding paragraph see Smith, *Loyalists and Redcoats*, 24-25; Robson, Expedition, 535-60; Journal of H.M. Sloop Cruizer, Captain Francis Parry, Martin to Clinton, March 20, 1776, Journal of HMS Mercury, Captain James Montagu, *Naval Docs.*, IV:369, 429, 290-92; Extract of a Letter from a Gentleman, North Carolina, to His Friend in this City, March 10, 1776, *Pennsylvania Evening Post*, March 26, 1776.

4. Robson, Expedition, 553-4; Parker to Philip Stephens, May 13, 1776, *Naval*

Docs., V:110.

5. Robson, Expedition, 553-5; Clinton to Martin, April 6, 1776, *Naval Docs.*, IV:691.

6. Journal of the Provincial Congress, Halifax, N.C., April 4-May 14, 1776, *Colonial Records*, 10:499-500, 511; *Annual Register* (London, R. Dodsley, 1776) 19, 156-57.

7. Journal of the Provincial Congress, Halifax, N.C., *Colonial Records*, 10:512.

8. Samuel Johnston to the Delegates in Congress at Philadelphia, April 13, 1776, *Colonial Records*, 10:495; Howe to Lee, April 10, 1776, "The Lee Letters," *Collections of the New York Historical Society*, (New York, Printed for the Society 1872), 4:398-400, hereinafter cited Lee Letters.

9. Lee Letters, 4:398-401; Schaw, *Journal of a Lady of Quality*, 187.

10. Edward McCrady, *South Carolina in the Revolution 1755-1780* (2 vols., New York, No Publisher, 1901), I:Chapter VII: "John Wells' Account of the British Attack on Charleston, June 29 to July 4, 1776;" and "Extract of a Letter from a Surgeon in Sir Peter Parker's Fleet, dated July 9, 1776," *Naval Docs.*, V:927-28, 1002-04.

11. For this and the succeeding paragraph see Martin to Germain, Snow *Peggy*, South Carolina, within the Bar off Charles Town, July 5, 1776, *Colonial Records*, 10:652-54.

12. For this and the next paragraph see Robson, Expedition, 535, 560; Smith, *Loyalists and Redcoats*, 30-31.

13. Martin to Samuel Martin Jr., July 6, 1776 and Martin to Germain, July 6, Martin Papers, XVI, 41361, ff. 293-94; Martin to Germain, August 7, 1776, *Colonial Records*, 10:735-37; Rawdon to Huntington, July 3, 1776, *Historical Manuscript Commissioners Report on the Manuscripts of the Late Reginald Rawdon Hastings, Esq., of the Manor House Asby de la Zouche*, (4 vols., London, H.M.S.O. 1928-1947), III:175, hereinafter cited *Hastings Mss.*

14. Journal of the Council of Safety, Halifax, July 21, 1776, *Colonial Records*, 10:682, 702, 708-11.

15. Martin to Germain, September 28, 1776 and Ashe to the Council of Safety, October 8, 1776, *Colonial Records*: 823-24, 840.

16. Martin to Samuel Martin, Jr., August 9, 1776, Martin Papers, XVI, 41361, ff. 295-6.

17. Martin to Samuel Martin, Jr., September 30, 1776, Martin Papers, XVI, 41361, ff. 297-300; Martin to Germain, September 28, 1776, *Colonial Records*, 10:823-24.

18. Carl Van Doren, *Secret History of the American Revolution*, (New York, The Viking Press, 1968), 28, hereinafter cited Van Doren, *Secret History*. North Callahan, *Flight from the Republic The Tories of the American Revolution*, (Indianapolis, The Bobbs-Merrill Company, Inc., 1967), 129-30.

19. This and the succeeding paragraph are based on L. B. Butterfield et al,

eds., *The Adam Papers*, (Cambridge, The Belknap Press, 1962, 4 vols.), 2:250, 3:399-400, 416-433; Ira D. Gruber, *The Howe Brothers and the American Revolution*, (Chapel Hill, University of North Carolina Press, 1972), 116-20.

20. This and the succeeding paragraph are based on Martin to Germain, November 8, 1776, *Colonial Records*, 10:899-900, 920, 962, 1003-13. Clark, *State Records*, 12, 439-443, 22, 880-889, 24, 263-264. The patriot governor Richard Caswell purchased most of Martin's furniture at a public auction. Alonzo T. Dill, *Governor Tryon and His Palace* (Chapel Hill, University of North Carolina Press 1955), 197; Martin to Samuel Martin, Jr., November 14, 1776, Martin Papers, XVI, 41361, f. 301.

21. This and the succeeding paragraphs are based on Martin to Samuel Martin, Jr., April 9, 16, 1777, Martin Papers, XVI, 41361, ff. 305-10.

22. Samuel Martin, Jr. to Martin, Martin Papers, May 11, 1777, XIX, 41364, ff. 34-55.

23. Martin to Germain, May 17, 1777, *Colonial Records*, 10:401-05; Martin to Samuel Martin, Jr., June 4, 1777, Martin Papers, XVI, 41361, ff. 311-12.

24. Martin to Samuel Martin, Jr., July 7, 1778, Martin Papers, XVI, 41361, ff. 313-14.

25. Oliver, *History of Antigua*, III:441; Martin to Samuel Martin, Jr., December 8, 1779, Martin Papers, XVI, 41361, ff. 315-18; Carl Van Doren, *Secret History*, 234; Haywood, *Tryon*, 198.

26. This and the succeeding paragraph are based on Martin to Samuel Martin, Jr., December 8, 1779, Martin Papers, XVI, 41361, 315-18.

27. Martin to Samuel Martin, Jr., May 12, 19, 1780, Martin Papers, XVI, 41361, ff. 319-22; *The American Rebellion, Sir Henry Clinton's Narrative of His Campaigns, 1775-1782*, ed. William B. Willcox (New Haven, Yale University Press, 1954), Chapter XI, hereinafter cited *American Rebellion*.

28. Smith, *Loyalists and Redcoats*, 131-33.

29. Martin to Germain, June 10, 1780, *Report on the Manuscripts of Mrs. Stopford-Sackville*; *The Siege of Charleston*, Tr. and Ed. by Bernhard A. Ulendorf, (Ann Arbor, University of Michigan Press, 1938), 57.

30. *Stopford-Sackville*, II:174, 176; Smith, *Loyalists and Redcoats*, 145-46.

31. Cornwallis to Germain, Camden, August [no date] and 21, 1780, *Stopford-Sackville*, 175-76.

32. Oscar T. Barck, Jr., and Hugh T. Lefler, *Colonial America*, Second Edition, (New York, Macmillan 1968), 614; R. D. W. Connor, *History of North Carolina* (Multi vols., Chicago, The Lewis Publishing Co. 1919), 2:469; Smith, *Loyalists and Redcoats*, 147-48; *The Cornwallis Papers, Abstracts of Americana*, Comp. by George H. Reese, (Charlottesville, University Press of Virginia, 1970), 27-28, hereinafter cited Reese, *Cornwallis*.

33. Smith, *Loyalists and Redcoats*, 148-49.

34. Franklin to Clinton, New York, October 28, 1780, *Report on American Manuscripts in the Royal Institutions of Great Britain*, (4 vols., London,

H.M.S.O. 1904-09), II:198, 467, 469-70, 481, 508, 521, 528-29, hereinafter cited *Royal Institutions Mms.*; *American Rebellion*, 237-38, 359-51; Carl Van Doren, *Secret History*, 234-35.

35. For this and the succeeding paragraph see Schaw, *Journal of a Lady of Quality*, 268; Reese, *Cornwallis*, 20, 56-57, 66, 68, 85, 149, 209-10; Charles Ross, ed., *Correspondence of Charles, First Marquis Cornwallis*, (3 vols., London, J. Murray, 1859), 1:54, hereinafter cited Ross, *Cornwallis*; Theodore Thayer, *Nathanael Greene, Strategist of the American Revolution*, (New York, Twayne Publishers, 1960), hereinafter cited Thayer, *Greene*; Smith, *Loyalists and Redcoats*, 150.

36. Thayer, *Greene*, 296-97; and for a more detailed and authoritative account see Don Higginbotham, *Daniel Morgan, Revolutionary Rifleman* (Chapel Hill, University of North Carolina Press 1961), Chapter 9; Smith, *Loyalists and Redcoats*, 151-52; Reese, *Cornwallis*, 57, 68.

37. This and the next paragraph are based on Smith, *Loyalists and Redcoats*, 152; Ward, *Revolution*, II:778-779.

38. Reese, *Cornwallis*, 67, 211.

39. Smith, *Loyalists and Redcoats*, 152-53; Benjamin F. Stevens, ed., *The Campaign in Virginia, 1781: An Exact Reprint of Six Rare Pamphlets on the Clinton-Cornwallis Controversy . . . , (2 vols., London, No Publisher 1888), 1:213-14; hereinafter cited Clinton-Cornwallis Controversy.*

40. Ross, *Cornwallis*, I:489.

41. Ross, *Cornwallis*, I:494, 509; Schaw, *Journal of a Lady of Quality*, 268.

Chapter IX

1. *Hastings Mss.*, III:193-94.

2. *Historical Manuscript Commissioners Report on Manuscripts in Various Collections* (8 vols., London, H.M.S.O. 1901-1914), 6:177. The Knox manuscripts are now in the Clements Library at Ann Arbor, Michigan.

3. Martin to Welbore Ellis, 28 South Milton St., London, March 7, 1782, Martin to unknown correspondent, London, November 7, 1781, *Royal Institutions Manuscripts*, II:414, 347; Thomas Macknight to Lord Dartmouth, July 19, 24, 1781, March 13, 1783, *Dartmouth Manuscripts*, II:478-80.

4. This and the succeeding paragraphs are based on DeMond, Loyalists, 202-204. North Callahan, *Flight from the Republic* (Indianapolis, the Bobbs-Merrill Company, Inc., 1967), 126 hereinafter cited Callahan, *Flight*. For a more detailed study on the compensation and pensions allowed for loyalists, see DeMond, *Loyalists*, Chapter X, and Transcript of the Manuscript Books and Papers of the Commission of Enquiry into the Losses and Services of the American Loyalists held under the Acts of Parliament of 23, 25, 26, 28, and 29 of George III, preserved among the Audit Office Records in the Public Record Office of England, 1783-1790. Volumes related to North Carolina loyalists are in the Department of

Archives and History, Raleigh, N.C. Other sources of manuscripts on the loyalists can be found in the Nova Scotia Historical Society Collection, Halifax, Nova Scotia, and the Haldimand Papers in the Canadian Archives, Ottawa.

5. DeMond, *Loyalists*, 205; Callahan, *Flight*, 132.

6. Schaw, *Journal of a Lady of Quality*, 268-69; Martin to Samuel Martin, Jr., Richmond Surrey, November 19, 1785, Martin Papers, XVI, 41361, f. 323; and for a statement on the value of the pound sterling see John J. McCusker, *Money and Exchange in Europe and America, 1600-1775*, (Chapel Hill, University of North Carolina Press, 1978), 142, 186, 219. The pound varied in value in the 18th century as it does in the 20th century.

7. Schaw, *Journal of a Lady of Quality*, 269; Oliver *History of Antigua*, II:240.

8. The Register Book of Burials in the Parish of St. George Hanover Square in the County of Middlesex beginning 1st of January 1762, Burials II:437, Archives of St. George Hanover Square, London, W. 1., hereinafter cited Register Book St. George Hanover Square, Oliver, *History of Antigua*, II:244-45, III:441.

9. Schaw, *Journal of a Lady of Quality*, 269, 270; Josiah Henry's obituary in *Gentleman's Magazine* (London, 1799), 1087; for Uncle Josiah's will see "Wills." *Collections of the New York Historical Society* (New York, 1900), 9:55.

10. Schaw, *Journal of a Lady of Quality*, 269; Register Book St. George Hanover Square, Tombstone Number 1423, Burial Ground, Bayswater Road, Tombstone Inscriptions.

11. A collotype reproduction of the original manuscript of *The Comic Adventures of Old Mother Hubbard and Her Dog* was made by Oxford University Press, *The Oxford Dictionary of Nursery Rhymes*, ed. by Iona and Peter Opie, (Oxford: 1951), 319-23.

12. Leonard Woods Labaree, *Royal Government in America, A Study of the British Colonial Systems Before 1783* (New York, 1958), 396, 398-400.

13. R. B. Sheridan, "The Rise of a Colonial Gentry: A Case Study of Antigua, 1730-1775," *Economic History Review*, XIII, No. 3, (April 1961), 342-57; Richard B. Sheridan, "The West Indian Antecedents of Josiah Martin, Last Royal Governor of North Carolina," *North Carolina Historical Review*, LIV (July 1977), 259n.

14. Unsigned, "William Legge," *DNB*, XI, 859; William L. Saunders, *Colonial Records*, VIII:xiii. Legge is Lord Dartmouth.

15. This and the succeeding paragraph are based on James M. Clifton, "Golden Grains of White: Rice Planting on the Lower Cape Fear," *North Carolina Historical Review*, L (October 1973), 369.

16. David Leroy Corbitt, *The Formation of the North Carolina Counties 1663-1943* (Raleigh: State Department Archives and History, 1950), 145.

Bibliographical Note

The largest collection of manuscripts pertaining to Josiah Martin is to be found in the Martin Papers in the manuscript collections of the British Museum. This collection contains personal letters, business papers, and genealogical material of the Martin family beginning in the sixteenth century. This valuable corpus of papers was acquired by the British Museum in the 1920's and thus escaped the attention of the historical commission who had been sent to the British Public Records Office in the 1880's to copy colonial records of North Carolina. The pioneering and monumental achievement to recover North Carolina's past was published as *The Colonial Records of North Carolina* from 1886 to 1890, and constitutes the second largest collection of Martin papers, especially those related to Josiah Martin's administration as governor of North Carolina. Fortunately by 1975 the Division of Archives and History had microfilmed the Martin Papers in the British Museum. Fugitive manuscripts about Martin can be found in the State Archives at Raleigh, North Carolina and in the manuscript collections of Duke University, Durham, and in the Southern Historical Collections at Chapel Hill. The Duke of Grafton Papers are at Bury St. Edmonds, and West Suffolk Record Office, England. The Germain Papers and the Knox Papers are in the Clements Library, at the University of Michigan, Ann Arbor. The Knox Papers have been collected and published in *Reports on Manuscripts in Various Collections*, (Dublin, 1909), and some of the Germain Papers can be found in the *Report on the Manuscripts of Mrs. Stopford-Sackville*, (2 vols., London, 1904-1910).

There are references to and about Governor Martin in manuscripts collected in the following publications: *Letters and Papers of John Singleton Copley and Henry Pelham, 1739-1776*, (Boston, 1914); Charles Ross, ed., *Correspondence of Charles First Mar-*

quis Cornwallis, 3 vols., (London, 1859); *The Manuscripts of the Earl of Dartmouth*, 3 vols., (London, 1887-1896); *Report on the Manuscripts of the late Reginald Rawdon Hastings, esq. of the Manor House, Ashby de la Zouche*, 4 vols., (London, 1928-1947); *The Papers of Sir William Johnson*, 14 vols., (Albany, 1921-1965), *The Lee Papers*, 4 vols., (*Collections of the New York Historical Society for the Year 1871, . . . 1872, . . . 1873, . . . 1874*), (New York, 1872-1875), and by the same society, *The Letter Book of John Watts*, (Albany, 1928); James Munro, ed., *Acts of the Privy Council of England, Colonial Series*, (London, 1912); the *Journal of the Commission of Trade and Plantations, January 1768-December 1775*, (London, 1937), and the *Report on American Manuscripts in the Royal Institutions of Great Britain*, 4 vols., (London, 1904-1909).

Other primary sources relating to Governor Martin can be found in Janet Schaw's *Journal of a Lady of Quality Being the Narrative of a Journey from Scotland to the West Indies, North Carolina, and Portugal, in the years 1774 to 1776*, ed. by Evangeline Walker Andrews and Charles McLean Andrews, (New Haven, 1927). The two provincial newspapers during Governor Martin's administration, *North Carolina Gazette* and the *Cape Fear Mercury* printed some of his proclamations and speeches. In London, the *Annual Register* and the *Gentleman's Magazine* are useful for those historians working in the eighteenth century.

There has been quite a bit of material published on the Regulator movement in North Carolina. In the past, historians have had to refer to the *Colonial Records of North Carolina* for some of the basic documents, but in 1971 the State Department of Archives and History at Raleigh published *The Regulators in North Carolina, A Documentary History, 1759-1776*, compiled and edited by William S. Powell, James K. Huhta, and Thomas J. Furnham. Those people who are tracing ancestors will still have to use the *Colonial Records* but this recent compilation will prove most useful to historians. Related to primary sources about the Regulators, in a sense, is Eli W. Caruthers's apology for the Regulators, *A Sketch of the Life and Character of the Reverend David Caldwell*, (Greensboro, 1842), because Caruthers interviewed many of the

Regulators when they were advanced in years. Thus, his work reflects eye witness accounts filtered through many years. The historian has to be skeptical about anyone's memory with the passage of time, but much of what Caruthers relates could not be found in official documents. Moreover, older people sometimes have sharper memories about things that happened fifty years before than they do in the most recent fifty minutes. Caruthers should be used with some objectivity, although some of his poignant tales tug at the heartstrings. After all, he was presenting the Regulators in the most favorable light.

There are many useful studies about the Regulators, and perhaps the first objective monograph was John Spencer Bassett's "The Regulators of North Carolina (1756-1771)," in *The Annual Report of the American Historical Association for 1894*, (Washington, 1895). There were apologists for both sides of the Regulator movement and the following are a select list of publications that the reader may find of some interest: William K. Boyd, ed., *Some Eighteenth Century Tracts Concerning North Carolina*, (Raleigh, 1927); Adelaide L. Fries, ed., *Records of the Moravians in North Carolina*, 7 vols., (Raleigh, 1922-1947); Arthur P. Hudson, "Songs of the North Carolina Regulators," *The William and Mary Quarterly*, 4:4, (October, 1947), 470-485; William E. Fitch, *Some Neglected History of North Carolina*, (New York, 1905); Marshall D. Haywood, *Governor William Tryon, and His Administration in the Province of North Carolina, 1765-1771*, (Raleigh, 1903); Archibald Henderson, "The Origin of the Regulation in North Carolina," *American Historical Review*, 21, (January, 1916), 320-332; Mary E. Lazenby, *Herman Husband, A Story of His Life*, (Washington, 1940); Lamar Middleton, *Revolt U.S.A.*, (New York, 1938); William S. Powell, ed., *The Correspondence of William Tryon and Other Selected Papers* (Raleigh: Division of Archives and History, Department of Cultural Resources, 2 volumes, 1980-1981), and David L. Swain, "The War of the Regulation," *North Carolina University Magazine*, 9:3 (October, 1859), 9:6 (February, 1860), 9:8 (April, 1860), 10:1 (August, 1860).

For those readers who wish to know more about the loyalists, they are referred to the pioneering work of Lorenzo Sabine, *Bio-*

graphical Sketches of Loyalists, (Boston, 1864), which is still one of the finest studies on the loyalists. Other studies on the loyalists that may prove useful are: Moses C. Tyler's two volume *Literary History of the American Revolution* (1897); Claude H. Van Tyne, *The Loyalists in the American Revolution*, (New York, 1902); Robert O. DeMond, *The Loyalists in North Carolina During the Revolution* (Durham, 1940); Hugh T. Lefler and Albert R. Newsome, *North Carolina: the History of a Southern State (Chapel Hill, 1954); Paul H. Smith, Loyalists and Redcoats* (Chapel Hill, 1964); and William H. Nelson, *The American Tory* (Oxford, England, 1961); North Callahan, *Flight from the Republic* (Indianapolis, 1967); Robert M. Calhoon, "The Floridas, the Western Frontier, and Vermont: Thoughts on the Hinterland Loyalists," in *Eighteenth Century Florida Life on the Frontier*, ed., Samuel Proctor (Gainesville, 1976); Carole W. Troxler, *The Loyalist Experience in North Carolina*, (Raleigh, 1976), and Carole W. Troxler, *The Migration of Carolina and Georgia Loyalists to Nova Scotia and New Brunswick*, (Ann Arbor: Xerox Publishing Co., 1976), Ph.D. thesis. Those readers who wish to study the primary sources on thoughtful loyalists are referred to the works of Samuel Seabury, Joseph Galloway, Robert Proud, James Allen, Jonathan Odell, and William Eddis. For a survey of the interpretations of the loyalist historians and the loyalists themselves, see *Allegiance in America: The Case of the Loyalists*, ed., G.N.D. Evans, (Reading, Mass., 1969). Transcript of the Manuscript Books and Papers of the Commission of Enquiry into the Losses and Services of the American Loyalists held under the Acts of Parliament of 23, 25, 26, 28, and 29 of George III, preserved among the Audit Office Records in the Public Record Office of England, 1783-1790. Volumes related to North Carolina loyalists are in the Department of Archives and History, Raleigh, N.C. Other sources of manuscripts on the loyalists can be found in the Nova Scotia Historical Society Collection, Halifax, Nova Scotia and the Haldimand Papers in the Canadian Archives, Ottawa.

Index